D1571188

SEASON OF YOUTH

SEASON OF YOUTH

The Bildungsroman from Dickens to Golding

Jerome Hamilton Buckley

HARVARD UNIVERSITY PRESS

*Cambridge, Massachusetts
and London, England*

© Copyright 1974 by the President and Fellows of Harvard College

All rights reserved

Second printing 1975

Library of Congress Catalog Card Number 73-85887

ISBN 0-674-79640-3

Printed in the United States of America

FOR
NICK, ELEANOR,
VICTORIA AND TOM

PREFACE

"HAPPY season of youth!" exclaimed Goethe, with enthusiasm and a little irony, "happy times of the first wish of love!" More than a century later Somerset Maugham countered the opinion with a sober cynicism: "It is an illusion that youth is happy, an illusion of those who have lost it; but the young know they are wretched, for they are full of the truthless ideals which have been instilled into them, and each time they come in contact with the real they are bruised and wounded." *Wilhelm Meister* and *Of Human Bondage*, the sources of these quotations, represent not only the range in tone and time of the present book but also the unity of its concern, for both are chronicles of youth, however that season is to be regarded; both are what we must call Bildungsromane, the one the prototype of the form, the other a standard early-modern example.

Though it glances at Goethe and the Continental antecedents of the genre, this study concentrates on the development of the Bildungsroman in England (and with Joyce in Ireland); and, in writing it, I have been constantly struck by the awkwardness of the German term as applied to English literature. I have therefore considered—and sometimes, for the sake of convenience and variation, accepted —several possible synonyms: the novel of youth, the novel of education, of apprenticeship, of adolescence, of initiation, even the life-novel. The first two of these are perhaps the least unsatisfactory alternatives, if "youth" can imply not so much a state of being as a process of movement and adjustment from childhood to early maturity, or if "education" can be understood as a growing up and gradual self-discovery in the school-without-walls that is experience. But none of the substitutes quite replaces the label Bildungsroman as I interpret it, attempt to describe it in my introductory chapter, and affix it to a remarkable sequence of English fiction from Dickens to William Golding. If the word ultimately escapes precise definition or neat translation, its meaning should nonetheless emerge clearly enough from an account of the novels themselves and the steady recurrence of certain common motifs in them. None of the novelists we shall examine claimed to be writing a Bildungsroman—some indeed could not have known the term at all. Yet each, after Goethe, was very much aware of the literary tradition in which he or she was working, and I have found it possible to establish frequent relationships and lines of influence between one author and the next and to say something of the development of the genre.

Since most of the English Bildungsromane are highly autobiographical, this book raises the problem of the prevalence of the confessional impulse in Romantic and modern culture and explores repeatedly the general uses of subjectivity. Yet the novels, individually, differ as sharply as the lives they reflect and appraise. A number of them—*Great Expectations*, for example, *Jude the Obscure, Sons and Lovers, A Portrait of the Artist as a Young Man*—are among the best and best-known works of English fiction and as independent entities they have accordingly received much criticism and appreciation from diverse points of view. Few, however, have been considered in any detail with reference to the conventions of the Bildungsroman. A generic study may, I believe, help explain the emphases, method, and peculiar difficulties of each. But since each of the novels, whatever its derivations, attains its own strength and integrity, I have chosen not to arrange my materials thematically but rather to approach each work separately, as an object to be measured in itself yet at the same time set in its chronological place in a developing tradition.

Though no previous history has covered quite the same area as this one undertakes to survey, much of the territory should be familiar to scores of my Harvard students who have followed the fortunes of the Bildungsroman with me in Humanities 153 and who, sharing much with the young protagonists of the fiction, have greatly enlarged my understanding of the genre. Some of the estimates of the novels and novelists have undoubtedly carried over from my lectures to the rather differently shaped chapters in which they now appear. Parts of the Dickens chapter, close to its present form, were delivered as a guest lecture at the University of California, Santa Barbara; the essays on George Eliot and Samuel Butler and some of the introduction were read at various times to the Harvard Victorians; and each successive section as written was given the indulgent attention of my wife, Elizabeth. I thank all of my auditors for their patience and encouragement.

I should like also to acknowledge a summer grant from the American Council of Learned Societies, which abetted my research, and support from the Clark Fund, Harvard University, which assisted in the preparation of my manuscript. I am grateful to have had at my disposal the great collections of the Harvard College Library and, more briefly, the resources of the British Museum. I have profited as always from the advice of friends and colleagues. And in writing of novels of "education," I have been conscious of many a more elusive debt to teachers of another time, in another country.

Cambridge, Massachusetts   J. H. B.
October 1973

CONTENTS

SEASON OF YOUTH

❧ I ❧

INTRODUCTION:
THE SPACE BETWEEN

I N the preface to *Endymion* Keats described his poem as a product of inexperience and immaturity, "a feverish attempt rather than a deed accomplished." Yet the long-drawn, tortuous romance, which by allegory depicts the awakening of the sympathetic imagination, marked, he knew, a necessary phase in his growth as a poet. Like Endymion, who at length finds the ideal enclosed in a human and earthly love, Keats too would eventually achieve a calm and steadying acceptance of life's anomalies. Meanwhile (it was then April 1818), he could explain his bewilderment and troubled sense of misdirection: "The imagination of a boy is healthy, and the mature imagination of a man is healthy; but there is a space of life between, in which the soul is in a ferment, the character undecided, the way of life uncertain, the ambition thick-sighted. . . ."

A month later, in a remarkable letter to his friend Reynolds, Keats developed the metaphor of a many-chambered mansion, to account for his own present state of mind and the general malaise of youth. The child, he wrote, lingers in "the infant or thoughtless Chamber" as long as he remains content with simple sensations and impressions. All too

1

soon, however, the assertion of the thinking principle drives him into the second room, "the Chamber of Maiden-Thought," where before long his new-found delight in ideas, the joyous liberty of speculation, is shadowed by his perception of the world's misery and pain, an awareness which gradually darkens the bright chamber and at the same time opens new doors, "all dark—all leading to dark passages." His perspective all lost, the youth now can see no balance of good and evil, no real harmony or purpose in man's life. "*We,*" said Keats, "are now in that state—We feel the 'burden of the Mystery.' To this point was Wordsworth come, as far as I can conceive when he wrote 'Tintern Abbey' and it seems to me that his Genius is explorative of those dark Passages. Now if we live, and go on thinking, we too shall explore them."[1] Keats's letters themselves help illuminate the dark transition, and his interest in what transpires in the chamber of maiden-thought foreshadows, as we shall see, the concern of a considerable body of Victorian and later prose fiction. But it was Wordsworth—to an even greater extent than Keats could know (for *The Prelude* remained unpublished till 1850)—who first gave prolonged and serious attention to each stage of the imagination, to boyhood, maturity, and the darker space between.

Speaking of *The Prelude* on its completion in 1805, Wordsworth declared it "a thing unprecedented in literary history that a man should talk so much about himself. It is not self-conceit that has induced me to do this, but real humility. I began the work because I was unprepared to treat any more arduous subject, and diffident of my own powers."[2] The introduction to Book I probes the diffidence in some detail, the ambition to produce a great epic, the fear of confusing the grand and the grandiose, and the too easy rationalizing of procrastination and inactivity:

> Thus from day to day
> I live, a mockery of the brotherhood
> Of vice and virtue, with no skill to part
> Vague longing that is bred by want of power
> From paramount impulse not to be withstood,
> A timorous capacity from prudence;
> From circumspection, infinite delay.
> Humility and modest awe themselves
> Betray me, serving often for a cloak
> To a more subtle selfishness. . . .

The object of the present poem is soon made explicit: "to fix the wavering balance of my mind" by reviewing the whole past, its defeats and successes, disenchantments and moments of exultation. And the long analysis has scarcely begun before we are given a clue to the resolution:

> There is a dark
> Invisible workmanship that reconciles
> Discordant elements, and makes them move
> In one society. Ah me! that all
> The terrors, all the early miseries
> Regrets, vexations, lassitudes, that all
> The thoughts and feelings which have been infus'd
> Into my mind, should ever have made up
> The calm existence that is mine when I
> Am worthy of myself![8]

By the end of Book XII in the earliest version, Wordsworth had long since dispelled the darkness of his initial misgivings; he had achieved, partly in the actual process of writing, the "healthy" imagination of his maturity and was ready to be-

gin his epic. At the time he could hardly have suspected that
The Prelude was actually already that major work, not
merely a preliminary exercise but itself the deed accomplished.

Wordsworth was in no sense a precocious writer. But in
tracing the "growth of a poet's mind,"[4] he began with recollections of early childhood on the assumption, psychologi-
cally acute, that the child was father of the man or, to shift
the metaphor, that the defined attributes of the child's
character would somehow build a bridge over the troubled
currents of adolescence to a more stable maturity. Memory
accordingly serves in *The Prelude* as the principal agent of
integration; a past emotion intensely remembered serves a
present purpose:

> So feeling comes in aid
> Of feeling, and diversity of strength
> Attends us, if but once we have been strong.[5]

The deepest strength stems from flashes of sudden insight,
"spots of time," scattered throughout existence but most
frequent and compelling in unself-conscious childhood,
moments when the soul, "lost"[6] to immediate selfish concern, catches a brief intimation of some ultimate pattern, a
perdurable grandeur in the natural world or an elemental
dignity in the human gesture. The shocks to the moral
being of the young man, especially the disillusion and
despair attendant upon the collapse of the liberal cause in
revolutionary France (here the substance of a consum-
mately fine political poetry), are to be understood intellectually, as the logical consequence of responses to events in
time. But the vital impressions that become the "spots of
time"—the strange cry of the dry wind as it pins the child's
body against a craggy ridge, the illusion of the hills wheel-
ing past as the boy stops short on his skates, the sight of a

girl struggling with dreary fortitude across a moorland waste—these are to be apprehended less by the intellect than by the passionate intuition. The memory of such perceptions is the "natural piety" that binds the poet's days each to each, the child to the youth and the youth to the mature man. So described and interpreted, the "spots of time" acquire a religious significance; each is a true "epiphany," a warranty of the soul's belonging to a larger life; like the encounter with the leech-gatherer, each seems almost "a leading from above, a something given," sent by a special act of grace "from some far region."

Yet the poet, as Coleridge reminded him, receives but what he gives; the revelation, though involuntary, comes to the prepared sensibility of one with the innate endowment of an artist, and the harmony that it establishes is no less aesthetic than religious. One passage of the poem indeed makes clear that the child's reaction to a spectacle of horror could be conditioned, even transformed, by his private experience of imaginative literature; it tells how a drowned man, "with his ghastly face," was drawn by grappling irons from the quiet waters of Esthwaite, and

> yet no vulgar fear,
> Young as I was, a Child not nine years old,
> Possess'd me, for my inner eye had seen
> Such sights before, among the shining streams
> Of Fairy land, the Forests of Romance:
> Hence came a spirit hallowing what I saw
> With decoration and ideal grace;
> A dignity, a smoothness, like the works
> Of Grecian Art, and purest Poesy.[7]

Here the response of the boy is already the shaping vision of the grown poet.

Though somewhat more general and less intimate in the revised manuscripts, *The Prelude* in all its forms is a highly

personal poem, an extended confession or apologia, and as
such indeed "a thing unprecedented," at least in English
verse. But like every autobiographer, even the most fla-
grantly indiscreet, Wordsworth deliberately selected his
materials, rejected what he had no need or wish to use,
and laid particular stress on the themes of most importance
to him or to the self-portrait he chose to paint. Thus,
though he prepared a convincing record of his political
sentiments in France, he passed over his French love affair
in total silence—unless the awkwardly intrusive tale of
Vaudracour and Julia in the 1805 version is to be read as
an oblique commentary on the liaison with Annette Vallon. Those who regard the relationship as crucial in Wordsworth's development deplore its omission; Herbert Read,
for example, who saw Annette as the first cause of much
later repression and sublimation, found *The Prelude* gravely
weakened by a studied hypocrisy. But the very name of
Annette Vallon was virtually unknown to Wordsworthians,
outside the poet's family circle, until our own century; and
the essential estimate of *The Prelude* as a poem should not
have been altered by the discovery of her existence. For
the work has its own integrity and speaks to us in its own
aesthetic terms; its chronicle of youth seems neither false nor
evasive; its argument is so coherent and self-sustaining that
we do not miss its exclusions. Our enjoyment of it as a partial autobiography is undoubtedly enriched by our knowledge of such facts of the poet's life as objective scholars have
been able to determine and by our interest in his personality
and the workings of his particular genius not only here but
throughout his other poetry. Yet the final appeal of *The
Prelude,* like that of the autobiographical novels that were
to follow, lies in the author's capacity to make his development seem representative as well as idiosyncratic. Words-

worth as the prime example of what Keats called the egotistical sublime, "which is a thing per se and stands alone,"[8]
was surely conscious of his difference, of his livelier sensibility and special dedication. But the sublimity transcends
the egotism; the larger relevance of the poem lies in the bold
assumption that the "I" may speak for all humanity and
that a painstaking account of the growth of the poet's own
mind will necessarily reveal much that is characteristic of
the whole mind of man.

In effect a sort of comic counterpart to the solemn *Pre-*
lude, *Don Juan* likewise follows a young man in his progress
from boyhood to the threshold of a poised maturity.
Though iconoclastic in attitude and reductive of all ideals,
Byron's masterpiece is, in some respects, more conventional,
less "unprecedented," than Wordsworth's. Its form looks
back to the sprawling epic medleys of the Italian renaissance.
The conduct of its narrative derives in part from the
picaresque tradition. The satiric technique owes not a little
to the examples of Dryden, Pope, and Swift. The unheroic
hero is the *ingénu* like Gulliver or Candide, eventually
sophisticated by his travels through a corrupt society. Nonetheless, the poem is also a new and strikingly original work,
highly personal and to a degree even autobiographical. Juan
of course is not Byron. But Juan's mother seems to be
sketched from the poet's wife, his early reading seems more
remembered than invented, the local color of the Greek and
Turkish cantos may be traced to the grand tour of 1810,
and the Norman Abbey affectionately described in Canto
XIII is clearly Byron's ancestral Newstead. Moreover, quite
apart from such incidentals relating to Juan and his adventures, Byron himself appears in the poem, from the beginning, as narrator, the controlling voice, humorous, sardonic,
sentimental on occasion, confiding and concealing, learned,

infinitely digressive, altogether inexhaustible. Though Juan
is decidedly no poet, the narrator, self-depicted, gives us a
portrait of the artist concerned with politics and war and
women but also with art itself, the logic of burlesque, the
morality of satire, the relation of truth to poetry, and the
pitiful inadequacy of the critics who have misconstrued his
intention. This Byron, or Byronic persona, finds an irony
of detachment rather than a natural piety the surest perspective in which to view his hero, his younger self, and the
world he has intimately known. By the last cantos Juan has
begun to approximate the maturity of the narrator; he is
becoming the ironic eye turned upon the follies of an
English aristocracy. The poem stops (it could never end)
before moving far in this new direction, but not before
suggesting to us that Byron in another age might have been
a master of prose fiction, an analyst of high society comparable to Thackeray or to Proust. As it is, *Don Juan*, like
The Prelude in a quite different way, anticipated rather
than directly influenced the Victorian autobiographical
novel of youth.

　If there had been any immediate influence from the
British Romantic period, we might have expected it to be
Waverley, which indeed has recently been described—
almost as if it were another *Way of All Flesh*—as "not a
romantic novel at all but an ironic novel of a young man's
education."[9] Scott does begin *Waverley*, after a brief family
history, with an account, largely autobiographical, of his
hero's early reading; but he presents no dramatic vignettes
of Edward's childhood or any clear impression whatever
of the growing boy. He is concerned merely to show a
danger which he feared he himself might not wholly have
escaped: "the dainty, squeamish, and fastidious taste acquired by a surfeit of idle reading, had . . . rendered our

hero unfit for serious and sober study" and therefore likely to give real life, when he encountered it, a "romantic tone and colouring." Then, at the end of five short chapters, which are to him a necessary prologue, Scott reveals his true intention; he apologizes for exploring the background in what his readers may think excessive and tedious detail, but promises now to carry his story straightway "into a more picturesque and romantic country."[10] The actual plot commences—and the autobiographical component virtually vanishes—with young Captain Waverley's setting off to join his regiment, and henceforth his mental and moral "education" is far less important to us than the places he visits, the vivid men and women he meets, and the historical events in which reluctantly he finds himself taking part—the elements, in short, that make the novel memorable. For Waverley himself, though perhaps not quite the "sneaking piece of imbecility" Scott called him, is scarcely an engaging character; he is naive, low-spirited, recessive, driven only fortuitously to action. His growth is little more than the vacillation his name suggests, and his maturity brings him a possible respite from bemused indecision but no real perspicacity or depth of insight. *Waverley* makes no effort to develop significantly the theme of initiation. Scott's interest and success clearly transcend the depiction of his anemic hero.

In any case, the most familiar model for the nineteenth-century novel of education was German rather than British. It was Goethe's *Wilhelm Meisters Lehrjahre*, published between 1794 and 1796 as a reworking of *Wilhelm Meisters theatralische Sendung*, begun and abandoned some years earlier. Though only a longish fragment as it survives, the *Sendung*, or *Mission*, has, as its title might indicate, a greater unity and a more distinct purpose; it is Wilhelm's object to seek self-realization in the service of art: as actor and

later manager of a stage company, he will make of the
German theater a primary agent of cultural change. In the
finished novel this aim must compete with many other intentions and values. The *Lehrjahre* consequently is a curious
medley, without center or consistency; dull exposition and
prosy asides jostle lively scenes from Bohemian life among
the itinerant troupers; wit collides with sentiment, short
dramatic ballads with long irrelevant interpolated tales and
large tracts of cloudy occultism. Scattered throughout the
whole are many details and impressions adapted from
Goethe's own experience: a childhood delight in puppets
(Wilhelm's account of which is so circumstantial that it puts
his mistress to sleep), the tension between visionary son
and hard-headed practical father, efforts at amateur acting
and first-hand observation of the vagaries of fellow-players,
response to the esoteric rituals of freemasonry, even the
aimless, lovesick wandering through the streets by night
(where the fictional Mariana substitutes for the actual
Lili Schönemann[11] as the object of troubled affection). And
in most scenes appears Wilhelm himself, sometimes the
protagonist, more often the spectator or auditor, a young
man whom Goethe viewed with marked ambivalence, now
as simply a poor dog ("ein armer Hund"), now as his own
true likeness ("mein geliebtes dramatisches Ebenbild").[12]

Carlyle, who in 1824 translated the *Lehrjahre* as *Wilhelm
Meister's Apprenticeship*, declared in his preface that Wilhelm was "a milksop, whom, with all his gifts, it takes an
effort to avoid despising."[13] The hostility arises no doubt
partly from Carlyle's half-concealed disgust with the
amorality of the youth's amours. But Wilhelm, nonetheless,
is in many respects a weak and indecisive hero, one who
takes far longer than Wordsworth "to fix the wavering

balance" of his mind. Yet like Wordsworth, who disliked
the novel, and unlike Waverley, whom he sometimes resembles, Wilhelm does have an active mind, and he speaks it often
and at length. Goethe undercuts with irony some of his
long sententious speeches, but the ideas in them are frequently Goethe's own and therefore to be heard with respect. Wilhelm is self-conscious, almost to the point of absurdity, in his quest for self-culture; he carefully weighs his
obligations to himself, as when he decides to join the players
on their visit to the count's castle: "Wilhelm, who had come
from home to study men, was unwilling to let slip this opportunity of examining the great world, where he expected
to obtain much insight into life, into himself, and the dramatic art."[14] Like the young Goethe's, his is the artistic
temperament, eager to achieve independence and self-expression, impatient with his father's mercantile mentality
and contemptuous of all deadening devotion to Commerce,
which in an early poem he has personified as "a shrivelled,
wretched-looking sibyl."[15]

Nonetheless, Wilhelm's "apprenticeship" to the stage
eventually proves, like Goethe's own dream of a vocation
in the plastic arts, a quite misdirected ambition. Wilhelm
does make an effective romantic Hamlet, perhaps because
the character, as he (or Goethe) conceives and projects it, is
so like his own. But soon after his production of the play,
he is willing to abandon the stage altogether in the belief
that his histrionic talents are strictly limited. And the theater
he rejects suddenly becomes an allegory of all the illusions
of his troubled youth. The true apprenticeship, we then see,
is spiritual rather than professional. When he has served his
term, he is formally released; through many dark passages,
he has been led into the light; and a mysterious abbé salutes
him, "Hail to thee, young man! Thy Apprenticeship is

done: Nature has pronounced thee free."[16] For the agency of his salvation, he learns, is a veritable *deus ex machina*, a secret society, emissaries of which, sent out from mountain fastnesses, have watched over and guided him since his boyhood. Wilhelm, who has known himself guilty of willful error, has actually been predestined to succeed; he is now prepared to move from conscious self-culture to a spontaneous understanding of life, and accordingly is ready for his initiation into the brotherhood of the elect. But as the novel follows him through new snarls of relationships and much windy rhetoric, it sacrifices most of its appealing realism to an abstract and unconvincing philosophy. Schiller was displeased with the denouement, and most later readers have found it unsatisfactory. Goethe, by way of elucidation, told Eckermann that "the whole work seems to say nothing more than that man, despite all his follies and errors, being led by a higher hand, reaches some happy goal at last."[17] Carlyle, however, with a greater irony and a dash of healthy skepticism, suggested that to less perceptive and less Germanic souls the intention and effect of the *Apprenticeship* would remain forever uncertain; few could ever decide "whether this is a light, airy sketch of the development of man in all his endowments and faculties, gradually proceeding from the first rude exhibitions of puppets and mountebanks, through the perfection of poetic and dramatic art, up to the unfolding of the principle of religion, and the greatest of all arts,—the art of life,—or is nothing more than a bungled piece of patchwork, presenting in the shape of a novel much that should have been suppressed entirely, or at least given out by way of lecture."[18]

Still, whatever its structural weakness or ambiguity of tone, *Wilhelm Meister* has established itself in literary history as the prototype of the Bildungsroman. Though that term was not in common usage until quite late in the nineteenth century, the genre was already popular in Germany among the Romantics and in England by the time of the early Victorians. The Bildungsroman in its pure form has been defined as the "novel of all-around development or self-culture" with "a more or less conscious attempt on the part of the hero to integrate his powers, to cultivate himself by his experience."[19] And the origins of its characteristic hero have been traced to a number of conventions and traditions: to the hero of the old moral allegories, to the picaresque hero who in his travels meets all sorts and conditions of men, to the Parzival figure learning slowly through his trials, to the "Renaissance man" bent on exercising to the full his many talents. In Germany the Bildungsroman soon produced several clearly marked variants: the *Entwicklungsroman*, a chronicle of a young man's general growth rather than his specific quest for self-culture; the *Erziehungsroman*, with an emphasis on the youth's training and formal education; and the *Künstlerroman*, a tale of the orientation of an artist. In England these categories have been far less rigid; the pursuit of self-culture has hardly ever been so deliberate or programmatic, and the process of education, though schooling may play a major role in it, has seldom begun or ended with prescribed courses of study. Moreover, the English Bildungsroman—I now use the label in its broadest sense as a convenient synonym for the novel of youth or apprenticeship—has also frequently been a kind of *Künstlerroman*. Its hero, more often than not, emerges as an artist of sorts, a prose writer like David Copperfield or Ernest Pontifex, a poet like Stephen Dedalus, an artisan and aspiring intellectual like Hardy's Jude, a painter like Lawrence's Paul Morel or Maugham's Philip Carey. Insofar as the word *Bildung* itself is related to *Bild* and *Bildnis*, it may connote "picture" or "portrait" as well as "shaping" or "formation"; and the Bildungsroman may then typically become what Joyce's title promises, *A Portrait of the Artist as a Young Man*, or rather, as Joyce develops his material, a study of the inner life, the essential temper, of the artist in his progress from early childhood through adolescence. In such novels, as certainly in Joyce's, the "artist" in question is often not far removed from the novelist, or at least from the novelist as he remembers himself to have been in his formative youth.

Though the Bildungsroman attracted many fewer writers in nineteenth-century France than in Germany or England,[20] the work of Stendhal deserves attention as an anticipation of later developments in the genre, especially the increase in autobiographical self-consciousness and the sharpening of focus on the motivation of the hero. From the beginning of his career in Paris, Stendhal was absorbed in the contemplation of his own personality; he made regular and copious notes on his conduct and appetites, measured his virtues and vices with a cold dispassion, catechized himself, communed with himself, and adopted in life and literature innumerable roles, aliases, and pseudonyms to express and exhibit himself and at the same time to conceal what he feared to betray. Through autobiography and fiction, and both commingling, he sought to create a coherent and intelligible self-image. His *Vie de Henry Brulard*, a detailed account of his own childhood and adolescence, achieves much of the detachment and objectivity of a novel —and it has indeed been considered the only real Bildungsroman of the century in France.[21] By irony and self-mockery Stendhal is able to view his past self as another person, yet one that in every way predicts his present being. Henry must despise his father, rebel against him, and turn to his

maternal grandfather, in order to establish a more congenial lineage and a prouder identity. He must insist on his
loneliness as a child, his distance from other boys, his greater
sensitivity to suffering, and his awareness of social hypocrisies, if he is to emerge eventually as the wise, humane
cynic who is the fifty-three-year-old Henry Brulard, who in
turn is Stendhal, whose real name was Henri Beyle. The
mature Brulard, obviously an artist in words, can pause
frequently to comment on the style as well as the substance
of his memoir; he seems, in the act of writing, to be creating
as much as recording his own life. The literal facts, he himself is the first to admit, may have been distorted or mis-
remembered; but all that matters ultimately to him is the
larger truth to temperament.

In *The Red and the Black,* where the direct autobiographical element is relatively small,[22] a similar temperament dominates the whole dramatic action. We first meet
Julien Sorel as a slim youth of eighteen, perched precariously, book in hand, above the rafters of a mill shed,
whence he is suddenly and cruelly routed by a clout on
the head from his illiterate father. (Alienation from his
father will lead him to adopt substitutes, the Abbé Pirard[23]
and others, and finally to imagine himself the illegitimate
son of some unknown aristocrat, a man nobler far in blood
and spirit than Sorel the carpenter.) Though we are told
little of Julien's childhood, we readily gather that literature
has long provided his one release from perpetual misery
and that an aptitude for study has spurred his ambition
to escape bodily from his home town, Verrières, and all
its crass venality and stifling false pieties. Eventually, after
the experience of adulterous love and the discipline of a
provincial seminary, he does set out for Paris, convinced
that at last he is "going to make his debut on the stage of the

great world."[24] In the city he assumes the role of the sophisticated dandy, suave, poised, possessed of an urbane hauteur
which he will preserve until the end when, on trial for his
life in Besançon, he will archly deride his country-bourgeois
accusers.[25] From the moment of his arrival in Paris, however, he has had few illusions about the manners and morals
of the beau monde; he recognizes its weakness, corruption,
and elegant inanity and is prepared to manipulate them to
his own advantage and advancement. The shrewd Marquis
de la Mole is quick to detect Julien's distinction: "Other
provincials coming to Paris admire everything, thought the
marquis; this one hates everything. They have too much
affectation, *he* has too little; and the fools take him for a
fool." Julien is in fact "an unhappy man at war with the
whole society." But to maintain his perspective on the general folly and to mask his own vulnerability, he is willing,
like Don Juan in England, to play the hypocrite and to
analyze his motives: "Yes, it will be amusing to cover with
ridicule that odious being I call 'me.' If I had faith in my
own impulses, I would commit some crime to distract myself."[26] Throughout the novel Byron's poem, which supplies more chapter epigraphs than any other source,[27] is
very much in Stendhal's mind; and Byron's unheroic hero,
especially as in the late cantos he approaches the condition
of Byron himself, provides a model of nonchalance, wit,
self-protective irony, and freedom from provinciality.[28]
However vicious some aspects of his egoism may be, Julien
in final adversity exhibits the signal virtue of self-possession. On his last day, permitted to walk briefly in the bright
sun, he is able to tell himself, "Well, then, everything's
going to be all right; I have no lack of courage."[29] If he has
learned nothing else in his sad, brief, ambitious career, he
has at least discovered the importance of self-assertion,

indeed self-creation, through defiant action and courageous gesture. Like Byron, like Stendhal himself, Julien is the existentialist to whom life's meaning, if it is to have meaning, must lie in the gallant response to the absurd challenge.

Wilhelm Meister and *The Red and the Black* differ sharply in manner and matter from each other and from the English Bildungsromane that followed—from *Great Expectations*, for example, or *The Way of All Flesh* or *Sons and Lovers*, each of which in turn has its own distinctive style and substance. Yet from all these books and many others we may abstract the broad outlines of a typical Bildungsroman plot and so determine the principal characteristics of the genre. A child of some sensibility grows up in the country or in a provincial town, where he finds constraints, social and intellectual, placed upon the free imagination. His family, especially his father, proves doggedly hostile to his creative instincts or flights of fancy, antagonistic to his ambitions, and quite impervious to the new ideas he has gained from unprescribed reading. His first schooling, even if not totally inadequate, may be frustrating insofar as it may suggest options not available to him in his present setting. He therefore, sometimes at a quite early age, leaves the repressive atmosphere of home (and also the relative innocence), to make his way independently in the city (in the English novels, usually London). There his real "education" begins, not only his preparation for a career but also —and often more importantly—his direct experience of urban life. The latter involves at least two love affairs or sexual encounters, one debasing, one exalting, and demands that in this respect and others the hero reappraise his values. By the time he has decided, after painful soul-searching, the sort of accommodation to the modern world he can honestly make, he has left his adolescence behind and entered upon his maturity. His initiation complete, he may then visit his old home, to demonstrate by his presence the degree of his success or the wisdom of his choice.

No single novel, of course, precisely follows this pattern. But none that ignores more than two or three of its principal elements—childhood, the conflict of generations, provinciality, the larger society, self-education, alienation, ordeal by love, the search for a vocation and a working philosophy—answers the requirements of the Bildungsroman as I am here seeking to describe and define it. Thus *Lord Jim* and *Emma, The Old Wives' Tale* and *The Ambassadors, Tom Jones* and *The Egoist,* though each splendidly develops some of the characteristic themes, all belong essentially to other categories of the novel. Yet, when we have made all such necessary exclusions, we still have left for consideration a large and impressive body of fiction, remarkable for its freshness and variety, both of style and content, within the recognizable genre.

In the dedication to his autobiographical *Sinister Street* (which carries as its epigraph the passage by Keats about childhood, manhood, and the space between), Compton Mackenzie defended the great length at which he had explored his hero's growth. "Yet are a thousand pages," he asked, "too long for the history of twenty-five years of a man's life, that is to say if one holds as I hold that childhood makes the instrument, youth tunes the strings, and early manhood plays the melody?"[30] After all, he insisted later, he had carefully picked and chosen among his memories: "If I were to set down all I could remember of my childhood, the book could not by this time have reached much beyond my fifth year." His intention, he said, was "not to write a life, but the prologue of a life,"[31] and the conditioning of childhood was clearly of first importance in his hero's development. To Byron, as to Fielding, the young child was little more than the small adult. To the authors of the Bildungsromane, as to Wordsworth, the child was an entity in himself responsive to experiences that might alter the entire direction of his growing mind and eventually influence for better or for worse his whole maturity. Not until the psychology of the child was taken seriously as an appropriate literary concern was the writing of the English Bildungsromane a possible enterprise.

The growing child, as he appears in these novels, more often than not will be orphaned or at least fatherless, like David Copperfield, Pip, Jude, Pater's Marius, George Ponderevo in *Tono-Bungay*, Philip Carey in *Of Human Bondage*, and Sammy Mountjoy in *Free Fall*. But if not deprived by death of a father, who presumably would have been a true guide and protector, he will almost certainly be repelled, like Richard Feverel and Stephen Dedalus and Paul Morel, by a living father who mistrusts and seeks to thwart his strongest drives and fondest desires. "A man," says Ernest Pontifex (when he has learned to talk like Samuel Butler), "first quarrels with his father about three-quarters of a year before he is born. It is then he insists on setting up a separate establishment. When this has been once agreed to, the more complete the separation forever after the better for both."[32] The loss of the father, either by death or alienation, usually symbolizes or parallels a loss of faith in the values of the hero's home and family and leads inevitably to the search for a substitute parent or creed, such as Julien Sorel expects to find in his mentors or Wilhelm Meister discovers in the masonic secret society. The defection of the father becomes accordingly the principal motive force in the assertion of the youth's independence. It links him immediately with the traditional heroes of romance and folklore, the exiled Joseph and the boy David, Romulus and Oedipus, Aladdin and Jack the Giant-Killer, each of whom, fatherless, must make his own way resolutely through the forests of experience.

The journey from home is also in some degree the flight from provinciality. But the English hero is much less aggressive than his French counterpart, "the young man from the provinces"[33] like Julian Sorel or the ruthless, self-seeking Eugène Rastignac of Balzac's *Père Goriot*. He first enters the city, as Pip or Ernest or Jude does, with bewilderment and naiveté; and the city plays a double role in his life: it is both the agent of liberation and a source of corruption. In nineteenth-century English poetry the city is likewise an ambiguous symbol. It may stand as a citadel of light, like Tennyson's Camelot, the protest of a civilization against wilderness, barbarism, and bestiality. But more often it may be the dark hell of James Thomson's City of Dreadful Night. In *The Prelude* the young Wordsworth finds London a crowded and exciting panorama of modern society, but also a lonely and strangely insubstantial place, a Bartholomew Fair, all illusion and confusion, in fact not unlike T. S. Eliot's urban Waste Land, "Unreal City, . . . I had not thought death had undone so many." In the Bildungsromane the city, which seems to promise infinite variety and newness, all too often brings a disenchantment more alarming and decisive than any dissatisfaction with the narrowness of provincial life.

The novel of youth, at least in the Victorian period, is frequently the equivalent of the Renaissance conduct book, insofar as one of its recurrent themes is the making of a gentleman. But in the busy world of middle-class progress the gentlemanly ideal becomes increasingly difficult to discover or define; struggle for survival in the atomistic modern city is hardly conducive to good manners and quiet consideration of others; the urban is seldom the urbane. In the jargon of the time, to "make good" is to make money;[34] and the gentleman, especially if his resources are limited, commands less respect than the financial "success."[35] Money therefore assumes a new and pervasive importance in the Bildungsroman. If Richard Feverel and Harry Richmond can take a considerable wealth for granted, most of the other heroes from Pip and Jude to Stephen Dedalus and Sammy Mountjoy must resist, sometimes ineffectually, the menace of a real poverty. The "great expectations" of Dickens's title are more or less delusive "prospects of inheritance."[36] A bankruptcy is central to the plot of *The Mill on the Floss*. Money-worries plague the Morel family in *Sons and Lovers*. And reckless speculation brings the collapse of Uncle Teddy's empire in *Tono-Bungay*. Mr. Overton, the narrator of *The Way of All Flesh*, who declares money more desirable than health or reputation and believes the loss of money the root of all evil, withholds Aunt Alethea's legacy until Ernest is mature enough to appreciate a beautifully managed portfolio. Goethe long before commented that his Wilhelm had been foolish to remain indifferent to his property and money: "He knew not that it is the manner of all persons who attach importance to their inward cultivation altogether to neglect their outward circumstances. This had been Wilhelm's case: he now for the first time seemed to notice, that, to work effectively, he stood in need of outward means."[37] Most of the later heroes, however, are less able than Wilhelm or Ernest to reconcile the outward and the inward, to see how the processes of money-making contribute to their true enrichment of spirit. The sensitivity that made for childhood alienation from father and home leads many to the larger repudiation of a materialistic society. The bitterness of Michael Fane in *Sinister Street* differs in degree rather than kind from a quite common disillusion; pondering the fate of a murderer, once his friend, Michael turns his rage and frustration against the whole money-driven urban world (and his mood seems doubly ominous when we remember that *Sinister Street* appeared in 1914): "Meats had sinned against the hive: this infernal hive, herd, pack, swarm, whichever word he felt to be the degradation of an independent existence. Mankind was become a great complication of machinery fed by gold and directed by fear. Something was needed to destroy this gregarious organism. War and pestilence must come. . . ."[38]

If he survives his trial by parents, by money, by the city, the hero, like the knights of the old romances, may still have to undergo further testing before his initiation is completed. "Love of any object," Sir Austin Feverel tells Richard, "is the soul's ordeal; and [women] are ours, loving them, or not." But Richard's ordeal is largely self-induced—by his wilful neglect of love and his determined dabbling in passion. And the central conflict in nearly every other Bildungsroman is likewise personal in origin; the problem lies with the hero himself. Thus David Copperfield has an errant heart, and Pip misdirects his ambitions and affections. Ernest Pontifex like Wilhelm Meister at first misconceives his vocation.[39] George Ponderevo is willing to abandon scientific truth for the promotion of the fraudulent Tono-Bungay. And Sammy Mountjoy deliberately compromises his freedom when he lets himself be governed by a selfish lust. Yet each of these young men experiences privileged moments of insight, epiphanies, spots of time, when the reality of things breaks through the fog of delusion. And each then feels a responsibility for change of heart and conduct. For each is what we should now call "inner-directed"; each is guided by a sense of duty to the self and to others, a sense perhaps inculcated or sharpened by parents and childhood conditioning, and perhaps never freely admitted, but nonetheless remaining latent and strong through all the rebellions of adolescence.

Yet even when he sees the error of his ways and judgments, the hero is by no means guaranteed a resolution to his problems at all comparable to the joyous denouement of *Wilhelm Meister*. Like *The Red and the Black*, some of the Bildungsromane—*The Mill on the Floss, Marius the Epicurean, Jude the Obscure, Jacob's Room*—end with the death of the protagonist. Others, like *The Ordeal of Richard Feverel* or *Tono-Bungay*, leave us speculating on the defeat of all positive emotion. Perhaps most—*Great Expectations, A Portrait of the Artist, Free Fall*, for example—conclude more or less uncertainly, with an open question about the hero's final choice. Only a few—*David Copperfield, The Way of All Flesh*, and *Of Human Bondage*—reach a recognizably happy ending. And of the last of these books, Somerset Maugham himself admitted that readers had found the ending "the least satisfactory part." Such a criticism should have been no surprise, for the marriage of the unfortunate Philip to a pleasantly robust Sally violates the logic of the plot; it is a wish-fulfillment introduced from without: "Turning my wishes into fiction, as writers will," Maugham confessed, "towards the end of it I drew a picture of the marriage I should have liked to make."[40]

Here we have a clue to the common difficulty of ending a Bildungsroman with conviction and decision. Like *Of Human Bondage*, the typical novel of youth is strongly autobiographical and therefore subject at any time to intrusions from areas of the author's experience beyond the dramatic limits of the fiction. As a rule it is a first or second book in which the novelist is still very close to his orientation, often indeed too close to achieve an adequate perspective. Since his career is still in progress, perhaps only beginning, he can hardly be sure that the initiation of a hero in many ways so like himself has been an unqualified success. He may, therefore, choose to leave the hero's future ambiguous; he may, in a sort of self-justification, seek to reward the hero beyond his deserts; or, again, he may evade the problem altogether by bringing the hero to an untimely death. But whatever course he follows, he will not find it easy to give his novel a cogent and organic ending.

There are of course many degrees of identification between author and hero and of detachment from each other. In his comments on *Of Human Bondage*, Maugham makes a distinction we should bear in mind when approaching any Bildungsroman: "It is not an autobiography, but an autobiographical novel; fact and fiction are inextricably mingled; the emotions are my own, but not all the incidents are related as they happened and some of them are transferred to my hero not from my own life but from that of persons with whom I was intimate."[41] As the ending of that book demonstrates, the involvement of the personal emotions of the novelist can impair the integrity of a novel. But it can also, if properly controlled, lend a peculiar vibrancy to character, setting, and incident. Maugham was right in believing that the last quarter of *The Red and the Black* suffers by its return to the objective, impersonal facts that originally suggested the story, for as soon as Stendhal feels bound by the given, he seems much less .ree to project the wonderfully real imaginary young man, derived largely from himself, who is Julian Sorel.

It is sometimes difficult, however, to draw a sharp line

THE SPACE BETWEEN 25

between autobiography and the autobiographical novel. *The Education of Henry Adams*, written in the third person and carefully shaped in contrived patterns, has much of the irony and detachment we normally associate with fiction; and Edmund Gosse's *Father and Son*, developed in vivid vignettes and dramatic episodes, even with snatches of dialogue, bears most of the earmarks of the Bildungsroman. Conrad's *Youth*, on the other hand, a tale narrated by Marlow (though actually "a piece of personal experience"),[42] is closer in tone to a memoir than to a novel. Looking back from an achieved maturity, Marlow speaks of his subject with a warm nostalgia: "I remember the drawn faces, the dejected figures of my two men, and I remember my youth and the feeling that will never come back any more—the feeling that I could last for ever, outlast the sea, the earth, and all men; the deceitful feeling that lures us on to joys, to perils, to love, to vain effort—to death; the triumphant conviction of strength, the heat of life in the handful of dust, the glow in the heart that with every year grows dim, grows cold, grows small, and expires—and expires, too soon, too soon—before life itself."[43]

But these are exceptions. The autobiographer is typically the older man, like Marlow, indulging in fond retrospect, often more than a little sentimental in his view of his youth, recalling what it pleases him to remember. The autobiographical novelist is usually a younger man, nearer in time to his initiation, self-protectively more ironic, still mindful of the growing pains of adolescence, reproducing as accurately as possible the turbulence of the space between childhood and early manhood. The autobiographer must account, at least to himself, for the omissions from his life story; he must be to a considerable degree self-conscious—through modesty, through fear of unwanted self-exposure,

through the desire not to be judged excessively egotistical;
and he must know that he can paint only a partial self-
portrait, for he can describe his experience only from his
own point of view, and his life changes even as he records
it. The autobiographical novelist is patently freer to conceal or reveal what he will of his past by assigning to his
hero some of his own acts and feelings and inventing as
many others as he chooses to complete a dramatic characterization. He thus has a distinct advantage over the direct
autobiographer. But he has a special responsibility as a
novelist to make his book aesthetically independent of its
author. Both the strength and the weakness of the Bildungsroman, insofar as it is subjective at all (and very few examples of the genre are not), lie in its autobiographical
component. It gains in immediacy and authenticity from the
novelist's intimate knowledge of his materials. It suffers
whenever the novelist's engagement leads to special pleading for a self-interest outside the frame of the fiction or
when the motivation of the hero is determined by forces
in the novelist's experience for some reason excluded from
the novel. In such cases, we must know something of the
author's life, as the most objective of his biographers have
been able to present it, if we are adequately to understand
and appraise his book.

Whereas Wordsworth had declared *The Prelude* "unprecedented" in its subjectivity, Walter Pater, writing
Marius the Epicurean some eighty years later, claimed that
it was one of his hero's "modernisms" to keep a diary or
journal in which he might confess to himself his private
thoughts and feelings. In the interim between the poem and
the novel there appeared innumerable examples in both
verse and prose of what Matthew Arnold was calling "the
dialogue of the mind with itself," a new and unabashedly

subjective literature. Perhaps the most successful of the autobiographical forms, because the most oblique and richly creative, was the Bildungsroman, which attracted most of the major Victorian novelists and a number of their twentieth-century successors. An examination of some representative Bildungsromane from about 1850 to the present should indicate how each writer in turn learned to accommodate a powerful personal vision to the developing conventions of the genre. And it should uncover, along the way, some fresh perceptions of the unpredictable vitality of youth.

⋅ẟ II ỗ⋅

DICKENS, DAVID AND PIP

On reading the first number of *David Copperfield* in May 1849, Thackeray wrote enthusiastically to Mrs. Brookfield: "O it is charming. Bravo Dickens. It has some of his very prettiest touches—those inimitable Dickens touches which make such a great man of him." His satisfaction, however, was not entirely disinterested, for he professed himself pleased to think that Dickens—though, of course, without acknowledgment—had been "copying, . . . taking a lesson from Vanity Fair" on how to improve his style by "foregoing the use of fine words." Nonetheless, the new serial seemed good enough in itself to put him upon his mettle and remind him that he must now look to his own "fame and name." "It's beautiful," he told William Brookfield; "it beats the yellow chap of this month hollow."[1]

The yellow chap was *Pendennis*, which had been appearing since the previous November. A forerunner of *David Copperfield* in some respects other than simply date of inception (Dickens's book was actually completed a few weeks earlier), *Pendennis* has been called "the first true *Bildungsroman* in English fiction."[2] And indeed it has many elements of the genre. It is Thackeray's effort to evoke the spirit of his own youth—though scarcely the letter, for the direct autobiography,[3] limited to memories of persons and places and occasional strokes of self-portraiture, does not

28

extend to decisive acts or crises of emotion. Insofar as he "develops" at all during a prolonged and protected adolescence, Pen moves from a naive provinciality to a bland worldliness, a Thackerayan acceptance of human nature and society: "I take the world as it is," he complacently reminds his friend Warrington, "and being of it, will not be ashamed of it. If the time is out of joint, have I any calling or strength to set it right?"[4] But, whatever it may have meant to Thackeray, Pen's attitude is less an earned philosophy than a ready rationalization of passivity and self-indulgence.

Though it presents a host of engaging minor characters and a good many animated episodes, *Pendennis* achieves no sustained focus on either hero or theme; it is in fact a singularly uneven novel. During its composition Thackeray had grown tired and listless ("My work," he said, "shows my dullness"), before the first magical chapters of *David Copperfield* drove him "to fetch up [his] languishing reputation."[5] Thereupon he introduced Pen to the rowdy realm of London journalism as he himself had first known it in the early 1830's; and the pulse of his narrative immediately quickened. Its progress, however, was abruptly halted, when his tale was less than half told, by a grave illness that forced him to suspend publication for three months. When he began again, he had difficulty in giving the serial its former vitality, and he more and more subordinated an interest in Pen's character to a concern with the intricacies of contrived plotting.

Much of the problem throughout the novel lies in Thackeray's sense of severe inhibition. When we first meet him, Pen is already seventeen years old; we are given no dramatic impression of a formative childhood; we are introduced, as at the beginning of *Wilhelm Meister*, to a

young man launched on his amorous career by a sentimental
entanglement with an actress. But we are warned, by the
preface to the finished book, not to expect a full or realistic
account of a young man's conduct: "You will not hear—it is
best to know it—what moves in the real world, what passes
in society, in the clubs, colleges, mess-rooms,—what is the
life and talk of your sons." Thackeray's claim that *Pendennis*, though it may "fail in art," has "the advantage of a
certain truth and honesty" is somewhat weakened by his
admission that "since the author of 'Tom Jones' was buried,
no writer of fiction among us has been permitted to depict
to his utmost power a MAN. We must drape him, and give
him a certain conventional simper. Society will not tolerate
the Natural in our Art."[6] Though intended to disarm
criticism, such a complaint does not encourage our confidence in the hero's credibility. Realism in fiction is at best
only approximate; but the successful Bildungsroman,
whether Victorian or modern, must not suggest that the
novelist feels seriously constrained by the conventions of his
time. In the last analysis the appeal of *Pendennis* has little
to do with the character of Pen.

The preface to *David Copperfield* is altogether different
in tone and purpose. Dickens has apparently worked with
zest at each successive number, and now, having completed
his serial, he is torn between pleasure and regret, "pleasure
in the achievement of a long design, regret in the separation from many companions." He has no apologies to make.
He confesses only his solid commitment to his subject matter, for "no one can ever believe this Narrative, in the
reading, more than [he] believed it in the writing." And
he knows, he says, that an author must feel "as if he were
dismissing some portion of himself into the shadowy world,

when a crowd of the creatures of his brain are going from him
for ever." This last comment is perhaps deliberately ambiguous: it may suggest not only the author's engagement
with his characters, but also his concern with materials of
a more personal significance. That the second meaning is at
least implicit, we may gather from a letter of October 1850
to his friend John Forster, where Dickens describes in similar imagery his coming to the end: "I am within three pages
of the shore; and am strangely divided, as usual in such
cases, between sorrow and joy. Oh, my dear Forster, if I
were to say half of what Copperfield makes me feel to-
night, how strangely, even to you, I should be turned inside
out! I seem to be sending some part of myself into the
Shadowy World."[7] The only clue in the novel itself to anything so private might have been a clause in small type on
the cover of each number: "Which He never meant to be
Published on any Account." But the "He" here of course
is not Dickens; it is David Copperfield the Younger of
Blunderstone Rookery, who is the modest narrator of his
own story.

The manuscript that Dickens himself "never meant to be
published on any account," at least during his lifetime, was
an autobiography begun several years before the novel[8]
and abandoned when it stirred memories too painful to
explore. After Dickens's death Forster printed enough of
the fragment to disclose the well-kept secret that the
wretchedness of David Copperfield at Murdstone and
Grinby's had had its close parallel in the novelist's own
despair when he had been consigned as a child to Warren's
blacking-warehouse:

> The deep remembrance of the sense I had of being utterly ne-
> glected and hopeless; of the shame I felt in my position; of the
> misery it was to my young heart to believe that, day by day,

what I had learned, and thought, and delighted in, and raised my
fancy up by, was passing away from me, never to be brought
back any more; cannot be written. . . . That I suffered in secret,
and that I suffered exquisitely, no one ever knew but I. How
much I suffered, it is, as I have said already, utterly beyond my
power to tell. No man's imagination can overstep the reality.
But I kept my own counsel, and i did my work. . . . For many
years, when I came near to Robert Warren's in the Strand, I
crossed over to the opposite side of the way, to avoid a certain
smell of the cement they put upon the blacking-corks, which
reminded me of what I was once.[9]

With only the slightest verbal change, or none at all, a good
many such passages found their way into the eleventh chapter of *David Copperfield*, where the dramatic context might
disguise their subjective origin.

Innumerable smaller details in the novel—David's childhood readings, for example, or his schooling at Salem
House Academy, which was actually Wellington House—
can be likewise traced to Dickens's own life. But only one
other experience, David's courtship of Dora, had apparently
a personal significance at all comparable in intensity to the
episode of the warehouse. Dora, pretty, flirtatious, demanding, spoiled by much attention, clearly derives from Dickens's first love, Maria Beadnell, estranged long since from
him by parental interference, petulance, and misunderstand-
ing. Twenty-two years after the separation and over four
years after the completion of *David Copperfield*, Dickens
confessed to Maria, by that time a matronly Mrs. Winter,
that the novel contained "a faithful reflection of the passion" he had once had for her. "People," he wrote, "used to
say to me [of David and Dora] how pretty all that was, and
how fanciful it was, and how elevated it was above the little
foolish loves of very young men and women. But they little
thought what reason I had to know it was true and nothing

more nor less."[10] And in a letter of about the same date to Forster, who had questioned the warmth of the relationship, he affirmed rather testily the strength of his past feelings for Maria. "No one," he insisted, "can imagine in the most distant degree what pain the recollection gave me in Copperfield. And, just as I can never open that book as I open any other book, I cannot see the face (even at four-and-forty), or hear the voice, without going wandering away over the ashes of all that youth and hope in the wildest manner."[11] Of the autobiographical sources of the fiction, we scarcely need more explicit testimony.

Nonetheless, though their lives touch at many points, David Copperfield is clearly not Charles Dickens. Neither as children nor as adults, except perhaps in their habits of observation, are they at all alike in temperament.[12] David, too, ultimately becomes a novelist; but we cannot imagine his ever becoming the restless inventive genius prepared, like Dickens, to announce, "I am the modern embodiment of the old Enchanters, whose Familiars tore them to pieces. I weary of rest, and have no satisfaction but in fatigue."[13] As the reversal of initials might imply, David is his creator's counterpart rather than his double; he is as quiet, serene, gentle, and self-effacing as Dickens was passionate, excitable, and aggressive. Though he also suffers intensely as a child, David transcends his miseries and bears few lasting scars. His experience is ordered in a positive direction; the grim yields to the hopeful. Thus his schooling under the sadistic Mr. Creakle and his servitude at Murdstone and Grinby's *precede* his happy days at the idealized academy of Dr. Strong, whereas the school to which Dickens was sent after his release from Warren's warehouse was considerably inferior to the one he had attended before his great humiliation. Unlike Dickens, David never for long feels abandoned and betrayed by father and mother; for, though an orphan, he is given a memorable series of substitute parents, from the evil Murdstones to the altogether good, gruff Aunt Betsey. In the novel, passages of fresh objective creativity mingle with the painful autobiographical fragments describing the blacking factory, and the light of comedy begins to dispel the darker shadows of self-pity: the irrepressible Wilkins Micawber, whose improvidence is above and beyond all recrimination, replaces the ineffectual John Dickens, who suggested his character but who himself could be remembered only with a measure of unforgiving resentment. David's detached view of the Micawbers in their perpetual difficulties diverts him from self-absorption at a time of crisis and so prepares him, when deliverance seems possible, to leave the warehouse behind without a smoldering sense of rancor and injustice. Later David is spared the frustration Dickens had known on parting from Maria; he is permitted to marry Dora. And even when Dora proves as incompetent a housekeeper as Dickens thought his own wife, Kate, and David knows that his marriage is a failure, he remains far tenderer and more patient than Dickens ever could have been in similar circumstances.[14]

David Copperfield, then, is to be read as David's autobiography, not Dickens's. Some of the trial titles sent to Forster suggest the literary tradition to which the first-person narrative should be related: *The Copperfield Disclosures, The Copperfield Confessions, The Last Will and Testament of Mr. David Copperfield*. Another, however, *The Copperfield Survey of the World as It Rolled*,[15] might seem to us more accurate, for David's personal confessions and disclosures occupy but a small part of a long book, and we are less immediately struck by them than by the gentle irony and good humor with which he introduces us to the people and places he has observed in the rolling world. From the beginning he feels compelled to account for an extraordinary, indeed quite Dickensian capacity as observer: "If it should appear from anything I may set down in this narrative that I was a child of close observation, or that as a man I have a strong memory of my childhood, I undoubtedly lay claim to both of these characteristics."[16] Though the novel is never egotistical, "I" and "My" dominate the early chapter headings, and in the first half of the novel the narrator is indeed usually at the center of the action; but in the last half, where the first person rarely enters the titles, David sometimes seems to have become simply the recessive spectator. Yet we miss the point if we forget that *David Copperfield* is designed as a Bildungsroman and fail to see that almost every character and incident may have some final relation to the development of the hero.

Like Wordsworth in *The Prelude*, David presents his autobiography as the product of a powerful memory working over his experience from childhood to early maturity. Though the suffering at Murdstone and Grinby's proves less traumatic than its parallel in Dickens's life, David describes it as something quite unforgettable: "I now approach a period . . . which I can never lose the remembrance of, while I remember anything; and the recollection of which has often, without my invocation, come before me like a ghost, and haunted happier times." Later, writing of the Yarmouth storm and the death of Steerforth, he confronts an ever-present reality: "As plainly as I behold what happened, I will try to write it down. I do not recall it, but see it done; for it happens again before me." The strength of the memories derives from the vividness of the original sense impressions; what has been observed intensely becomes forever a part of the observer. Thus sound, sight, and smell recreate the scene of David's mother's funeral:

> If the funeral had been yesterday, I could not recollect it better. The very air of the best parlour, when I went in at the door, the bright condition of the fire, the shining of the wine in the decanters, the pattern of the glasses and the plates, the faint sweet smell of cake, the odour of Miss Murdstone's dress, and our black clothes. Mr. Chillip is in the room, and comes to speak to me.[17]

Often, as in Proust—though David's effort at recall requires no Proustian deliberation—the present impression will help recover the buried past. The scent of a geranium leaf strikes David "with a half comical, half serious wonder as to what change has come over [him] in a moment," for it brings back years later a vision of Dora in a straw hat with blue ribbons, and a little black dog in her arms, against a bank of bright blossoms. And the splash of the rain on the road by the Wickfield house reminds him, on his return after long absence, of the mood in which he once used to regard vagrants limping into town on wet evenings, a mood "fraught, as then, with the smell of damp earth, and wet leaves and briar, and the sensation of the very airs that blew upon [him] in [his] own toilsome journey."[18] Such moments of recollection are virtually "spots of time," suggesting to David a unity, or at least a continuity, amid all the diversity of his experience.

Occasionally the pressure of the present impression is so intense that it, too, seems to him a sort of memory of some lost larger life, carrying with it a sense of *déjà vu*, "a feeling . . . of what we are saying and doing having been said and done before, in a remote time—of our having been surrounded, dim ages ago, by the same faces, objects, and

circumstances—of our knowing perfectly well what will
be said next, as if we suddenly remembered it!"[19] The feeling, twice related to the fleeting awareness that he has
neglected or misunderstood Agnes Wickfield, is accom-
panied by a certain bewilderment, a half-conscious sense
of misdirection, intimating that he has misread the signposts
of his life. David has much of the poet's sensibility, a delight
in sensuous concretions, a fascination with the miracle
of memory, but he shows nothing of Wordsworth's concern
for the development of the artist as such or the shaping of
an aesthetic theory. His autobiography describes the education, through time remembered, of the affections; his
growth lies in the ordering of his "undisciplined heart."

David experiences a moment of great qualitative depth, a
half-understood troubling self-revelation, when he hears
Annie Strong's defense of her marriage to the elderly
schoolmaster. Annie might at one time, she confesses, have
given herself to the indolent, self-seeking Jack Maldon, had
not the love of Dr. Strong persuaded her that "there can
be no disparity in marriage like unsuitability of mind and
purpose" and so protected her from "the first mistaken
impulse of [her] undisciplined heart."[20] The phrase lingers
with David, like the perpetual judgment on his own life and
conduct, and he applies it before long to the disparity of
temperament between himself and his childwife:

"The first mistaken impulse of an undisciplined heart." Those
words of Mrs. Strong's were constantly recurring to me, at this
time; were almost always present to my mind. I awoke with them,
often, in the night; I remember to have even read them, in dreams,
inscribed upon the walls of houses. For I knew, now, that my
own heart was undisciplined when it first loved Dora; and that
if it had been disciplined, it never could have felt, when we were
married, what it felt in its secret experience.

Later, when Dora lies dying, he remembers all his unspoken dissatisfactions, and his "undisciplined heart is chastened heavily." Finally, in bereavement, "left alone with [his] undisciplined heart," he must learn to redirect his impulses and energies.[21]

As in Annie's use of the term, describing the possible appeal of Maldon, the undisciplined heart is clearly associated with a wayward sensuality, which is so central to a number of relationships as to constitute a major theme in the novel. David's frail mother seems "very fond" of the monstrous Mr. Murdstone and submits only too eagerly to his possessive embrace:

> He drew her to him, whispered in her ear, and kissed her. I knew as well, when I saw my mother's head lean down upon his shoulder, and her arm touch his neck—I knew as well that he could mould her pliant nature into any form he chose, as I know, now, that he did it.

Aunt Betsey, disciplined at last by kindness to Mr. Dick and true affection for David, has years ago made an impulsive marriage to a wastrel. Little Em'ly, at the cost of all that should be dear to her, is attracted to the ruthless Steerforth, the irresistible Byronic *homme fatale*. Steerforth in turn can exploit her innocence as if in "a brilliant game, played for the excitement of the moment, . . . in a mere wasteful careless course of winning what was worthless to him," and yet, in a mood of dejection that David is unable to fathom, he can also deplore his lack of discipline: "I wish with all my soul I had been better guided! . . . I wish with all my soul I could guide myself better!"[22] Rosa Dartle is consumed forever by a sexual frustration she herself has wilfully nurtured. And Uriah Heep, "umble" as he is, blatantly avows his designs upon Agnes. All of these should

have taught David his lesson; instead they provide parallels
to his experience, an ambiance in which undisciplined
choice may prove disastrous.

David's most serious mistaken impulse is his immediate
and complete commitment to Dora, at the first sight of
whom he feels his fate sealed forever. On entering Mr.
Spenlow's house, he hears a voice making introductions:

> It was, no doubt, Mr. Spenlow's voice, but I didn't know it, and
> I didn't care whose it was. All was over in a moment. I had ful-
> filled my destiny. I was a captive and a slave. I loved Dora
> Spenlow to distraction!
>
> She was more than human to me. She was a Fairy, a Sylph, I
> don't know what she was—anything that no one ever saw, and
> everything that everybody ever wanted. I was swallowed up in
> an abyss of love in an instant. There was no pausing on the
> brink; no looking down, or looking back; I was gone, headlong,
> before I had sense to say a word to her.[23]

In itself this passage has the charm and vitality of extravagant youth; though we know that first love so delirious
often proves illusory, we nonetheless feel it beautiful and
harmless, especially if the lover is such a pleasant young
man as David seems to be. In the context of the whole novel,
however, the passage has darker overtones; it indicates a
precipitancy that may injure others as well as David, a
naiveté that threatens to leave him defenseless and amorphous. With it should be contrasted the first description of
Agnes Wickfield, which appears in a much earlier chapter:

> Although her face was quite bright and happy, there was a tran-
> quillity about it, and about her—a quiet, good, calm spirit,—
> that I have never forgotten, that I never shall forget. . . .
>
> I cannot call to mind where or when, in my childhood, I had
> seen a stained glass window in a church. Nor do I recollect

its subject. But I know that when I saw her turn around in the grave light of the old staircase, and wait for us, above, I thought of that window; and I associated something of its tranquil brightness with Agnes Wickfield ever afterwards.[24]

Though the idealization and especially the placing of the girl in an angelic stained-glass attitude make it difficult, here and sometimes elsewhere, to believe in Agnes as a flesh-and-blood creation, David gives priority to the object rather than to his own immediate response. The sight of Agnes does not intoxicate him; he will only gradually come to know his love. But Agnes will remain the model of the calm considerateness he must achieve in his own heart if he is to reach his maturity. From the beginning, as Dickens's plan notes make clear, Agnes is to be understood as "the real heroine" of the novel.[25]

Like other Victorians, David endures a dark night of despair before he finds hope and purpose and even true identity; he moves through the "pattern of conversion"[26] traced by Carlyle in *Sartor Resartus* and seen with variations in *In Memoriam* and later, after *David Copperfield*, in other Bildungsromane and in the autobiographies of John Stuart Mill and John Henry Newman. After the deaths of Dora and Steerforth and the emigration to Australia of the Peggottys and the Micawbers, David wanders disconsolately through Italy and Switzerland. "Absence," the chapter devoted to his three-year exile, differs in style from the rest of the narrative; it is the one section given over to sustained analysis and introspection, a subjective, almost lyrical account of a crisis which, in accordance with Dickens's working notes, must be "dreamily described."[27]

In his Everlasting No David sees his whole life now "a ruined blank and waste, lying wide around [him], unbroken, to the dark horizon." He is once again the homeless alienated orphan, like the child in the warehouse, but now without the will to find distractions from his sorrow. His despondency hardens into despair, and he comes to think death the only possible escape. He passes the great shrines of history in a trance, "as a dreamer might," observing nothing. "Listlessness to everything, but brooding sorrow," he explains, "was the night that fell on my undisciplined heart." The first faint break in the darkness comes when suddenly, as he descends into an Alpine valley, he is stirred by "some long-unwonted sense of beauty and tranquillity," a feeling far less intense than Wordsworth's epiphany at the Simplon Pass, yet sufficient, when he enters the valley village, to make him responsive, with a quite Wordsworthian reverence, to the singing of shepherds as if he were hearing the voice of "great Nature" herself. A letter from Agnes then helps restore his perspective on the purposes of human life and society, somewhat as the more mystical letters from Hallam in *In Memoriam* help affirm the continuity of the living soul. As Tennyson sees the darkness dissolve, so, in reading, David feels "the night . . . passing from [his] mind." Again like Tennyson, who resolves to "take what fruit may be/Of sorrow under human skies," he now cultivates "the human interest" he has "lately shrunk from," and before long he has many friends in the Swiss valley. His Everlasting Yea, as *Sartor* prescribed, is the discovery of his life's work; already a writer, he becomes the dedicated novelist—presumably first of all the author of a Bildungsroman:

> I worked early and late, patiently and hard. I wrote a Story, with a purpose growing, not remotely, out of my experience, . . . and the tidings of my growing reputation began to reach me from travellers whom I encountered by chance. After some rest and change, I fell to work, in my old ardent way, on a new

fancy, which took strong possession of me. As I advanced in the execution of this task, I felt it more and more, and roused my utmost energies to do it well.[28]

Having made the saving adjustment to work and society, David has conquered self-indulgent sorrow and is prepared at last to discipline his affections.[29] In a new self-knowledge he recognizes his lifelong love of Agnes, which was strong, he now admits, even when, in blindness, he "bestowed his passionate tenderness upon another object." Returning to England consciously "a better man" for the change he has undergone, he can eventually tell Agnes, "There is no alloy of self in what I feel for you."[30] Agnes is indeed his necessary complement; she is both the clear-eyed understanding for which he has always groped and the unselfish fortitude necessary to give his sensibilities purpose and direction. In marriage to Agnes, David achieves the integration of personality to which the hero in the novel of youth typically aspires.

"Of all my books," said Dickens, "I like this the best. . . . Like many fond parents, I have in my heart of hearts a favourite child. And his name is *David Copperfield*."[31] From other comments it seems clear that his fondness extended from the book to the character, perhaps with the sense of satisfaction that through art David could be granted "the one happiness" Dickens felt he had missed in life. Yet he could hardly have considered the bland David of the last chapters an adequate surrogate for his tempestuous self, and he knew from his own experience that a young man's development might be troubled by a guilt and inner conflict which David had never suffered. When he returned to the Bildungsroman as a genre ten years later, he was ready to deal not in wish-fulfillment but in forces precluding a tranquil resolution, in errors of pride and self-interest, far more insidious than the well-intentioned but undisciplined heart.

Dickens himself was the first to compare *Great Expectations* with *David Copperfield.* In October 1860 (the serial publication began in December), he told Forster: "The book will be written in the first person throughout, and during the first three weekly numbers you will find the hero to be a boy-child, like David. Then he will be an apprentice. . . . To be quite sure I had fallen into no unconscious repetitions, I read David Copperfield again the other day, and was affected by it to a degree you would hardly believe."[32] Though popular from the beginning, *Great Expectations* was never as dear to Dickens as his "favourite child." Yet, largely because he approached it with complete dispassion and no vestige of self-pity and proportioned it with matchless logic, it strikes most modern readers as the better book, and many indeed as Dickens's finest work. Some would agree with Bernard Shaw that it altogether "wiped out" *Copperfield.* Others, less exuberant, might prefer Humphry House's description of *Great Expectations* as "the pendant to the first part of *David Copperfield,* the more mature revision of the progress of a young man in the world."[33] But even the first part of *David Copperfield* differs sharply in tone and method from *Great Expectations,* and the whole of it—by no means expunged—remains remarkable for its own distinct qualities. Still, considered simply as a study of a young man's progress—that is, as a Bildungsroman—*Great Expectations* is undoubtedly the more impressive novel, for its narrower, sharper focus allows a much fuller characterization of the narrator, who is once again the protagonist. Like David, Pip, in telling his story, has the virtues of Dickens the novelist; but unlike David, who is relatively reticent, Pip in his acute self-analysis reveals much of the temper of Dickens the man.

As in *David Copperfield*, many of the settings in *Great Expectations* are drawn from scenes familiar to Dickens since his boyhood. Pip's village has been identified as Cooling; the nearby town is clearly Rochester; the hulks were the prison ships once anchored at Chatham; we can trace the original of Miss Havisham's weird Satis House; and we may be sure that the marshes have been evoked in all their gray miasma by one who knew the ooze of real Thames mud beneath his feet. Yet there is none of the direct autobiography that from time to time invades *Copperfield*. Pip's conduct at no point coincides precisely with that of Dickens; the personal has become oblique, distant and ironic. We may find the true measure of the difference between the two novels in an incidental comment by the blacksmith Joe Gargery, who, to the great embarrassment of Pip, has just arrived in London. When Pip's friend Herbert asks him if he has seen anything yet of the city, Joe replies, "Why, yes, Sir, . . . me and Wopsle went off straight to look at the Blacking Ware'us. But we didn't find that it come up to its likeness in the red bills at the shop doors: which I meantersay, . . . as it is there drawd too architectooralooral."[34] Here the warehouse that Dickens previously could not bring himself to mention except under the fictional guise of Murdstone and Grinby's is reduced from a menace to a joke by a fearless, almost self-mocking disengagement. In *Great Expectations*, of course, the parallel to David's misery in the warehouse, or to Dickens's, is Pip's revulsion from the forge after a brief acquaintance with the faded pomp of Satis House:

> I had believed in the forge as the glowing road to manhood and independence. Within a single year all this was changed. Now,

it was all coarse and common, and I would not have had Miss Havisham and Estella see it on any account. . . . What I had dreaded was, that in some unlucky hour I, being at my grimiest and commonest, should lift up my eyes and see Estella looking in at one of the wooden windows of the forge. I was haunted by the fear that she would, sooner or later, find me out, with a black face and hands, doing the coarsest part of my work, and would exult over me and despise me.[35]

But whereas David's feeling of degradation was intended to elicit our deepest sympathy, Pip's distaste and dread, presented with a relentless detachment, are far more ignoble than the work of which he is ashamed. The mature Pip's account of his unhappy apprenticeship is decidedly not to be confused with an apologia for the young Dickens.

Yet, for all its objectivity of manner, *Great Expectations* comes closer than *Copperfield* to being a portrait of the author. Not only does Pip, like David, have a keen Dickensian memory, apparent in the vividness of the physical details he recalls and in scattered remarks on the persistence of an emotion through time ("To the present hour, the weary western streets of London on a cold dusty spring night, with their ranges of stern shut-up mansions and their long rows of lamps, are melancholy to me from this association").[36] He also shares with Dickens—and not with David—several obsessive drives and passions,[37] which as narrator he describes with cogency and great candor. He has an excessive respect for the power of money, a naive confidence that he can somehow buy real security and peace of mind. He loves against all reason a proud beauty who never can or will adequately reciprocate his affection: Estella, clearly modeled on the actress Ellen Ternan, whom the mature Dickens could neither acknowledge nor relinquish. And he nervously strives to conceal his past in the dread that public knowledge of his humble beginnings might debar him from the society of "gentlemen" toward which he too aggressively aspires. Pip's sense of guilt and his involvement, conscious and unconscious, with criminals surely reflects Dickens's remembrance of his father's humiliation before the law and his lifelong awareness of the thin line between respectability and illicit impulse. Pip's vanity and wilful self-delusion echo a fiercer pride tempered by a stronger imagination. And his restless ambition dimly mirrors a more alarming, because unremitting and ultimately self-destructive, energy.

But whatever was subjective in origin, the product of an acute self-knowledge, has been assimilated to a beautifully controlled work of art. If *Great Expectations* comments dramatically on Dickens's uncertainties and moral misgivings, it nonetheless, in the very act of doing so, abundantly illustrates his aesthetic confidence and power. It moves in three equal parts with a dialectical precision: the first presents Pip in a state of relative innocence and naiveté, driven at length from Eden[38] by his worldly "expectations"; the second depicts his corruption in the city, where his hopes, though realized, prove delusions; the third records the utter loss of material wealth and the concomitant recovery of spiritual integrity. From the beginning all persons and places are sharply defined as separate objective entities. The setting in Chapter I is seen with a painter's eye and sketched with a draftsman's economy: "The marshes were just a long black horizontal line then, as I stopped to look after him; and the river was just another horizontal line, not nearly so broad nor yet so black; and the sky was just a row of long angry red lines and dense black lines intermixed." When we first meet her a few pages later, Mrs. Joe is cutting bread—and the action is individual and idiosyncratic, an index to her whole self:

> My sister had a trenchant way of cutting our bread-and-butter for us, that never varied. First, with her left hand she jammed the loaf hard and fast against her bib—where it sometimes got a pin into it, and sometimes a needle, which we afterwards got into our mouths. Then she took some butter (not too much) on a knife and spread it on the loaf, in an apothecary kind of way, as if she were making a plaister—using both sides of the knife with a slapping dexterity, and trimming and moulding the butter off round the crust. Then, she gave the knife a final smart wipe on the edge of the plaister, and then sawed a very thick round off the loaf: which she finally, before separating from the loaf, hewed into two halves, of which Joe got one, and I the other.[39]

Throughout the novel even the simplest gesture, as here, is likely to have symbolic import, for the whole is as much unified by recurrent symbols and chains of imagery as by solidity of structure. Our attention is drawn to the hard, heavy hands of Mrs. Joe, who boasts that she has brought Pip up "by hand," meaning by bottle-feeding, but suggesting also by systematic cuffing. And we watch for the expressive hands of other characters, subtle variations on the theme: the "coarse hands" of the boy Pip, the nervous hands of Estella knitting, the murderous hands and scarred sinewy wrists of her lost mother, Magwitch's strong outstretched hand, Biddy's always clean hands, Miss Havisham's bony hands pressed to her left side (which immediately remind Pip of the younger convict), the hand of the lawyer Jaggers washed of dirty business with a lemon-scented soap.[40] Such details are reproduced with a literal accuracy, but it is the logic of poetry and not of a workaday realism that accounts for their presence and the design into which they are woven. Like a poem, the novel exacts our

willing suspension of disbelief by its texture, the coherence
of its symbols, and the sense that it is exploring through
metaphor a real and pertinent psychology. We can thus
accept the improbable fantasy of Satis House, where Miss
Havisham strikes Pip at one moment as a witch, at another
as his fairy godmother; and we scarcely question the unlikely melodrama of Pip's struggle with Orlick at the lime
kiln as if with a devil at the gate of Hell.[41] *Great Expectations* boldly invokes any device, realistic or not, that will
advance its central object, the depiction of its hero's development.

That Dickens was aware of the particular conventions of
the Bildungsroman, though unfamiliar with that label, is, I
think, apparent from his statement that, when beginning
the new book, he reread *David Copperfield* to make sure
he would not indulge in unconscious repetition. What he
wished not to repeat was not, I assume, personal detail (for
it was no longer his intention to be circumstantially autobiographical), but rather the same use of the standard motifs
of the genre as it was defining itself in nineteenth-century
fiction. *Great Expectations* as a Bildungsroman shares many
characteristics of the form with *Copperfield* and still more
with *The Red and the Black*, which Dickens perhaps never
read. But it gives each element fresh interpretation and new
vitality.

Pip, like many other apprentice-heroes, is an orphan, but
that condition instills no conventional independence or self-
assertion. Instead, it is the source of a distinct resentment
and a sorry lack of initiative:

> Within myself, I had sustained, from my babyhood, a perpetual
> conflict with injustice. I had known, from the time when I could
> speak, that my sister, in her capricious and violent coercion, was
> unjust to me. I had cherished a profound conviction that her

bringing me up by hand, gave her no right to bring me up by jerks. Through all my punishments, disgraces, fasts and vigils, and other penitential performances, I had nursed this assurance; and to my communing so much with it, in a solitary and un-protected way, I in great part refer the fact that I was morally timid and very sensitive.[42]

Like other orphans, Pip must find a substitute father; but he has not far to look, for one is literally thrust upon him in the opening scene as he lingers over the graves of his departed parents. Magwitch's first positive act is to protect the child by assuming guilt for the theft from Mrs. Joe's pantry. Thereafter he lives and works only for his "boy," and if his money proves nearly disastrous to Pip, his love is ultimately the agent of Pip's redemption.

Pip travels the familiar highway from the provinces to the city. But he has less vivid reasons for leaving his native village than Julien Sorel's for deserting mean-souled Ver-rières. His early faith that the forge is "the glowing road to manhood and independence" is far nearer the truth than the illusions that shatter it, and he can eventually look back on his naive farewell to the country only with deep irony: "No more low wet grounds, no more dykes and sluices, no more of these grazing cattle—though they seemed, in their dull manner, to wear a more respectful air now, and to face round, in order that they might stare as long as possible at the possessor of such great expectations—farewell, monoto-nous acquaintances of my childhood, henceforth I was for London and greatness: not for smith's work in general and for you!"[43] The city, as in other Bildungsromane, proves a sad disappointment; but its menacing drabness is now caught with an incomparable intensity. The dismal offices of Little Britain, the forlorn houses of Barnard's Inn, the crowded streets, the ominous riverside are more than setting; all relate expressionistically to the mood and theme of the novel. Pip wryly recalls his mixed feelings on arrival in London: "We Britons had at that time particularly settled, that it was treasonable to doubt our having and our being the best of everything: otherwise, while I was scared by the immensity of London, I think I might have had some faint doubts whether it was not rather ugly, crooked, narrow, and dirty."[44] He can scarcely afford to admit what a dreary foggy dust-hole he considers the lodgings Mr. Jaggers has procured for him. The most candid opinion of the apartment, even after Pip has tried at reckless expense to make it presentable, comes from Joe on the occasion of his unwelcome visit: "For the present may be a wery good inn, according to London opinions, . . . and I believe its character do stand i; but I wouldn't keep a pig in it myself—not in the case that I wished him to fatten wholesome and to eat with a meller flavour on him."[45] Joe fears that the close stale atmosphere of London may be injurious to the health; actually Pip's life in the city threatens his body less than his whole moral being.

The chief agent of his corruption is money, a familiar theme here given unusual prominence. Money seems to be the central objective of most of the Londoners Pip meets, from his predatory houseboy to Mr. Jaggers, with his sharp eye to business, and Wemmick, with his awesome regard for portable property. But even before coming to the city, Pip has a "first decided experience of the stupendous power of money" when he sees it utterly confound Trabb's boy. So dazzled is he himself by his great expectations that he is willing for the moment to take the mercenary, hypocritical Pumblechook at face value as "a sensible practical good-hearted prime fellow."[46] Pip might have learned a lesson from Joe's angry retort to Mr. Jaggers that no money could possibly compensate him for the loss of his apprentice. Instead, he shares (at least until he knows he is sharing it) Magwitch's assumption that money can buy all things desirable. Magwitch desires most a well-bred son, and he comes to believe that that is precisely what his money has bought. Pip's ambition is strikingly similar: to buy for himself the status of a gentleman.

From the moment he hears Estella call him "a common labouring boy" with "coarse hands" and "thick boots,"[47] Pip is ashamed of all things "coarse and common" in his background and in his present life at the smithy. To be worthy of the disdainful Estella, whom he identifies at first sight as "a young lady," Pip must clearly improve himself—"Biddy," he tells his honest confidante, "I want to be a gentleman." His unknown benefactor has the same ambition for him, and eventually Mr. Jaggers comes to rescue him from the laboring village: "Well, Mr. Pip, I think the sooner you leave here—as you are to be a gentleman—the better." Pip's deliberate pursuit of his objective recalls Wilhelm Meister's dedication to self-culture. But whereas Wilhelm's ideal was reasoned and coherent, Pip's is ill conceived and naively developed. It rests on a contemptible snobbery, which leads Pip to repudiate the best man he has known ("I wished Joe had been rather more genteelly brought up," or again, "I wanted to make Joe less ignorant and common that he might be worthier of my society"). Biddy recognizes his unkindness and reminds him, "Yet a gentleman should not be unjust neither." And Herbert Pocket commends to him the principle that "a true gentleman in manner" must be "a true gentleman at heart," for "no varnish can hide the grain of the wood." Herbert himself, with his nonchalance and charm and "natural incapacity to do anything secret and mean," provides an immediate gentlemanly example Pip might well emulate.[48] But Pip has his own more superficial notions of the role he is determined to play. His idea of a gentleman is not unlike Carlyle's concept of the Idle Dilettante, the mannered rather than mannerly spender of unearned income, content to "go gracefully idle in Mayfair," untroubled by the drudges supporting his existence. Pip may or may not be a Carlylean dandy (we are not told what sort of appearance he affects), but the livery he designs for his houseboy—a "blue coat, canary waistcoat, white cravat, creamy breeches," and high boots—suggests a taste more flamboyant than discreet. On first coming to London he is told that he is "not designed for any profession" and will "be well enough educated" if he can hold his own "with the average of young men in prosperous circumstances." He assumes without question that this golden mediocrity satisfies a gentlemanly requirement; but when his expectations evaporate and he is forced to consider a vocation, he is overcome with dismay: "I have been bred to no calling, and I am fit for nothing."[49]

At no time does it occur to him that the gentleman, as Newman defined the ideal for the Victorians,[50] must be tolerant, open to new ideas, devoted to the free play of the intellect, sympathetic, considerate of the feelings of others. On the contrary, in spite of his better instincts, he forces himself to accept the credentials of the brutish Bentley Drummle, a thick-skulled sadist with a pedigree and a good deal of money, whom he both envies and despises. Magwitch, however, is entirely satisfied with Pip's success, and on his return from Australia is eager to claim credit for making it possible: "Yes, Pip, dear boy, I've made a gentleman on you! It's me wot has done it! . . . I lived rough, that you should live smooth; I worked hard that you should

be above work." Later, tracked down, caught and man-
acled, Magwitch can console himself, "I've seen my boy,
and he can be a gentleman without me." Pip thinks he knows
better, for he has already decided to give up the money that
sustains his social pretensions. But love and devotion have
now changed the young man's scale of values, and Magwitch is actually not far wrong: without him, without his
money, Pip has at last a chance to become a real gentleman.
Eventually he approaches that objective, when, to tell his
story, he sets his experience in perspective and candidly
deplores "all those wretched hankerings after money and
gentility that . . . disturbed [his] boyhood."[51]

Pip the narrator differs more sharply from Pip the
adolescent than the mature David Copperfield from his
younger self. Though the young David has to learn the
value of the disciplined heart, he commands a large measure
of sympathy from the beginning; if sometimes impercipient,
he is essentially kind and good, a gentleman by nature and
without deliberate effort. Pip as autobiographer has a more
complex development to describe, a conquest of selfish
pride and self-delusion, snobbery, hypocrisy, and timorous
feelings of guilt. So eager is he to trace the effects of his
shortcomings that he is reluctant to mention his virtues.
His tale accordingly has the quality of a dramatic monologue; we must deduce his whole character from what he
leaves unsaid as well as from his frank confession, and we
must establish the necessary continuities between his past
and the present in which he is writing. George Orwell complained that the child Pip speaks a perfect English rather
than the broad Essex of his companions.[52] But most of Pip's
speech throughout the novel is recorded in indirect discourse properly consonant with the educated style of the
narrator, and the few direct quotations, it seems to me, fit

better into place in the same language than if the mature man had tried to present the child as a third person objectively distinct from himself. The concentrated purpose of *Great Expectations* is to depict the moral growth of a single character, the painful initiation, as he himself remembers it.

Magwitch in his last illness may have wondered "whether he might have been a better man under better circumstances," but "he never justified himself by a hint tending that way, or tried to bend the past out of its eternal shape."[53] Pip in the retrospect that is his story is likewise able to examine his whole experience without evasion, excuse, or denial. But as he presents himself in the process of growing up, he is much given to apology and self-deception; he is eager at any given moment to forget or escape his past and to rationalize his present course of action; and he is slow to learn the truth that "all other swindlers upon earth are nothing to the self-swindlers."[54] Yet he has been shaken as a child by a terror that remains for years to haunt his imagination:

> Since that time, which is far enough away now, I have often thought that few people know what secrecy there is in the young, under terror. No matter how unreasonable the terror, so that it be terror. I was in mortal terror of the young man who wanted my heart and liver; I was in mortal terror of my interlocutor with the iron leg; I was in mortal terror of myself, from whom an awful promise had been extracted; I had no hope of deliverance through my all-powerful sister, who repulsed me at every turn; I am afraid to think of what I might have done on requirement, in the secrecy of my terror.[55]

And the terror, exacting the pledge of secrecy, leads to an abiding sense of guilt. Pip has aided a criminal, made himself involuntarily an accomplice, and so begun a career in

which he will one day find himself "encompassed by all
this taint of prison and crime." When his sister is assaulted
with the convict's leg-iron, he persuades himself not to
reveal the source of the weapon: "the secret was such an
old one now, had so grown into me and become a part of
myself, that I could not tear it away."[56] But he feels partly
guilty of the attack as well as the concealment, for he has
often wished to see Mrs. Joe silenced and has now inad-
vertently supplied the means. Later Orlick, the real as-
sailant, makes him face up to the possibility of his guilt in
thought if not in word or deed. By that time, however, he
is ready to abandon self-swindling and to confront the inexorable truths of his development.

Orlick has been construed as Pip's double, the agent
carrying out his subconscious wishes, and so a witness to the
fact that Pip has good reason to experience criminal guilt.[57]
But to pursue such an argument is to suggest that Pip's sins
are offenses against society rather than moral failures, and
Pip the narrator, who seems to me a trustworthy guide,
makes it emphatically clear that they are the latter. Pip
indicts himself for ingratitude, selfishness, and emotional
dishonesty. He declares himself in his snobbery "capable of
almost any meanness towards Joe or his name." He recognizes an "ungracious condition of mind" in his being
ashamed of home and of Joe's occupation—"ungracious"
perhaps with the overtone of meaning "cut off from heav-
enly grace and charity." He is vain about his few calculated
gestures of magnanimity, as when, home for his sister's
funeral, he asks if he may sleep in his own little room—"I
felt that I had done rather a great thing in making the
request."[58] His departure the next morning shows him at his
worst, not the criminal but the deficient human being; he

has been annoyed at Biddy for asking if he really means
to keep his promise to return, and he now bids farewell
showily to her and to Joe:

> "Good-bye, dear Joe!—No, don't wipe it off—for God's sake,
> give me your blackened hand!—I shall be down soon and often."
> "Never too soon, sir," said Joe, "and never too often, Pip!"
> Biddy was waiting for me at the kitchen door, with a mug of
> new milk and a crust of bread. "Biddy," said I, when I gave her
> my hand at parting, "I am not angry, but I am hurt."
> "No, don't be hurt," she pleaded quite pathetically, "let only
> me be hurt, if I have been ungenerous."
> Once more, the mists were rising as I walked away. If they
> disclosed to me, as I suspect they did, that I should *not* come
> back, and that Biddy was quite right, all I can say is—they were
> quite right too.[59]

Pip needs no instruction in moral cowardice and following the course of least resistance; as a child, "quite an un-
taught genius,"[60] he has discovered baseness for himself.
But he is certainly abetted in meanness of spirit by Estella,
who engenders in him false pride, false hopes, and a woeful
contempt for his origins. Estella entices and rebukes, tor-
tures and torments, and Pip is aware of "all the pain" she has
cost him and of being "always miserable" in her presence.
She speaks with the cold logic of Louisa in *Hard Times:*
love is a fancy she can not comprehend, "a form of words,
but nothing more." She has, she insists, no heart, "no soft-
ness, . . . no—sympathy—sentiment—nonsense." Herbert,
who is normally generous in his judgments, describes her
as "hard, haughty and capricious to the last degree."[61] Pip
knows only too well the validity of this indictment; but
from the moment he first sees Estella, he feels bound to her
beyond all rational argument or persuasion, and she remains through all his growing years a fever in the blood,

an image of what he selfishly desires and cannot have. The intensity of the commitment is paralleled in the English Bildungsroman only by Philip Carey's abject surrender to Mildred in *Of Human Bondage* and Sammy Mountjoy's ruthless determination to possess Beatrice in *Free Fall.* "The unqualified truth," Pip admits, "is that when I loved Estella with the love of a man, I loved her simply because I found her irresistible. Once for all; I knew to my sorrow, often and often, if not always, that I loved her against reason, against promise, against peace, against hope, against happiness, against all discouragement that could be. Once for all; I loved her none the less because I knew it, and it had no more influence in restraining me, than if I had devoutly believed her to be human perfection."[62] But love in such terms, appetite without sympathy, proves destructive and demeaning; Pip cannot reach his moral maturity until he can recognize the claims of a love which involves disinterested charity, and so rid himself of his old obsession.

Yet even when most deluded, he retains enough judgment to be frequently dissatisfied with his conduct. He knows in his heart that Biddy is "immeasurably better than Estella"[63] and that life at the forge is healthier than the death-in-life of Satis House, and he suffers a serious ambivalence of emotions, what he calls a "confused division of mind," as he faces his moral choices. Whether or not he often chooses badly, the fact that he experiences conflict and remorse is itself some indication of his potential for spiritual change. Though he has a strong recurrent sense of guilt, his errors are largely sins of omission, and these coexist with undeniable positive virtues. If he neglects Joe, he is nonetheless loyal to Herbert, whose career in business he manages quietly to advance; and Herbert in turn values his friendship, with no expectation of personal advantage.

He is alert, quick to associate ideas and impressions, sensitive to the patterns of memory that unify his experience. He has, as long as he is not thinking of Estella, a pleasant sense of humor; he enjoys the absurdities of Mr. Wopsle's Hamlet and joins convivially in Wemmick's wedding party. And despite his unkindness to Biddy, he readily discerns and rejects the brutal and the fraudulent, Drummle, Pumblechook, and the grasping hangers-on at Miss Havisham's. The city is clearly a force of corruption, but it also sophisticates Pip in ways not wholly bad, by widening his range of knowledge and giving him glimpses into the complexities of modern society. Whatever his moral condition, he will not be able to return for long to the simplicities of the village.

Pip's regeneration begins when his fear of Magwitch becomes a fear for Magwitch, when his selfish recoil from his protector yields to an anxious and selfless solicitude; as he hides the convict from the law, he risks his own comfort and safety in a way he himself would not have believed possible. He can now feel compassion also for Miss Havisham, who asks him to forgive her: "My life," he tells her, "has been a blind and thankless one; and I want forgiveness and direction far too much to be bitter with you."[64] But he must be tested further. Orlick at the lime kiln forces him in extremity ("I felt," Pip says, "that I had come to the brink of my grave")[65] to an honest and dreadful confrontation of his whole past. Finally a narrow escape from drowning, when the river police capture Magwitch, dissolves his last grain of repugnance and pride: "in the hunted, wounded, shackled creature, . . . I only saw a man who had meant to be my benefactor, and who had felt affectionately, gratefully, and generously, towards me with great constancy through a series of years. I only saw in him a

much better man than I had been to Joe."[66] At the trial
he endures the horror of standing by Magwitch as the
judge pronounces the death sentence and the audience rises
and points down at both of them. He tends the prisoner
lovingly until the end and then falls into his own little
death, a serious illness that leaves him for weeks in delirium.
From this he eventually recovers, as if reborn, feeling, he
says, like a child again. For watching over his progress is
his childhood friend and foster-father, Joe, whom he now
recognizes for what he is, if not a perfect gentleman, then
something finer, "this gentle Christian man." Joe at last
carries him down to an open carriage and drives him into
the country, where he rejoices in the fullness of life, much
as the self in Tennyson's debate "The Two Voices," emerg-
ing from the dark night of the soul, is admonished by the
fields bathed in the light of a Sunday morning:

> The day happened to be Sunday, and when I looked on the love-
> liness around me, and thought how it had grown and changed,
> and how the little wild flowers had been forming, and the
> voices of the birds had been strengthening, by day and night,
> under the sun and under the stars, while poor I lay burning and
> tossing on my bed, the mere remembrance of having burned and
> tossed there, came like a check upon my peace. But, when I heard
> the Sunday bells, and looked around a little more upon the out-
> spread beauty, I felt that I was not nearly thankful enough—
> that I was too weak yet, to be even that—and I laid my head on
> Joe's shoulder, as I had laid it long ago when he had taken me
> to the Fair or where not, and it was too much for my young
> senses.[67]

By losing himself, Pip thus retrieves his identity; his redis-
covery of his first affections is his passport to maturity.

Physically rehabilitated, Pip goes back to the village in
the hope of offering his once "errant heart" to Biddy (the

epithet recalls *David Copperfield*, though Pip's wayward-ness has been far more self-conscious and deliberate than David's). His story is now near its end; the result of the proposal will, he says, be all he has "left to tell."[68] Biddy, however—the irony is most appropriate—has just married Joe, and Pip accordingly goes abroad alone as a representa-tive of Herbert's import-export company. When he returns to England eleven years later, he finds the Gargerys the happy parents of a son named in his honor, but assures them that he himself will not marry and that he has conquered his old obsessive love for Estella: "That poor dream, as I once used to call it, has all gone by, Biddy, all gone by!"[69] Here would be a wholly satisfying conclusion to the novel, a final testimony to Pip's mature self-knowledge.[70]

But Dickens has given us two endings beyond this logical stopping-place, neither, I think, altogether adequate. The first, more laconic and surely stronger than the alternative, shows us Pip, on another visit, with little Pip in London, where he is greeted by Estella, now widowed and remar-ried, who mistakes the child for Pip's own. Pip does not linger long enough to correct her impression, but he is nonetheless, he tells us (with a slight and rather unpleasant resurgence of self-regard), pleased to have seen her: "I was very glad afterwards to have had the interview; for, in her face and in her voice, and in her touch, she gave me the assurance that suffering had been stronger than Miss Havisham's teaching, and had given her a heart to under-stand what my heart used to be." The second and standard ending, supplied when Bulwer Lytton thought the original too severe, brings Pip to reunion with Estella in the dank ruined garden of Satis House. The scene, though skillfully contrived to echo the imagery of Pip's first departure from the marshes, is neither probable nor convincing. Though we gather that Estella has suffered and "been bent and broken . . . into a better shape," we are given no reason to believe that she has ever learned the meaning of selfless love. Pip's attraction to her is acceptable only if we discount the significance of his "conversion." Yet the logic of the novel as a whole demands that Pip, properly to complete his initiation, sacrifice Estella along with all his other false expectations. And the technique of the narrative itself points in the same direction. Pip as narrator would certainly have had something "left to tell" in the last pages if he knew he would woo and win Estella when he found it was too late to marry Biddy. Moreover, unless he is deceiving us from the beginning, it is difficult to see how he could arraign Estella so consistently and emphatically throughout his story and all the while assume that she will provide its happy denouement. Fortunately the existence of the alternatives allows us to choose the one that does little harm to the integrity of the book, and to ignore the other as an inorganic afterthought.

With *David Copperfield* and *Great Expectations* Dickens gave the English Bildungsroman both personal intensity and objective power. From his own strenuous experience and his sharp insight into the processes of his mind and memory, he drew moods and incidents which his creative imagination worked into new forms. His mastery in both novels of first-person narration enabled him to give each an inward dimension by dramatizing the consciousness of the narrator, by letting David or Pip interweave memories and past fears with present observations or pause to consider the mysteries of time which help shape his identity. In Pip especially he created a rounded character, interesting as hero and persuasive as narrator. Though not a professional novelist like David, Pip commands an equally fine prose style, less serene and meditative, but wittier, more ironic, more precise in both description and analysis. We do not know what Pip read during his period as Idle Dilettante in London, but we can credit his claims to literacy: "through good and evil I stuck to my books," and again, "Notwithstanding my inability to settle to anything, . . . I had a taste for reading, and read regularly so many hours a day."[71] Whatever he may have read, he clearly learned from some sources how to write—though very few of the books he encountered could have been nearly so well written as his own story.

❧ III ❧

GEORGE MEREDITH:
HISTORIES OF FATHER AND SON

Dismissing Dickens as "a caricaturist who aped the moralist," George Meredith once predicted (with a singular lack of prescience), "If his novels are read at all in the future, people will wonder what we saw in him."[1] We need not now—as all too many modern readers have done—turn the prophecy against the prophet. Yet we cannot but remark how deeply Meredith, especially in his Bildungsromane, *The Ordeal of Richard Feverel* and *The Adventures of Harry Richmond*, was indebted to Dickens, and we must suspect that his determined hostility, expressed on many occasions, arose largely from his effort to establish his own independent idiom. The method of narration and even the plotting of *Harry Richmond*, the relation of the characters to one another, recall *David Copperfield*,[2] and the theme, the shattering of foolish fond illusions, resembles that of *Great Expectations*. Similarly, in *Richard Feverel* the dominant Sir Austin invites comparison with Mr. Dombey,[3] secondary figures like the motherly Mrs. Berry or the ingenuous Ripton Thompson seem drawn from Dickens originals, and even a background shadow like Mr. Beazley is sketched in something akin to Dickensian shorthand (for Meredith himself not infrequently stooped to caricature): "Our old friend Ripton sat in a room apart

63

with the confidential clerk, Mr. Beazley, a veteran of Law, now little better than a Document, looking already signed and sealed and shortly to be delivered."[4]

The impact of Stendhal and Goethe is less obvious, though Meredith was openly sympathetic to both. He was familiar, we know, with *The Red and the Black* and apparently admired its psychological acuteness,[5] and Richard Feverel's role-playing may have been suggested by Julien Sorel's. Since Goethe from the beginning was one of his heroes, it is not surprising to find some possible traces of *Wilhelm Meister*[6]—Richard's delighted discovery (like Wilhelm's) that he is a father, Kiomi (the child of nature in *Harry Richmond*, somewhat like the less robust Mignon), Harry's sense of misdirection (like Wilhelm's), and his painfully slow growth by the process of trial and error. But the demonstrable influence of Goethe or Stendhal or even Dickens is less important than the fact that Meredith was aware of early examples of the Bildungsroman and the uses of the genre. Sir Austin Feverel, whose knowledge is largely vicarious, draws less on life itself than on a literature of adolescence as he maps out in his notebook the "progressionary phases" of youth "from Simple Boyhood to the Blooming Season, The Magnetic Age, The Period of Probation, from which, successfully passed through, he [is] to emerge into a Manhood worthy of Paradise."[7] And Harry Richmond's source seems likewise literary—it may indeed be *Wilhelm Meister*—when he writes of his own divided emotions: "It is, I have learnt, out of the conflict of sensations such as I then underwent that a young man's brain and morality, supposing him not to lean overmuch to sickly sentiment, becomes gradually enriched and strengthened, and himself shaped for capable manhood."[8] Meredith like Dickens put a good deal of himself into each of his

Bildungsromane, and like Dickens he relied on the conventions of the form to give his personal experience perspective and objectivity.

Richard Feverel and *Harry Richmond* are both novels of "education" describing a development from childhood through adolescence. Both are concerned with apprenticeship to life rather than to a trade; the shaping conflicts are largely emotional; there is no real economic struggle in either—though money plays as conspicuous a part in *Harry Richmond* as in *Great Expectations*. The heroes are too affluent to be the usual deprived "young men from the provinces," but each does begin life on a country estate, to which eventually he must return. Though the city as such is not a prime objective, both have some taste of urban corruption; Richard falls from grace in London, and Harry oscillates between the rural goodness of Riversley and the more sophisticated settings of his father's extravagance. As in earlier novels of youth, each in his Magnetic Age and Period of Probation experiences a sexual awakening and the customary tensions between love and lust—but with a difference: Meredith is considerably bolder in his treatment of sexual relations than his predecessors in the English Bildungsroman,[9] and at the same time he grants his female characters a much greater intelligence and a far sounder moral instinct. As a result the sentimental vagaries of Richard and Harry are to be measured not so much against the purposefulness of mature men as against the perceptions of sensitive and sensible women, Lucy Feverel, Lady Blandish and Clare Forey, Janet Ilchester, Aunt Dorothy and the Princess Ottilia, each depicted with precision and unflagging sympathy. But even more prominent in both books is another motif common to the genre, the hero's need to come to terms with his father or to free

himself from his father's possessive grasp (Richard and
Harry are both semi-orphans: neither, growing up, remembers his mother).[10] The second edition of *Harry Richmond* significantly bore the subtitle of *Richard Feverel*, "A
History of Father and Son." The two novels differ greatly
in method, style, and plot, but the symbiotic relationship of
father and son in each is central to the novelist's concern
and is probed with an insistency that often betrays its autobiographical origin.

On his mother's death George Meredith at the age of five
was left to the mercies of his improvident father, Augustus,
tailor, of Portsmouth. Twenty-five years later George's wife
deserted him, and his son Arthur at the age of five was in
turn left to *his* anxious care. In *Richard Feverel*, completed
in the spring of 1859, about a year after the separation, he
presented aspects of himself as both father and son. In
Harry Richmond (which ran as a serial in the *Cornhill* from
September 1870), he identified his own feelings with the
son and then proceeded quite dispassionately to probe the
character of the father,ʼ a man even more indulgent and
neglectful than Augustus had been. In both novels, despite
a characteristic reticence about his own affairs, he revealed
the necessity of apologia and self-appraisal. But in neither
did he disclose the sense of insecurity, embarrassment, and
even shame he felt as a tailor's son associating with gentlemen. Thanks to a certain hauteur, as a boy he had been
called "Gentleman Georgy";[11] as an adult he saw the irony
of such a title and was too proud to endure it.

The problem of the gentleman—a major issue, as we have
seen, in *Great Expectations*—scarcely arises in *Richard
Feverel* or *Harry Richmond;* Richard with lordly nonchalance takes his status for granted, and Harry as heir apparent to Riversley knows "the advantages of being bred a

gentleman"[12] and refuses to admit that his father is too much of a bounder to deserve that name. The theme, however, is explicitly developed in *Evan Harrington; or, He Would Be a Gentleman* (1861),[13] a novel too limited in scope of time and action to qualify as a Bildungsroman, but highly suggestive as a fragment of autobiography. Evan, already in his late adolescence when the story begins, is the son of a renowned tailor, newly deceased, named after Augustus Meredith's own flamboyant father, the tailor Melchisedec, and known by the same sobriquet, the Great Mel. Like Augustus, Evan has three sisters, each of whom through marriage has improved her social standing; and he himself, though expected to carry on the tailoring business, is painfully aware that the craft will necessarily militate against his efforts to prove himself a gentleman. His ambition to be such is prompted less by snobbery than by his desire to make himself acceptable to the aristocratic Rose, daughter of Sir Franks Jocelyn. And in pursuit of this objective, his conduct ceases to be a reflection of the deportment of Augustus and becomes an idealized fulfillment of Meredith's own wishes. For Rose is clearly a portrait of Janet Duff Gordon, whose family provided the novelist an entrée into an urbane society, where he felt alternately stimulated and slighted. Like Meredith, Evan has inherited both "Presence" and "Port," and he must learn which of these to cultivate if he is to reach a true maturity: Presence involves the grand manner, the airs and affable graces of Melchisedec; Port is the honest candor, forthrightness, and commonsensical realism of his mother. Fortunately, after some wavering, he chooses Port. The true gentleman, he discovers, is no snob; he is simply the man who acts with consideration and nobility or spirit. By a deed of self-sacrifice and generosity, Evan gains self-respect and the courage to face his origins;

he makes the Jocelyns his debtors and actually receives them
in the tailor's shop, where, appropriately, he wins his Rose.
Meredith likewise recognized the superiority of Port in the
assertion of his essential dignity; yet he was all his life too
responsive to dreams of grandeur not to acknowledge the
insidious appeal of Presence.

As *Evan Harrington* develops a familiar theme in new
terms, so *Richard Feverel*, Meredith's first real novel,[14] gives
the conventions of the Bildungsroman fresh interpretation.
On its first appearance, *Feverel* perplexed and antagonized
most of the few reviewers who troubled to notice it at all;
but *The Times* found it original as well as obscure, and the
Spectator saw in it "more of vigorous thought, imagination, wit, humour, and pathos, than would make the fortune
of a score of average novels."[15] It remains a strikingly inventive book, bewildering in its range of tone, dazzling in
its self-conscious verbalization. The action itself counts for
far less than the impact of action on the mental life of the
characters, and the third-person narrative is frequently interrupted by analysis of motives and unspoken thoughts.
Yet there is also a great deal of dialogue, stage-managed
with appropriate gestures, taut, implicative speech, fragments, broken sentences, as if the speakers, understanding
each other, need not explain themselves. Letters—from
Richard to Ripton, from Adrian to Lady Blandish, from
Lady Blandish to Austin Wentworth—provide subjective
variations, and Clare's pathetic diary dramatically affords
us a poignant view of her despair. The aphorisms of Sir
Austin, issued as *The Pilgrim's Scrip* and quoted constantly,
are often no more than tediously clever, but they are sometimes more ironic than Sir Austin himself suspects, and
even shrewdly perceptive, for the sentimentalist, we learn,

can detect foibles in others that he cannot see in himself. At any rate, the epigrams ascribed to Sir Austin give abstraction and generalization, of which Meredith was overfond, a plausible place in the framework of the novel. The style throughout, apart from the aphorisms, is highly metaphoric and allusive sometimes to the point of affectation. We may be amused to hear the deserted Mrs. Berry called Penelope and her errant husband "the wandering Ulysses of Footmen." But we must be baffled by the title of Chapter XXII, "A Shadowy View of Coelebs Pater Going about with a Glass-Slipper," unless we know of Hannah More's didactic novel *Coelebs in Search of a Wife;* and even then we might be confused by the "Pater" since Coelebs is an orphan attempting to fulfill the wishes of his dead parents, and we still might not see the immediate relevance of Cinderella's glass-slipper, apart from the fact that the Pater who is Sir Austin is offering not himself but his son, whom he considers a princely prize.

Similarly we may be put off by the artifice with which Meredith describes Richard's sudden interest in Italian politics:

Lady Judith had nobler [work] in prospect for the Hero. He gaped for anything blindfolded, and she gave him the map of Europe in tatters. He swallowed it comfortably. It was an intoxicating cordial. Himself on horseback over-riding wrecks of Empires! Well might common sense cower with the meaner animals at the picture. Tacitly they agreed to recast the civilized globe. The quality of vapour is to melt and shape itself anew, but it is never the quality of vapour to reassume the same shapes. Briareus of the hundred unoccupied hands may turn to a monstrous donkey with his hind legs aloft, or twenty thousand jabbering apes. The phantasmic groupings of the young brain are very like those we see in the skies, and equally the sport of the wind. Lady Judith blew. There was plenty of vapour in him, and it always resolved into some shape or other. You that mark those clouds of eventide, and know youth, will see the similitude; it will not be strange, it will barely seem foolish to you, that a young man of Richard's age, Richard's education and position, should be in this wild state. Had he not been nursed to believe he was born for great things? Did she not say she was sure of it? And to feel base, and yet born for better, is enough to make one grasp at anything cloudy. Suppose the Hero with a game leg. How intense is his faith in quacks! with what a passion of longing is he not seized to break somebody's head! They spoke of Italy in low voices. "The time will come," said she. "And I shall be ready," said he. What rank was he to take in the liberating army? Captain, colonel, general in chief, or simple private? Here, as became him, he was much more positive and specific than she was. Simple private, he said. Yet he saw himself caracoling on horseback. Private in the cavalry, then, of course. Private in the cavalry over-riding the wrecks of Empires. She looked forth under her brows with mournful indistinctness at that object in the distance. They read Petrarch to get up the necessary fires. Italia mia! Vain indeed was this speaking to those thick and mortal wounds in her fair body, but their sighs went with the Tiber, the Arno, and the Po, and their hands joined. Who has not wept for Italy? I see the aspirations of a world arise for her, thick and frequent as the puffs of smoke from cigars of Pannonian sentries![16]

This extraordinary passage, weaving in and out of Richard's mind and Lady Judith's and the author's own, now facetious, now serious, always mannered, crackling with irony, precedes by only a page or two the sustained lyricism of the description of a mountain storm, which for the moment cleanses Richard of all selfish illusion, a passage as direct and sensuous as the other is involuted and cerebral. Both appear in the same chapter, "Nature Speaks"; together they suggest the new resources of style and manner Meredith brought to the Bildungsroman, the means by which he sought to present the complexities of character and theme.

The autobiographical elements are also introduced in a new way, diffused throughout the novel, seen from diverse points of view and measured by the author himself, sometimes with almost complete dispassion, sometimes with excessive involvement. Sir Austin's task is Meredith's at the time of writing: the education of his only son after the defection of his wife. Meredith imbues Sir Austin with much of his own bitterness, and his anger introduces a note of rancor, which he himself must have come to dislike. A revised and somewhat pared-down version of *Richard Feverel* considerably blunts the attack on Mary, Lady Feverel, and so reduces the degree of what we must regard as special pleading for the novelist's personal interest. But Mary Meredith, even as she enters the first version, is not simply the object of contumely and recrimination; some positive aspects of her person and character contribute to the portraits of the lovely Lucy and the accomplished Lady Blandish. And from the beginning Sir Austin is treated with less sympathy than satire. Insofar as he is a partial self-portrait of the author, he represents Meredith's acknowledgment of his own pride, rigidity, and intolerance—evils that the composition of the novel apparently failed to exorcise, for even after its completion Meredith refused to allow his repentant wife to see their son or to communicate in any way with the boy.[17] Detachment and engagement thus curiously commingle in the depiction of Sir Austin, and the success or failure of the education he designs for Richard is at best uncertain—a measure probably of Meredith's diffidence about his own ability to provide intelligently for Arthur.

Richard's "education" is not simply the process of learning to live that is a necessary part of every young man's initiation; it is also a strict regimen of study, exercise, and gentlemanly deportment, known to the Feverel circle as the System. The novel accordingly, unlike most other English Bildungsromane, may also be considered an *Erziehungsroman*, even though the education here proves in the end far from exemplary. The System dictates that Richard, like the young John Stuart Mill, be tutored at home, where he may escape the corruptions of school and college, and that he be protected, as far as possible, from the influence of undesirable companions. He must not know temptation till he is mature enough to evaluate it: specifically, since Satan's agent was Eve, he must be kept, especially during the Magnetic Age, at a safe distance from women. He must, in other words (Sir Austin's words), be shielded from "the Apple-Disease" till he has advanced to "a certain moral fortitude"; this is the first principle of what the cynical Adrian, convinced that the Eden tree was a grapefruit rather than an apple, calls "the Great Shaddock Dogma." At seventeen Richard moodily questions "all manly pursuits and aims" and the very purpose of life itself. But his adolescent Weltschmerz is no indication that the System has failed: "On the contrary, it had reared a youth, handsome, intelligent, well-bred, and, observed the ladies, with acute emphasis, innocent. Where, they asked, was such another young man to be found?" The System prepares Richard to recognize immediately the artless beauty of Lucy, when he beholds her, "a daughter of earth," gathering dewberries, and to dispense with the subterfuges of courtship in declaring his love. "Then truly," we are assured, "the System triumphed, just ere it was to fail."[18]

Sir Austin, however, refuses to accept the triumph; his vanity wounded by Richard's choosing for himself, he determines to separate the lovers and "to pursue his System by plotting."[19] His designs henceforth are merely selfish and eventually ineffective; the System, at least from his point of view, perishes altogether when Richard in defiance elopes with Lucy.[20] "You see, Emmeline," he tells Lady Blandish, "it is useless to base any System on a human being."[21] He has mistakenly thought his son above and beyond other creatures, and he now discerns human weakness. But the irony of his remark lies in the fact that he has based the System not on Richard at all but on his own image of himself. "The moral," Meredith explained in a letter, "is that no System of the sort succeeds with human nature, unless the originator has conceived it purely independent of personal passion."[22] Sir Austin from the beginning has acted more from hate than love; he has made the education of Richard the means by which he will avenge the wrong done to him by Lady Feverel. Even so, if he were able to transcend his self-interest in due time, he might welcome the moment when what is objectively good in the System seems triumphant. Instead, his invincible pride forces him to go on endlessly exploiting the System to purely selfish ends.

Sir Austin is a supreme egoist. At Raynham Abbey, his estate, he presumes to play God. He is flattered to know his son guilty of burning Farmer Blaize's rick, insofar as the secret allows him "to act, and in a measure to feel, like Providence." By night he walks the Abbey corridors, looks in on his sleeping kinsmen, and fancies he can read their hidden motives; he becomes, as Adrian irreverently puts it, "a monomaniac at large, watching over sane people in slumber."[23] In his own estimation he is the perfect rationalist, "opposed to anything like spiritual agency in the affairs of men," convinced that his independent reason can dispose of all error and illusion. When he rationally determines that Richard has no real talent as a poet, he suggests that the poems be at once destroyed—and he has no understanding that

Richard's abject compliance with his wish brings an end to "all true confidence between Father and Son."[24] He prides himself on being a Scientific Humanist, whose intelligence, apparently omniscient and infallible, is ready to schematize all life and nature, to reduce a complex emotion to a tidy aphorism. When unable or unwilling to sacrifice his pride to a humbling charity, he invokes Science to excuse his inaction; he tells Lady Blandish why he cannot immediately forgive Richard:

> "That I should save him, or anyone, from consequences, is asking more than the order of things will allow to you, Emmeline, and is not in the disposition of this world. I cannot. Consequences are the natural offspring of acts. My child, you are talking sentiment, which is the distraction of our modern age in everything— a phantasmal vapour distorting the image of the life we live."[25]

The sentiment that distorts Sir Austin's perspective is self-pity, the need to generalize from his own unhappy experience, until his disappointment in love seems to him but an exquisite intensification of the trial all men must suffer and a special prototype of his son's ordeal. No gift of laughter restores a sense of proportion in which he may see the absurdity of his self-deceiving role; like most of Meredith's later egoists, he is virtually untouched by the Comic Spirit.

Egoism also blights the character of Richard, so conspicuously indeed that he sometimes seems more anti-hero than hero.[26] Taught that he must endure the Feverel ordeal *by* women, he is too self-absorbed to realize that he himself is actually an ordeal *to* the women about whom he should be most concerned. He is unconsciously cruel to his cousin Clare, who, pathetically frustrated, dies of love for him. He has no understanding of the unhappily married Lady Judith, whose sympathy he has won. He is unaware that Bella Mount, engaged to seduce him, has come to feel real affection; he regards her as simply part of his education in sensuality. Most seriously of all, having tried her patience to the breaking point, he abandons Lucy in her greatest need, to seek self-gratification under a foolish, false code of honor. He willfully deludes himself with sentimentalism, as when, in the midst of his affair with Bella, he muses on his neglected wife: "Dear tender Lucy! Poor darling! Richard's eyes moistened. Her letters seemed sadder latterly. Yet she never called to him to come, or he would have gone. His heart leapt up to her."[27] From childhood he is arrogant, hot-tempered, quick to take offense; at the age of seven he refuses to submit to the indignity of a medical examination ("I won't! Damned if I do!"); a little later he fights Tom Blaize, the farmer's son, and, "with the aid of Science," teaches him Feverel superiority. His friend Ripton knows his angry strength, and the rustic Tom Bakewell, at the time of the rick-burning, bows to his imperious will, "He's a young gentleman as 'll mak' any man do as he wants 'em."[28] Pride is the attribute that as the Hope of Raynham, a being lifted by endowment and the System above other men, he has learned most assiduously to cultivate. When his father seeks to break through his fierce reserve, "the spirit of his pride and old Rebellion" counsels him to resist. His mood is not unlike that of Lucifer in Meredith's most memorable sonnet, who, rising in "his hot fit of pride," is pricked by "memory of the old revolt from Awe"; and the similarity in language is scarcely accidental.[29]

As Sir Austin likes to play God, so Richard enjoys playing the devil, though perhaps not Prince Lucifer. At any rate, he salutes Bella as his "bright Hell-star," calls her a fellow-devil, and praises her for teaching him "how devils love."[30] But the excitements of devilry are a rather late discovery. Richard's favorite role is one more appropriate to a youth who is to be strenuously tried and tested: the knight errant. As he rows on the river, where he is shortly to meet Lucy, he dreams of the possibility in the drab modern world of "some high knightly deed which should draw down ladies' eyes from their heaven, as in the days of Arthur!"[31] During their courtship he tells Lucy that in other times he would have been a knight and won honor and glory for her. On his honeymoon Lady Judith predicts that he "will become a knight-errant," for he has "the characteristics of one"; and the notion at once flatters his ego: "His thoughts flew off with him as knight-errant hailed shrilly at exceeding critical moments by distressed dames and damsels. Images of airy towers hung around. His fancy performed miraculous feats."[32] Chivalry may be dead, he decides on coming to London, but there may still be "something to do"; he resolves to enlist Ripton's support for a knightly crusade to retrieve fallen women. But he succeeds only in delivering his lost mother to Mrs. Berry's rooming house, whereupon he—or the novelist—forgets all about her. Otherwise, his knight-errantry proves an empty gesture, a pose which diverts him from his duty to his wife and before long to his son. When he exiles himself to the Continent in search of similar roles, Mrs. Berry shrewdly appraises his conduct and character: "He's off in his 'eroics," she tells the sensible Austin Wentworth, "he want to be doin' all sorts o' things."[33]

Nonetheless, despite his heroics, despite his egoism, Richard remains until near the end an attractive and promising young man. He is forthright, vigorous, generous, and, for all his self-conscious role-playing, essentially honest. The impulses on which he acts so precipitantly are often sound. His excesses of enthusiasm, his wild daydreaming, are a necessary part of his charm, and the appeal of his naiveté and masculine grace to the several women of his ordeal is wholly understandable. Ripton has questioned his knowledge of life and London as he boldly plans his elopement; but the doubt vanishes at once before the intelligence, wit, and self-possession with which he befuddles his uncles at dinner: "his gaiety, his by-play, his princely superiority to truth and heroic promise of overriding all our Laws, his handsome face, the lord and possessor of Beauty that he looked, as it were a star shining on his forehead, gained the old complete mastery over Ripton."[34] Such a youth, in full command of self and situation, seems an achieved success, even an argument for Sir Austin's System.

In the end, however, the success proves illusory; the hero has fallen in tragic defeat, and Lady Blandish, remembering all that might have been, must tell Austin Wentworth that "Richard will never be what he promised." This final collapse may be traced directly to Richard's misguided chivalry, his will to receive full satisfaction from Mountfalcon for wrongs done to both Lucy and Bella. But it is clearly foreshadowed, before the novel is half over, by the nervous exhaustion he suffers when first parted from Lucy. At that time, brought down by a faintness induced by "excitement of blood and brain," he becomes seriously ill. The pressures of the System have clearly been too strong to resist; his self-assurance is crushed "under the heel of Science." His father at first considers the illness a "providential stroke": when the youth recovers, he will think no more of the girl. And Richard, who has "forgotten what he lived for," does beg pardon for his disobedience. Yet his mental state before long alarms even Sir Austin: "It was not natural. His heart seemed to be frozen; he had no confidences; he appeared to have no ambition—to have lost the virtues of youth with the poison that had passed out of him."[35]

We may compare this "Crisis in the Apple-Disease" with
what John Stuart Mill, describing how his emotional life
was stifled by another system, called "A Crisis in My Mental
History." At the age of twenty Mill experienced a period of
deep dejection, purposelessness, and alienation from his
father; and some of the terms of his self-analysis recall—
or perhaps anticipate—the account of Richard's depression:

> I seemed to have nothing left to live for. . . . I sought no com-
> fort by speaking to others of what I felt. If I had loved any one
> sufficiently to make confiding my griefs a necessity, I should
> not have been in the condition I was. . . . My father, to whom
> it would have been natural to me to have recourse in any prac-
> tical difficulties, was the last person to whom, in such a case
> as this, I looked for help. Everything convinced me that he had
> no knowledge of any such mental state as I was suffering from,
> and that even if he could be made to understand it, he was not
> the physician who could heal it. My education, which was wholly
> his work, had been conducted without any regard to the pos-
> sibility of its ending in this result. . . . The fountains of vanity
> and ambition seemed to have dried up within me, as com-
> pletely as those of benevolence.[36]

But the great difference between Richard and the young
Mill, as he presents himself, is that the education of the
latter, whatever its limitations, prepared him for a life work,
the mission of a philosophical reformer, to which he could
return with new spirit when he had passed his mental crisis.
The System, on the other hand, provides no outlet for
Richard's restless intellect; it leaves him without an apprenticeship, without a career. When he recovers from his
illness, he summons the courage to elope with Lucy and
then returns to the indulgence of his aimless sentimentalism.
Within a few weeks of his wedding he is ready to heed Lady
Judith's plea that he direct his energies into "some definitely

useful channel";[37] and immediately a "vague shapeless ambition" begins to displace his love for Lucy as the center of his concern. Later he persuades himself that the rescue of erring women is his vocation; but Bella, who is apparently beyond retrieval, sees clearly that what he still wants most is "something to do." In Germany he envies—in Carlylean accent—young laborers of his own age on their way to work: "Not cloud-work theirs! Work solid, unambitious, fruitful!"[38] but his musing on their steady purpose merely dissipates his own resolution. He himself remains a prey to indolence and sudden willful impulse.

Only when Austin brings him news of his son does he set aside his fantasies and yield to "something of a religious joy," shadowed soon by self-conscious anguish and shame. Then, as "great Nature spoke" consolation to David Copperfield wandering in despair in the Swiss Alps, so "Nature speaks" to Richard through a fierce storm in the forest high above the Rhine.[39] There the sense of living, breathing earth fills him "with awful rapture," amid such "grandeurs and mysteries" as Wordsworth knew among the Cumberland hills. There, too, the smell of fresh meadow-sweet, where he knows the plant should not grow, brings him to a dazed stop; and we remember perhaps the meadow-sweet hanging thick from the banks of the weir when he first met Lucy. He is now one with nature, brought back to elemental life by the dripping darkness that bathes the whole forest. His immediate link to the living world is a tiny leveret he has lifted from a cleft; he experiences a strange sensation, the sort of shock to the flesh that D. H. Lawrence would later describe with a similar intensity and wonder:

> It ran up one arm with an indescribable thrill, but communicated nothing to his heart. It was purely physical, ceased for a

time, and recommenced, till he had it all through his blood, wonderfully thrilling. He grew aware that the little thing he carried in his breast was licking his hand there. . . . Now that he knew the cause, the marvel ended; but now that he knew the cause, his heart was touched and made more of it. . . . Human tongue could not have said so much just then.

The scene closes with the break of dawn and a remarkable inner illumination, a spot of time; passing a shrine with Virgin and Child, Richard feels his strength ebb from him:

> He was in other hands. Vivid as lightning, the Spirit of Life illumined him. He felt in his heart the cry of his child, his darling's touch. With shut eyes he saw them both. They drew him from the depths; they led him a blind and tottering man. And as they led him he had a sense of purification so sweet he shuddered again and again.

He is at last purged of both shame and proud illusion, and presumably ready to return to Lucy.

So elaborately set is this "epiphany" and presented with such lyric conviction, we should expect it to play a decisive part in Richard's development and in the logic of the novel. But once back in England and aware of Mountfalcon's designs, Richard forgets the lesson of the earth, gives his egoism priority over his affection, and finds a new "mad pleasure in the prospect of wreaking vengeance"[40]—and the narrative moves abruptly to its unhappy conclusion. Since Richard's last lapse is, after all, in character and since Meredith has scattered tragic hints throughout the novel, or at least ominous shadows like that cast by the cypress near the lake at Raynham, some readers have defended the ending as necessary, inevitable, and even organic.[41] But whatever may be the darker implications of theme or plot, the ironic stance of the novelist scarcely prepares us for a final tragedy. Despite the dangers of arson, the rick-burning is labeled "the Bakewell comedy." The elopement is thought of as a new comedy, and the description of the wedding breakfast and of Adrian's delivery of the cake is surely comic writing of a high order. The last third of the novel is undoubtedly grimmer, but there is sardonic comedy in the seduction scene at Bella Mount's, and more than a little satire in the German interlude with Lady Judith. Finally, though Bella's last letter is serious and surely has dire consequences, Meredith cannot forbear telling us that it is written "in a sloping feminine hand, and flourished with light strokes all over like a field of the bearded barley"—an image Tennyson had used to comic effect in *The Princess*.[42] Egoism, in the Meredithian sense, is almost by definition a comic theme; and at no point in the novel are we asked to regard Sir Austin the egoist as a tragic figure. Richard, on the other hand, despite his egoism, commands our sympathies and our confidence that he will learn by his mistakes and somehow achieve a mature sense of proportion. We are disappointed and pained rather than surprised by his foolish challenge to Mountfalcon, but its result comes to us as a shattering shock; Lucy's sudden death seems arbitrary, and Richard's utter irrevocable defeat, almost gratuitously cruel: "Have you noticed the expression in the eyes of blind men? That is how Richard looks, as he lies there silent in his bed—striving to image her on his brain." The hero's development is thus permanently arrested rather than completed. Richard is left at the end, as his father was at the beginning, with a son to educate; but unlike his father, he has now no energy to devise any sort of System. And we cannot but feel that even a misguided gesture would be preferable to a total paralysis of the will. Richard's experience has brought him great pain but no tragic insight; his moral perception is ultimately no more acute than Sir Austin's; he has attained no real liberation.

As Meredith's later "history of father and son," *Harry Richmond* enjoys a great advantage over *Richard Feverel:* unity of tone and point of view. Though reworking some of the same motifs, the narrative is related in the first person by the hero, whose conscious purpose is to trace the gradual changes from childhood through adolescence "in his manner of regarding his father and the world."[43] Since the whole must be presented in Harry's relatively simple idiom, Meredith is restrained from encroaching upon the novel and digressing from it. Harry grows in self-awareness until by the end he can describe his own egoism and so vanquish it: "In reality the busy little creature within me, whom we call self, was digging pits for comfort to flow in, of any kind, in any form. . . ." Having recounted his adventures at length, he disarmingly tells us of the folly of talking too much about himself:

> The pleasant narrator in the first person is the happy bubbling fool, not the philosopher who has come to know himself and his relations toward the universe. The words of this last are one to twenty; his mind is bent upon the causes of events rather than their progress. As you see me on the page now, I stand somewhere between the two. . . .[44]

But such self-consciousness is not comparable to that of the intrusive author in *Richard Feverel.* Harry is no virtuoso either as intellectual analyst or as shaper of lyrical prose. Occasionally he writes with a greater flair for imagery than we expect of him—as when he remarks of his friend Heriot, a sort of coarser Steerforth, "His talk of women still suggested the hawk with the downy feathers of the last little plucked bird sticking to his beak."[45] But for the most part his style rolls efficiently forward, avoiding, as Meredith's typically does not, poetic trope and simile and all the flowers of rhetoric. So free of sustained metaphor indeed is the narrative that when Harry, idealizing his father, sets him "on a pedestal," he literally sees him right there: that is, he actually finds him masquerading as an equestrian statue, gilded from head to foot, mounted on a bronze charger. Thus the image is translated into the fact, and the dead metaphor becomes a live symbol, for Richmond Roy's act embodies all his outrageous showy pretense.

By withholding himself, even stylistically, from Harry's autobiography, Meredith is able to distance and objectify memories of his own life. *Harry Richmond* reveals none of the bitterness and indecision that pervade *Richard Feverel;* there is now no wife to be punished for desertion, and the rearing of a child is no longer the novelist's immediate unsolved problem.[46] Richmond Roy recalls Meredith's father and grandfather; like Augustus he lives far beyond his means, goes to debtor's prison, and alternately pampers and neglects his son; like the Great Mel, who fancied himself a descendant of kinsmen of the Tudors, he claims royal blood and builds a career on his grand illusions. But he is a resounding amplification, rather than a faint echo, of both Merediths, in his own right an independent creation, one of the most vigorous characters in Victorian fiction. Janet Ilchester, whom Harry eventually marries, derives, like Rose Jocelyn in *Evan Harrington*, from Janet Duff Gordon; but unlike Rose, she is depicted not as a remote ideal, but with cheerful realism as a healthy daughter of the squirearchy, for Meredith is now able to see his old infatuation with Janet in clear perspective. Other personal details, especially memories of a boarding school, an early year in Germany, and possibly a country love-affair[47] (appearing in the novel as Harry's attachment to Mabel Sweetwinter), are presented with a similar detachment, a complete freedom from subjective bias. Meredith explains his own youth and perhaps to some degree defends it, not by confession or author's commentary, but dramatically, through the experience of his hero.

As a novel *Harry Richmond* succeeds by exuberant overstatement. Harry moves through a sprawling panorama, crowded with incidents and thronged with characters.[48] He admits to "an extraordinary appetite for wealth," and the sums involved in his adventures reach staggering proportions, far beyond the expectations of Pip or the combined fortunes of Miss Havisham and Magwitch. On his twenty-first birthday he receives seventy thousand pounds as a mere token of what he may hope eventually to inherit. At a German university he entertains his fellow students "on a vast scale" and is denounced by the philosophical Dr. Julius von Karsteg as "one of the main drainpipes of English gold." His grandfather, who controls mines in Wales, is "virtually, in wealth and power, . . . a prince."[49] And his father, who himself owns nothing, is as wildly extravagant as the royal dukes of the Regency to whom he claims relationship. Harry lives in the world of the gentleman's Grand Tour and the magnanimous gesture; he must find his real self amid expensive distractions, in many situations and in scene after elaborately contrived scene.

If for most of his youth Harry seems amorphous and irresolute, it is simply that he is overshadowed by the forces, full of passionate intensity, contending for his soul: his father and his grandfather. The opening chapter (the only section in the third person, since the narrative here is based on hearsay rather than the hero's remembered observation) describes a noisy clash between the two over the possession of the child, and the rest of the novel extends and finally resolves that conflict. Early in his own story Harry tells us that he feels like "a kind of shuttlecock flying between two battledores."[50] Throughout his growth he is slowly defined by his attitude toward each in turn, and he does not reach his maturity till he can finally assert his independence of both. Meredith feared that he had made him "perhaps dull toward adolescence and young manhood, except to one *studying* the narrative."[51] But to such a student the close evolution of character, set against a plot in perpetual motion, should be of abiding interest.

Harry's grandfather, Squire Beltham, is a generous and indulgent guardian, yet possessive in his affection, eager to give the boy the Beltham name, concerned above all to have an heir to Riversley, one preferably married to his favorite Janet, with children to carry on his line. Harry repeatedly turns to him for support and security, but again and again is repelled by his vindictiveness toward Richmond Roy, who has become the obsessive object of the old man's hate. When, for example, Harry comes home with a gift of hock he and his father have brought from the Rhineland, the squire responds with characteristic violence and then typically fails in his efforts to buy Harry's approval:

> The four-and-twenty bottles of Hock were ranged in a line for the stable-boys to cock-shy at them under the squire's supervision and my enforced attendance, just as revolutionary criminals are executed. I felt like the survivor of friends, who has seen their blood flow.
>
> He handed me a cheque for the payment of debts incurred in my recent adventures. Who could help being grateful for it? And yet his remorseless spilling of the kindly wine full of mellow recollections of my father and the little princess, drove the sense of gratitude out of me.[52]

The squire's great moment is the climactic scene of the novel: the final exposure of Roy, or rather the breaking, for the pretender is then as surely broken as the wine bottles. But he himself never recovers from the vehemence of the attack—indeed with its delivery he gives up a major purpose in living. And his tirade, though true in all particulars, is so vicious in spirit that it forever alienates what is left of his grandson's respect.

Roy's solicitude for Harry is no more selfless than the squire's. By marrying his son to a princess, he expects to secure his own position in a royal establishment. Yet Harry so craves a father's affection that he is reluctant seriously to question designs he knows he cannot wholly trust. And Roy is in fact a most persuasive charlatan, at times deluding even himself into a belief in his perfect rectitude. When he carries off Harry as a small child from Riversley, he proves a delightful companion, inventive, vivacious, full of games and roles and enchanting stories. Later we see how he has charmed many others, especially women—both the squire's daughters, a young Welsh heiress, Lady Denewdney, Julia Bulsted, the Margravine of Sarkeld. As he bluffs his way without a sou through Parisian society, his deportment, we are told, is "a mixture of the ceremonious and the affable such as the people could not withstand."[53] Gossip from the few he does not convince and attacks from exasperated creditors merely spur him to new feats of daring, new displays of impervious composure. At least until the last confrontation with Beltham, he is amazingly resilient and dramatic, a man larger than life, as grandiloquent as Micawber, as resourceful in evasion as Falstaff, as energetic in deception as Uncle Teddy of *Tono-Bungay*. At the height of his career he has a megalomaniac's conviction that he is a providential molder of destinies: "While others deemed him mad, or merely reckless, wild, a creature living for the day, he enjoyed the conceit of being a profound schemer, in which he was fortified by a really extraordinary adroitness to take advantage of occurrences: and because he was prompt in an emergency, and quick to profit of a crisis, he was deluded to imagine that he had created it."[54] No wonder that a personage of such attributes should be to his son both an object of intense hero-worship and a source of shattering disillusion.

Having won Harry's confidence, Roy proceeds to inculcate his own false values. He gives the child a misleading "taste of grandeur" and fills him with extravagant dreams of unearned wealth and station. He skillfully plays on the young man's pride, conceit, and willingness to follow the course of least resistance. Harry eventually finds himself tacitly consenting to the deception of the Princess Ottilia, despite his sense of being self-deceived by the plot. As early as the statue scene, where Roy appears more buffoon than hero, Harry has doubts about his father's wisdom and integrity. But his mistrust is repeatedly overruled by his love, and the interaction of his feelings does much to shape the course of his development. Standing by Roy's side, as they sail to Ostend, he is suddenly ashamed of his "recent critical probings of his character" and seized with old sentiment: "My boy's love for him returned in full force." Not long after, however, at the time of Roy's efforts to impress the German prince, he has no such sympathy: "At no other period of our lives were we so disunited. I felt in myself the reverse of everything I perceived in him."[55] Again and again he deplores his father's double-dealing and despises his "sententious volubility," but is nonetheless unable to escape the magician's spell:

My glorious future, he said, was to carry a princess to England and sit among the highest there, the husband of a lady peerless in beauty and in birth. . . . I had the option of being the father of English nobles or of German princes; so forth. I did not like the strain; yet I clung to him. . . .

In spite of myself, I caught the contagion of his exuberant happiness and faith in his genius. . . . It struck me that he had really found his vocation, and would turn the sneer on those who had called him volatile and reckless. . . .

He shook me by both hands. I was touched with pity, and at the same time in doubt whether it was an actor that swayed me; for I was discontented, and could not speak in my discontent; I was overborne, overflowed.[56]

Harry's liberation coincides with Roy's decline, his stepping beyond the bounds of his charm. For Roy, despite the large gestures that suggest the broad strokes of caricature, is a complex rounded character, three-dimensional, subject to change from within. Even before the squire unmasks him he has begun to deteriorate. He is more and more excitable, increasingly dependent on stimulants, less able to distinguish fact from fantasy. As he rushes off to London to be politically "in the thick of the fray," Harry comments, "It was not a moment for me to catechize him, though I could see that he was utterly deluded." To the rest of the world he is still a comic figure; to Harry he now acts out a tragedy: "I chafed at his unteachable spirit, surely one of the most tragical things in life; and the proof of my love for him was that I thought it so, though I should have been kinder had he amused me, as in the old days." He is no longer amusing; he has grown dangerous. When he tries to blackmail the prince by announcing Ottilia's engagement to Harry, he is viciously intent upon having his will at any cost: "Never," writes Harry in frightened retrospect, "did power of earth or of hell seem darker to me than he at that moment, when solemnly declaiming that he was prepared to forfeit my respect and love, die sooner than 'yield his prince.' " After Beltham's cruel, though strictly honest diatribe, Roy, stripped of his illusions, collapses both mentally and physically. We last see him taken in Harry's embarrassed charge from a banquet at the city hall, where he has delivered a sad, insane speech on the iniquity of princes. Harry is almost destroyed by his father and with him, but he never wholly repudiates him; standing by his side in defeat, he tries hard to remember the royal impostor at his kingly best. And in the end, like Pip, he is saved by his love, or at least by letting himself be reconciled "to the idea of that strange father of mine."[57]

Harry's guide to his moral maturity, to a selfless love and understanding, is neither Roy's wild imagination nor the squire's belligerent practicality; it is a subtle refinement and fusion of both, the example—reflecting Meredith's respect for the female intelligence—of the Princess Ottilia and Janet Ilchester. As he is torn between father and grandfather, so he wavers between the two young women, the one gently idealistic, the other tenderly commonsensical: "I thought of Janet—she made me gasp for air; of Ottilia, and she made me long for earth. Sharp, as I write it, the distinction smote me. I might have been divided by an electrical shot into two halves, with such an equal force was I drawn this way and that, pointing nowhither."[58] But Harry overstates the difference; unlike the male contenders for his loyalty, Janet and the Princess meet on the grounds of sympathy, principle, and mutual respect. Other women stir his emotions: Mabel Sweetwinter, as fresh as an English meadow, appeals to his adolescent sentimentality; and Kiomi, the gypsy girl, "a superb savage," arouses his sexual appetites. Janet and Ottilia are essentially on the side of

reason, able to see themselves and their worlds in due perspective, able with the clarity of the Comic Spirit to discern
the consequences of willful egoism. The Princess teaches
Harry, who has been egregiously self-indulgent, his first
lesson in renunciation; she chills his self-love by placing
her duty to her family and her people above her personal
desire, and only with difficulty does he convince himself that
her quiet integrity is not to be coerced or compromised.

Janet's code and conduct are more familiar, more earth-
bound, but no less admonishing. When under the spell of his
father's romancing, Harry complains that Janet touches
"neither nerve nor fancy." Yet when weary of pretense
and extravagance, he attempts to recover his identity by
returning to Riversley and to Janet, who will see him as he
really is: "Some love for my home, similar to what one may
have for Winter, came across me, and some appreciation
of Janet as well, in whose society I was sure to be at least
myself, a creature much reduced in altitude, but without the
cramped sensations of a man on a monument. My hearty
Janet! I thanked her for seeing me of my natural height."[59]
Harry must be much less condescending than this, and his
need for honest appraisal more acute, before he can claim
Janet as his bride. But he does eventually learn by experience and example and is at last aware of the different person he has "grown to be."[60] He comes then to know and
to cherish Janet's courage, realism, and unaffected grace as
values far stronger than the illusions he once lived by.

Through marriage Harry at the end of his story obtains
most of the estate that Squire Beltham in his last burst of
temper denied him. He will now settle down with Janet in
the country, where (some readers have feared),[61] without
his father to mislead him, he may become a complacent
member of a dull squirearchy. But whether or not his

capacity for change will give his future some positive direction is really quite another matter, certainly not the subject of the Bildungsroman that engaged Meredith's attention. In the end Harry's initiation is complete; he has achieved independence and a measure of self-knowledge.

Even so, he must give us final word of Richmond Roy, for the relationship of father and son has been central to his development and the main theme of his narrative. Janet has endeared herself to Harry by a signal act of compassion; in his absence she has found Roy in a state of violent insanity and nursed him through weeks of delirium. Nonetheless, out of deference to the squire, she has denied him access to Riversley. When she and Harry are off on their wedding trip, however, Roy takes possession of the house and fills it with fireworks to celebrate their return. On their arrival they find Riversley in flames and Roy himself presumably—though his body is never found—burned to death in the holocaust.

The scene functions less effectively as fact than as symbol. Presented entirely in the two last paragraphs of the novel, it is too abrupt and melodramatic to convince or move us; we are too stunned to pity the deluded man who has accidentally destroyed himself, and we are perplexed by the casual matter-of-fact tone in which Harry reports the event. Yet there is a kind of poetic justice in Roy's perishing by his own highly characteristic ceremonial gesture, the placing of fireworks fit for a prince and princess, "such a display as only he could have dreamed of." And it is perhaps necessary to assure us that Roy himself, not just his influence, is literally dead, for his vitality was once so great that we might otherwise almost expect him even in defeat to recover his wits long enough to set Harry off again upon immature madcap adventures.

⊰ IV ⊱

GEORGE ELIOT: A DOUBLE LIFE

In 1855 Marian Evans convinced George Henry Lewes by a single piece in the *Westminster Review* that she was a writer of "genius." Yet Lewes could scarcely have predicted from the vitriolic essay, an attack on the popular Evangelical preacher John Cumming, that she would one day prove a novelist as remarkable for her compassion as for her analytic rigor.[1] Looking back, however, from the spring of 1860, when George Eliot completed *The Mill on the Floss*, he might have seen a foreshadowing of her attitude in an article on the morality of *Wilhelm Meister*, which she had written at about the same time as her exposé of Cumming. Goethe, she had argued, took no moral side either for or against his characters; he delighted simply in "living, generous humanity—mixed and erring, and self-deluding, but saved from utter corruption by the salt of some noble impulse, some disinterested effort, some beam of good nature, even though grotesque or homely."[2] She herself found it difficult to remain so neutral, and her Bildungsroman is certainly less detached than Goethe's. But she strove in her fiction to control her acerbity, to practice tolerance and understanding, and to suspend censorious judgment of the erring and the self-deluded, the homely and the unheroic. She was no longer so self-righteous in her intellectual commitments, or so assured in her rejections, as she had been in the days of the higher journalism. While still at work on *The Mill*, she described her changed disposition: "Many things," she told a friend, "that I should have argued against ten years ago, I now feel myself too ignorant and too limited in moral sensibility to speak of with confident disapprobation: on many points where I used to delight in expressing intellectual difference, I now delight in feeling an emotional agreement."[3] Though these remarks specifically concern her altered regard for religion, even for Evangelical Christianity, the mood carries over to the whole moral life of her novel. The most intellectual novelist of her time was also the most considerate of human feelings.

Had its composition been delayed a few months, *The Mill on the Floss* might have immediately preceded *Great Expectations* as a serial in Dickens's *All the Year Round;* for Dickens, who was among the first to identify the writer using the pseudonym "George Eliot" as a woman, was eager to have her contribute to his new weekly.[4] George Eliot in turn admired Dickens and appreciated his largeness of spirit, though, like Meredith, she mistrusted his influence and wished to pursue independently her own fictional objectives. Minor characters in *The Mill*, especially Bob Jakin with his fat mother and little wife, "Mrs. Jakin the larger and Mrs. Jakin the less," and his dog Mumps, suggest indebtedness to Dickens; and Bob's cozening of niggardly Aunt Glegg as he disposes of his yardgoods has all the irrelevance and something of the charm of a Dickensian comic interlude.[5] But, quite apart from the question of "influence," George Eliot revealed a skill in depicting childhood unequalled since *David Copperfield* and, at least according to Henry James, unsurpassed anywhere in English fiction.[6] Like Dickens she was able to enter the child's mind without adult condescension, to appreciate the

"strangely perspectiveless" intensity with which a child endures his present griefs and disappointments, and to understand how—as Wordsworth insisted—every moment of
childhood suffering leaves some trace which blends itself
"irrecoverably with the firmer texture of our youth and
manhood."[7] In this respect, as in others, *The Mill on the
Floss* deserves to stand beside *Great Expectations:* Maggie
Tulliver's miseries as a willful nine-year-old are no less
real than Pip's traumatic terrors; her wincing from the rebukes of her aunts at dinner is comparable to Pip's discomfort across the table from Pumblechook and Mrs. Joe;
her dream of joining the gypsies is as convincingly self-protective as the romance with which Pip invests the spectral
dreariness of Satis House. Neither novel distorts its picture
of the child's life with false idealization; yet each curiously
intimates that the end of childhood is somehow an expulsion
from Eden. Pip leaves his early home—and a measure of innocence—as he travels through the rising mists to London;
and the world, as in *Paradise Lost*, lies all before him. When
Maggie fetches her brother Tom from school to face their
father's illness and bankruptcy, she departs with him into
the forest of adult experience: "They had gone forth
together into their new life of sorrow and they would never
more see the sunshine undimmed by remembered cares.
They had entered the thorny wilderness and the golden
gates of their childhood had for ever closed behind them."[8]

  The Mill on the Floss differs from *Great Expectations* and
the other Bildungsromane we have examined in that it sets
out to describe the initiation of not one but two principal
characters. Pip like Richard Feverel goes to his ordeal alone;
Maggie and Tom, together in childhood, must confront the
adult world together, must choose their separate paths, and
must finally be reunited in death. Like the other novels,

The Mill has a strong autobiographical component. Maggie, we gather from topical allusions, was born in 1819, and Tom, three years earlier—the precise birth dates of Marian Evans[9] and her brother Isaac; and a good many episodes and even much of the setting (though it is transferred for purposes of plot to a coastal county) apparently reflect their early life in Warwickshire. George Eliot's later sonnet sequence, "Brother and Sister," readily identifiable as personal reminiscence, describes "the twin habit of that early time" in detail close at almost every point to the novel. Brother is protective, demanding, conscious of male superiority, quick tempered, rigid in his concept of justice; when he takes Sister fishing, he scolds her for neglecting the line but warmly lauds her success in hooking a silver perch. Sister is worshipful, eager for praise, sensitive to impressions; she rambles "puppy-like" with Brother across the daisied meadows, past the gypsy camp, along the river's edge, and together they learn

> the meanings that give words a soul,
> The fear, the love, the primal passionate store,
> Whose shaping impulses make manhood whole.

Later she will remember those hours as "seed to all my after good," much as Wordsworth recalled his boyhood as "fair seed-time" of the soul. Though schooling and the ways of the adult world end the intimacy of the children, Sister trusts that Brother, too, has gained from their relationship:

> His years with others must the sweeter be
> For those brief days he spent in loving me.[10]

Before much of *The Mill* was written, George Eliot denied that there would be any portraits from life in it,[11] and

Tom indeed is not literally Isaac Evans. But we see the young Marian's affection for Isaac in Maggie's love of Tom; and in Tom's rejection of Maggie after her flight with Stephen, we can surely detect Isaac's relentless respectability, prompting his repudiation of Marian when he learned of her liaison with Lewes. Similarly Maggie is not intended as a portrait of the artist as a young woman. But we know enough of the young Marian Evans to recognize a close temperamental affinity and to discover many details drawn from her experience. Like Maggie, she was attracted as a child to Defoe's *History of the Devil*,[12] read widely in the Latin classics, studied Euclid and logic, and found in Thomas à Kempis a profound revelation. Like Maggie, she was devoted to her father and nursed him through long illness. Though her parents bore only slight resemblance to Mr. and Mrs. Tulliver, her attitude toward her maternal relatives, the Pearsons, clearly inspired her brilliant study of the Dodsons. Her infatuation with John Chapman may have influenced her depiction of Stephen Guest, and her friendship with François D'Albert may have suggested Maggie's interest in Philip Wakem. Maggie, of course, is physically beautiful as Marian decidedly was not. She suffers no comparable religious struggle leading to a loss of faith. Though intelligent, she is not really, like Marian, a dedicated intellectual, and she gives no indication, even in her speech, that she could ever have become a trenchant essayist or a great novelist. Even so, the similarities are sufficiently numerous and striking to convince us that the narrator in the opening chapter, leaning on the bridge, looking at the child Maggie, is the author silently, sympathetically, confronting her own past self.[13]

The epigraph on the title-page, which is also the epitaph of Maggie and Tom and the last line of the novel, "In their death they were not divided," underlines the fact that *The Mill on the Floss* is by design a double life, a sort of contrapuntal Bildungsroman, comparing and contrasting hero and heroine as each moves into young adulthood. Most of the tentative titles proposed while the writing was still in progress, *The Tulliver Family*, *The House of Tulliver*, *The Tullivers, or Life on the Floss*, indicated that more than one protagonist was involved; and even *Sister Maggie*, the most frequently mentioned, implied a brother's judgment or point of view. On completing the manuscript, George Eliot clearly affirmed her intention; the three published volumes, she told John Blackwood, would have "the psychological unity that springs from their being the history of two closely related lives from beginning to end."[14] Accordingly the attention given to Tom's schooling and to Tom's job, which some readers have thought excessive,[15] rests on the premise that Tom as well as Maggie merits our concern. In our estimate of the novel, we must not ignore the declared duality of purpose. We must not allow our understandable preference for Maggie to obscure the dominant theme of at least three quarters of the book, the symbiotic relationship of sister and brother.

The Mill on the Floss pays far more heed than any earlier Bildungsroman to the secret springs of family life, its understandings and constraints, its possessiveness and limited freedoms, its unspoken and often inarticulate loyalties. For the first time it complicates the motif of antagonism between father and son—here also between mother and daughter—by a self-conscious application of the "laws" of heredity, and in so doing it anticipates *The Way of all Flesh*, *Jude the Obscure*, and *Sons and Lovers*, in each of which "inherited characteristics" play a significant role. When we first meet Mr. Tulliver, he is telling Mrs. Tulliver of his plans for

Tom's education and rather ruefully comparing the boy's mental capacities with Maggie's:

> "What I'm a bit afraid on is, as Tom hasn't got the right sort o' brains for a smart fellow. I doubt he's a bit slowish. He takes after your family, Bessy."
> "Yes, that he does," said Mrs. Tulliver, accepting the last proposition entirely on its own merits; "he's wonderful for liking a deal o' salt in his broth. That was my brother's way, and my father's before him."
> "It seems a bit of a pity, though," said Mr. Tulliver, "as the lad should take after the mother's side i'stead o' the little wench. That's the worst on't wi' the crossing o' breeds: you can never justly calkilate what'll come on't. The little un takes after my side, now: she's twice as 'cute as Tom. Too 'cute for a woman, I'm afraid," continued Mr. Tulliver, turning his head dubiously first on one side and then on the other.[16]

Tom proves indeed a Dodson in his sense of property and his way with money, his lack of imagination, his self-righteous deportment, and his unswerving honesty. Yet he has his father's stubborn will and vengeful temper, and he is ultimately less merciful than Aunt Glegg, who is ready to receive the disgraced Maggie whom he has rejected. Maggie, on the other hand, though full of forgiveness and never vindictive, is decidedly a Tulliver, impulsive, generous, excitable, full-blooded, tall and awkward as a growing girl, handsome as a young woman, yet never conventionally pretty like her mother or her dainty cousin Lucy. Her first speech, as she enters disheveled and muddied from her play by the river, aligns her against the orderly Dodsons: she will not make a counterpane for Aunt Glegg, "I don't want to do anything for my Aunt Glegg—I don't like her." By the same token she feels drawn to her father's sister, the kindly, improvident, prolific Aunt Gritty. And Mr. Tulliver for his part is so devoted to Maggie that he shows special consideration for Gritty in the hope that Tom will one day follow his example in the practice of brotherly love. Though each character is free to make his moral choices and must be held responsible for his decisions, the disposition of each is in large part predetermined, the product of his mixed inheritance.

If Maggie must suffer as an imprudent Tulliver, Tom can be expected to control his energies and resources more efficiently, for "nobody had ever heard of a Dodson who had ruined himself: it was not the way of that family."[17] Better equipped than the Tullivers to face the struggle for survival, the Dodsons better exemplify the provincial ethic described in the learned first chapter of Book IV, "A Variety of Protestantism Unknown to Bossuet":

> Here, one has conventional worldly notions and habits without instruction and without polish—surely the most prosaic form of human life: proud respectability in a gig of unfashionable build: worldliness without side-dishes. . . . The religion of the Dodsons consisted in revering whatever was customary and respectable. . . . The Dodsons were a very proud race, and their pride lay in the utter frustration of all desire to tax them with a breach of traditional duty or propriety. A wholesome pride in many respects, since it identified honour with perfect integrity, thoroughness of work, and faithfulness to admitted rules. . . . A conspicuous quality in the Dodson character was its genuineness: its vices and virtues alike were phases of a proud, honest egoism, which had a hearty dislike to whatever made against its own credit and interest. . . .

Anticipating *Middlemarch*, which George Eliot subtitled "A Study of Provincial Life," *The Mill on the Floss* introduces a new theme to English fiction. Dickens and Meredith see the city as a center of corruption and temptation, but neither attempts a close analysis of the provincial mentality that their heroes, city-bound, are leaving behind. *Great Expectations* evokes the marshes, the village and the country town with incomparable vividness; but the setting of *The Mill*, less detailed visually, is far more precise in terms of social and intellectual history. The temper of St. Ogg's in all its complacency and aggressive respectability emerges as distinctly as the mood of the mean-souled, avaricious Verrières in *The Red and the Black*, though George Eliot's view is calmer and more judiciously balanced than Stendhal's. Henry James was reminded of Balzac (if Balzac had been less solemn) "by the attempt to classify the Dodsons socially in a scientific manner." And E. S. Dallas in an early and perceptive review found "the odious Dodson family, . . . these mean, prosaic people," stunningly representative of "the sort of life which thousands upon thousands of our countrymen lead." Too careful a social analyst wholly to condemn her provincials, George Eliot was distressed by Dallas's reading. "I have certainly fulfilled my intentions very badly," she said, "if I have made the Dodson honesty appear 'mean and uninteresting,' or made the payment of one's debts appear a contemptible virtue. . . . I am so far from hating the Dodsons myself, that I am rather aghast to find them ticketed with such very ugly adjectives."[18] Yet the novel both labels and dramatizes the "oppressive narrowness" that conditions the lives of Tom and Maggie.

George Eliot herself was at one time a young woman fresh from the provinces, eager as *Westminster* essayist to establish her sophistication and her freedom from all parochialism. Yet she allows Maggie and Tom no escape from the provincial setting and only occasional transcendence of the provincial ethic. Neither ever tastes the liberation of the

great city, the challenge of cultural difference, the cosmopolitan diversity of manners and opinions. But each experiences something of the city's materialism in provincial St.
Ogg's, where the successful Dodsons belong and the failing
Mr. Tulliver has no place. After two dreary years of school-
teaching, Maggie basks briefly in the favor of a moneyed
small-town society and for the moment is almost seduced
into believing that the fuller life she craves may lie in
Lucy's comfortable world. After the disgrace of his father's
bankruptcy, Tom dedicates himself, body and soul, to the
most respected pursuit in St. Ogg's, the rapid acquisition
of capital. Forgetful of the religious struggles that molded
its past, St. Ogg's is resolutely devoted to the present, the
eighteen thirties, when the Industrial Revolution has
brought new machines and new modes of production and
the resourceful entrepreneur flourishes, while the less adapt-
able businessman flounders.[19] St. Ogg's proves pharisaical
and cruel to Maggie, but it is not the ultimate villain of the
novel, for Maggie is too strong to be destroyed by the
tyranny of public opinion. And it is not, as some readers
have alleged, really "decadent." The flood does not come
upon it as a judgment, for it survives the flood, and when
the waters recede, "the wharves and warehouses on the
Floss [are] busy again, with echoes of eager voices, with
hopeful lading and unlading."[20]

As we might expect, St. Ogg's has only the crudest notion of what constitutes a lady or a gentleman. The one
clear requirement, best met by Lucy Deane and her suitor,
the provincial dandy Stephen Guest, is apparently idle
affluence. Tom feels that Maggie has somehow degraded
herself by serving as a teacher. "I wished my sister to be a
lady," he tells her, "and I would always have taken care of
you, as my father desired, until you were well married."[21]

At Lucy's Maggie is, not reluctantly, "introduced for the first time to the young lady's life";[22] yet her past suggests an intellectual restlessness not to be satisfied for long with the mere amenities of polite conversation. Tom himself has been sent to Mr. Stelling's school where he must learn Latin and Euclid, which, as Philip Wakem informs him, belong to a general culture and are therefore a necessary "part of the education of a gentleman."[23] But even in such terms, which are beyond the usual grasp of St. Ogg's, the gentlemanly ideal has little relevance to the needs or demands of the tradesman's life; and Tom's education is largely ineffectual, for Tom is no scholar and, unlike Maggie, has no real respect for books or ideas. Yet, in spite of himself, he acquires at Mr. Stelling's something of the deportment of a gentleman and a confident, cultivated speech, which sufficiently impresses his father.[24]

We learn nothing of Maggie's education at Miss Firniss's boarding school, where presumably she was disciplined in less intellectual, ladylike pursuits, which she must have heartily disliked. Nor are we given any details about her teaching career, apart from incidental references to the "dreary situation" and the "third-rate schoolroom, with all its jarring sounds and petty round of tasks."[25] Tom's rise in trade, on the other hand, is described as circumstantially as if he were the single protagonist of the Bildungsroman. The narrator denies that Tom is simply "the spooney type of the Industrious Apprentice," since he has "a very strong appetite for pleasure."[26] But his desire is subject to his will, and he subordinates all else to the recovery of the family fortunes. Eventually he berates Maggie, "You struggled with feelings, you say. Yes! *I* have had feelings to struggle with, but I conquered them. I have had a harder life than you have had, but I have found *my* comfort in doing my duty." [27] His work is joyless and obsessive. If he has once secretly nursed a sentimental regard for Lucy, he now has no time for love. His confession startles even his money-minded Uncle Deane: "I want to have plenty of work. There's nothing else I care about much."[28] He has made his adjustment to the materialism of St. Ogg's with almost frightening efficiency, and his initiation seems complete.

So cold, calculating, self-righteous, and unregretful does Tom appear that many readers have found him repulsive and at least one sensitive critic has declared him altogether detestable and Maggie's love for him incomprehensible, "almost like a piece of perverseness, an aberration."[29] Maggie on one occasion delivers as severe an indictment:

> "Don't suppose that I think you are right, Tom, or that I bow to your will. . . . You have been reproaching other people all your life—you have always been sure you yourself are right; it is because you have not a mind large enough to see that there is anything better than your own conduct and your own petty aims. . . . You have no pity; you have no sense of your own imperfection and your own sins. It is a sin to be hard; it is not fitting for a mortal—for a Christian. You are nothing but a Pharisee."[30]

But Maggie speaks here only on special provocation. Her affection for Tom is far stronger than her anger, and it is neither perverse nor incomprehensible. Shortly after her outburst she sees Tom in his best light, in his short moment of triumph when his long self-denial finally absolves his father's debt; and she feels that his goodness far outweighs his faults. The author makes clear from the beginning Tom's virtues as well as his vices. Though as a boy he thinks all girls "silly," Tom is "very fond of his sister" and means "always to take care of her."[31] He is imposed upon by

Mrs. Stelling when asked to mind her infant daughter, and
he might be expected to hate "the little cherub," but, we
are told, he is "too kind-hearted a lad for that—there [is]
too much in him of the fibre that turns to true manliness,
and to protecting pity for the weak."[32] His first impulses
at the time of his father's bankruptcy are right and generous;
he will see that the servant Luke's loan is immediately re-
paid and that his uncle Moss's promissory note is destroyed.
"There were subjects, you perceive," the narrator comments
admiringly, "on which Tom was much quicker than on the
niceties of classical construction, or the relations of a mathe-
matical demonstration."[33] Later when he scolds Maggie
for needlessly humiliating herself, we are asked to see in
his rebuke "some tenderness and bravery mingled with
the worldliness and self-assertion."[34] Though he fails Maggie
in her time of distress, Tom is cruelly misguided rather
than essentially vicious. We should be able to understand
George Eliot's insistence that she had painted Tom "with
as much love and pity as Maggie."[35] And we should credit
his essential quality sufficiently to believe him capable of
a final moment of insight which suddenly reverses the
direction of his life, a moment in which he catches the
full import of Maggie's devotion: "It came with so over-
powering a force—it was such a new revelation to his
spirit of the depths in life that had lain beyond his vision
which he had fancied so keen and clear—that he was
unable to ask a question."[36]

While Tom has tried to live by self-reliance and without
love, Maggie from early childhood has craved affectionate
or admiring attention. "The need of being loved," we learn
at the outset, is "the strongest need in poor Maggie's nature."[37] Later, on her visit to Tom's school, Philip Wakem
is struck by her dark eyes "full of unsatisfied intelligence

and unsatisfied, beseeching affection."[38] The intelligence leads her to books, but the desire to be thought quick and clever is almost as compelling as her delight in knowledge; aware as a child that she will not be praised like Lucy for daintiness or grace, she attempts, as when she discusses Defoe with Mr. Riley or geometry with Mr. Stelling, to impress with her intellectual capacity. When she reaches young adulthood, she has become a woman of great physical attraction ("this tall dark-eyed nymph with her jet-black coronet of hair"), and though she claims to dislike compliments, she is grateful to Stephen Guest for making her conscious of the fact.

D. H. Lawrence would one day commend Maggie's abundant vitality and declare that he saw in "the smooth branches of the beech trees" a reminder of her arms.[39] George Eliot might have been both pleased and alarmed by so sensual a response to her heroine, for she seems clearly, especially in the last books of the novel, to have identified with Maggie, and Maggie's beauty is apparently a belated fulfillment of the wishes of the young Marian Evans. A distinctly subjective note enters the analysis of Maggie's emotion; the novelist takes sides, and the connotative vocabulary registers her own attitude as much as her character's:

> Sometimes Maggie thought she could have been contented with absorbing fancies; if she could have had all Scott's novels and all Byron's poems! Then, perhaps, she might have found happiness enough to dull her sensibility to her actual daily life. And yet . . . they were hardly what she wanted. She could make dream-worlds of her own—but no dream-world would satisfy her now. She wanted some explanation of this hard, real life: the unhappy-looking father, seated at the dull breakfast-table; the childish, bewildered mother; the little sordid tasks that filled the hours, or the more oppressive emptiness of weary, joyless leisure; the need

of some tender, demonstrative love; the cruel sense that Tom
didn't mind what she thought or felt, and that they were no
longer playfellows together; the privation of all pleasant things
that had come to *her* more than to others: she wanted some key
that would enable her to understand, and, in understanding, endure, the heavy weight that had fallen on her young heart.[40]

This passage immediately precedes—or introduces—the description of Maggie's discovery of Thomas à Kempis and
the way of renunciation, an event we know to have been
autobiographical in origin. Here and elsewhere, as Virginia
Woolf and F. R. Leavis among others have pointed out,
George Eliot falters when she asks "poor Maggie" to share
in her "young heart" the hungers of her own adolescence.[41]
At such moments a too closely engaged sympathy may lead
to the distortions of self-pity. Maggie is not to be allowed
a new career as a successful writer; there will be no deliverance in human time from the "sordid tasks" of her narrow
world. The child Maggie could be delineated with perspective and very little sentimentality. Pathos, delivered in af-
fective language, somewhat blurs the later image; Maggie
as a young woman necessarily escapes most of the irony
that touches—and helps define—the other characters.[42]

Nevertheless, the "mature" Maggie has her immaturities,
of which George Eliot is not wholly unaware. She has not
outgrown her early tendency to lapse suddenly, like little
Sister in the sonnet sequence, into dreamy reverie. When
she is literally "borne along by the tide" with Stephen, she
is at the same time being lulled into semi-consciousness by
the drift of her daydreaming. Her absent-mindedness encourages frequent flights from reality, and the indulgence
in such "fantasy life" may, as a recent critic suggests, be the
mark of a neurotic personality.[43] But Maggie's weakness in
this respect is simply a product of her strength, of her qual-

ity as a human being; her fantasies arise from a sympathetic imagination that can find no adequate release in the world of the mill or St. Ogg's. Both the need to establish harmony in the present and the desire to escape to a less troubling order are apparent in her sensitive response to music. When she was a child a tune from Uncle Pullet's snuff box was enough to reconcile her to angry Tom, and Christmas carolers beneath her windows could seem like angel voices in the heavens. At the time of her father's collapse she feels most keenly the loss of the family piano and the deprivation of music, and she is described as "a creature full of eager, passionate longings for all that was beautiful and glad, thirsty for all knowledge, with an ear straining after dreamy music that died away and would not come near to her."[44] Later, stimulated by a musical evening at Lucy's, she casts aside her self-denying austerity and confesses, "I think I should have no other mortal wants if I could always have plenty of music."[45] Maggie's "sensibility to the supreme excitement of music," the author comments, is an aspect of "that passionate sensibility" which makes "her faults and virtues all merge in each other."[46]

Maggie, for better or for worse, is an enthusiast, whether the object of her commitment is music or philosophy. For a considerable period of her unhappy youth, it is the latter; she gives herself completely to the cult of renunciation she has learned from Thomas à Kempis. Her interest in the *Imitation of Christ*, as we know, was shared by George Eliot, even at the time of writing *The Mill*, but the fervor of her commitment is parallel only to the earlier devotion of Marian Evans to an extreme Evangelicalism.[47] Maggie sees the sacrifice of selfish pleasure as the source of true happiness, and resigned acceptance as the key to all virtue. Yet she is neither joyful nor wholly sinless in her negations. Characteristically she throws "some exaggeration and wilfulness, some pride and impetuosity, even into her self-renunciation," with the result that she often loses "the spirit of humility by being excessive in the outward act."[48] Her self-denial is far less mature and purposeful than the sort of self-discipline that leads Princess Ottilia, acting from a sense of duty, to renounce Harry Richmond. It is rather, as Philip perceives, "a narrow asceticism" or again "a narrow self-delusive fanaticism," which stupefies, not quickens the spirit, for "it is stupefaction," he explains, "to remain in ignorance—to shut up all the avenues by which the life of your fellow-men might become known to you."[49]

When Philip assails her ascetic creed, Maggie half-recognizes the truth of his attack and half-suspects him of advancing his own self-interest. In effect he is speaking for George Eliot, who deplored the unnecessary stifling of the intelligence. Philip indeed is the only character in the novel properly equipped to appreciate Maggie's intellectual capacities and to value the strength and delicacy of her feelings. He is also the only one who really escapes the provincialism of St. Ogg's and can bring a broad general culture to bear on his judgments of art and life. Sensitive and made more so by his handicap, tender, high-strung, occasionally petulant, Philip awakens Maggie's protective instinct, her gratitude and even warm affection, but not her love. He is her faithful confidant, aware that he is cherished as such, yet also aware that, unlike Stephen Guest, he exerts little or no sexual attraction. The difference in Maggie's response to the two young men manifests itself, appropriately enough, in their singing at Lucy's. Philip chooses an aria by Bellini, pleading a deathless constancy, which he renders in a plaintive tenor. Maggie is "touched, not thrilled by the song." But Stephen scoffs at sweetly tenored sentiment and, by way of antidote, in a vibrant bass rolls out the cavalier lyric "Shall I, wasting in despair, / Die because a woman's fair?" The very air of the music-room pulses to the sound, and Maggie, "in spite of her re-sistance to the spirit of the song and to the singer, [is] taken hold of and shaken by the invisible influence—[is] borne along by a wave too strong for her."[50]

Stephen is a Victorian schoolgirl's notion of a dashing gallant. His every gesture is underlined with epithets of decorous boldness. His is "a violent well-known ring at the doorbell resounding through the house." He enters with a "bright strong presence and strong voice." He charms his female companions with "a half-ardent, half-sarcastic glance under his well-marked horizontal eyebrows." He hums a tune "in his deep 'brum-brum,' very pleasant to hear," and sings "with saucy energy." He guides a lady's arm "with a firm grasp" and habitually smiles "down from his tall height." From the beginning many readers have thought this provincial paragon a quite unworthy mate for a young woman of Maggie's intelligence and sensibility, though few have been so severe as Swinburne, who considered him a mere "thing" to inspire "bitter disgust and sickening dis-dain."[51] George Eliot herself has been censured for drawing Stephen with obvious approval, as if, mature in so much else, she failed utterly to recognize his limitations, or as if such a man might once have fulfilled the dreams of Marian Evans. A few critics have insisted that the portrait is satiric, for there is indeed an unmistakable irony in his introduction: "Mr. Stephen Guest, whose diamond ring, attar of roses, and air of nonchalant leisure, at twelve o'clock in the day, are the graceful and odoriferous result of the largest oil-mill and the most extensive wharf in St. Ogg's."[52] But the irony soon yields to amused sympathy, and before long serious regard replaces the amusement. Beside either Tom or Philip, Stephen remains a shadowy two-dimensional figure, described frequently as vigorous, but charged with no inner vitality. Had he been more fully realized, he might have been the male counterpart of Rosamond Vincy in *Middlemarch*, likewise the selfish product of provincial money and an education in the superficial graces. George Eliot is able to see Rosamond in perspective and to detect a streak of "commonness" in the intelligent Dr. Lydgate, whom she ensnares. If we are not to think Maggie similarly vulgar in her tastes (and the long exposition of the novel gives us no reason or wish to do so), we must regard Stephen simply as an unsuccessful device to advance the plot. We must accept the premise of Maggie's sexual attraction to him and assume that he can indeed offer her a "great temptation"[53] to ignore the call of duty.

A modern reader finds it difficult to grasp the enormity of the transgression. Maggie drifts dreamily out to sea with Stephen and, bemused and bewildered, is taken aboard a Dutch freighter; but next day, wide awake in the cold hard light of morning, she rejects Stephen's proposal to elope and, reasoning with herself, resolves to return home. She has in fact resisted the tempter and refused to betray Lucy and Philip; and her "sin" exists only in the minds of the scandal-mongers of St. Ogg's, to whom she is in all respects morally superior. But by her own standards she has been guilty of passivity, of allowing her enjoyment of the dreamy moment to subdue her free will. When Stephen first intimates that the tide has carried them too far to return and has in effect made their decision for them, Maggie protests, "You have wanted to deprive me of any choice." In the morning when he argues that to all appearances they have already eloped, she replies firmly, "Don't try to prevail with me again. I couldn't choose yesterday." To Maggie consent means deliberate and complete commitment. She cannot, she explains, deny all other loyalties and affections for the love of Stephen: "I have never consented to it with my whole mind. . . . It has never been my will to marry you."[54] As in Golding's *Free Fall*, the freedom of choice is too precious to barter.

When Stephen leads her—literally—down the garden path to the rowboat "without any act of her own will," Maggie is aware only of the present. She has forgotten her "self"— or, as we are told in a curious phrase, "Memory was excluded"[55]—for her essential self is simply what she can remember; it is all that the past has made her. Moral choice presupposes the wakeful free will, but past experience offers precedents to guide and even to limit the choosing. "If the past is not to bind us," Maggie asks Stephen, "where can duty lie?"[56] From her girlhood she has yearned for a sense of continuity. At the time of her father's bankruptcy she is distressed not so much by the imminence of poverty as by the thought that "the end of our lives will have nothing in it like the beginning."[57] Later she tells Philip that she desires "no future that will break the ties of the past."[58] Despite her attraction to Stephen, she knows that their life together could have "no sacredness," since to accept his proposal she would have to "let go the clue of life,"[59] her loyalty to others and her respect for her own antecedents. Though finally in disgrace, she insists on staying in St. Ogg's, when she might well begin anew elsewhere, for she cannot endure the prospect of rootlessness, of being "cut off from the past." At the end, just before the flood waters invade her room, she recoils from the temptation to ask Stephen to return; she will not once again exclude memory: "the sense of contradiction with her past self in her moments of strength and clearness," we are told, "came upon her like a pang of conscious degradation."[60]

Maggie's sensibility is distinctly Wordsworthian, and the phrasing that describes it in the last scene clearly echoes the passage in *The Prelude* that explains how "diversity of strength / Attends us, if but once we have been strong," a passage that George Eliot underlined in her own copy of the poem.[61] Maggie's natural piety, like Wordsworth's, is the force of memory that links past and present and so integrates and "educates" the personality. Piety so conceived is a major theme of *The Mill*, just as it is central to George Eliot's autobiographical sonnets, where Sister remembers her childhood with Brother and impressions which

> Were but my growing self, are part of me,
> My present Past, my root of piety.[62]

Maggie's earliest memory, she tells Philip, is of standing beside Tom by the riverbank. Though far from blissfully happy, her childhood had an intensity which her later experience can scarcely match; and Tom is at the center of her most vivid recollections. Ultimately Tom's approval matters more to her than Philip's affection or Stephen's love. Reconciliation with Tom, though won only in the last extremity, restores the past and with it the coherence and continuity she has most ardently sought.

The end of Maggie's life and Tom's does indeed, then, have something in it like the beginning. A pattern is complete; as the epigraph promised, in their death they are not divided. Yet the reunion, however necessary to the design of this double Bildungsroman, is effected only by completely ignoring or bypassing the moral and intellectual sources of the estrangement; and the scene is concluded with an unconvincing and sadly damaging sentimentality:

The boat reappeared—but brother and sister had gone down in an embrace never to be parted, living through again in one supreme moment the days when they had clasped their little hands in love, and roamed the daisied fields together.[63]

Lewes told the publisher John Blackwood that George Eliot's eyes grew "redder and swollener every morning" as, approaching the end of the novel, she lived through "her tragic story." "But," he added with deep satisfaction, "there is such a strain of poetry to relieve the tragedy that the more she cries, and the readers cry, the better say I."[64] Yet all her tears could not establish the reality of the resolution she had contrived. True tragedy must be inevitable and organically related to character and incident; the drowning of Maggie and Tom remains essentially a pathetic and gratuitous accident.

So pained was Henry James by the catastrophe that he wondered whether it was merely "a tardy expedient for the solution of Maggie's difficulties."[65] We know now that it certainly was not, since George Eliot, on first planning The Mill, made a careful study of murderous inundations before choosing the Trent River in Lincolnshire as a likely model for the flooding Floss. We have also her later assurance that she had looked forward to the tragic denouement "with attentive premeditation from the beginning."[66] And there are indeed throughout the novel many references to rivers, floods, and drowning, and a good deal of water imagery and symbolism.[67] Though we are not inclined to credit the alarms of so foolish a woman, Mrs. Tulliver voices her constant fear that Tom and Maggie will be "brought in dead and drownded some day."[68] Tom and Bob Jakin as children talk of past floods and how useful an ark will be to meet future ones. Maggie as a little girl recounts—almost prefiguratively—Defoe's tale of a witch's ordeal: "if she's drowned—and killed, you know—she's innocent, and not a witch, but only a poor silly old woman. But what good would it do her then, you know, when she was drowned? Only, I suppose, she'd go to heaven, and God would make it up to her."[69] The legend of St. Ogg, developed at some length, involves a blessing to protect his boat from the menace of the flood tides. Maggie, at sea with Stephen, dreams of being abandoned by St. Ogg and left to drown in troubled waters. Philip has also dreamed of Maggie's slipping helplessly down a waterfall; and he himself dislikes boating and teasingly warns Maggie not to "be selling her soul to that ghostly boatman who haunts the Floss—only for the sake of being drifted in a boat forever."[70] Nonetheless, despite all these carefully placed clues and intimations of tragedy, the ending, however deliberate in intention, does have the effect of a hasty expedient. The flood is a physical force outside the psychological framework of the action. It has no real relation to Maggie's dilemma;[71] it encroaches upon her melodramatically, an agent from without, just as she has resolved not to betray her past affections by calling back Stephen. Maggie is in the midst of prayer—"O God, if my life is to be long, let me live to bless and comfort"—when she is startled by a sudden cold stream beneath her feet; though she surely has not expected it, she is, we are told, "not bewildered for an instant"[72]—she knows it is the flood. The ironies here are more frightening than the novelist could have foreseen. It is not clear whether uncontrolled nature, an actual grim *deus ex machina*, is intended to mock the prayer or to fulfill it. The title of the last book, "The Final Rescue," suggests that death alone will provide release and transcendence. Yet even if we accept the flood as a possible means of reconciling Tom and Maggie, their deaths may still seem but a cruel accident. Until the last half-page of the narrative another sort of rescue would have been conceivable; the large boat passing by might have offered assistance instead of mere warnings of disaster.

George Eliot herself confessed that the conclusion of *The Mill on the Floss* seemed to her unduly compressed and precipitant. But it is unlikely that a more leisurely pace would have made the "tragedy" more convincing. Any tragic ending would probably remain as unsatisfactory as the revised happy ending of *Great Expectations*—but for a quite different reason. Dickens feels sufficiently detached from his hero—whom he nevertheless resembles—to offer him the sort of future most of his readers might wish him to have. George Eliot has identified herself too closely, too emotionally, with Maggie to know precisely what to do with her. She cannot grant Maggie a second life like her own in London without compromising the natural piety that binds the girl to the past. She is apparently reliving through Maggie her own early sense of responsibility and her reluctance to break family ties. Yet she cannot imagine Maggie's finding the meaningful career in St. Ogg's that she herself could not find in Warwickshire. On the other hand, if we have seen in the first chapter of the novel the narrator looking back on her childhood, meeting the eyes of her younger self as Maggie, we surely cannot credit Maggie's death. Like *Sons and Lovers* and Joyce's *Portrait*, which are subjectively engaged in a similar way, *The Mill on the Floss* describes the beginning of a life necessarily still incomplete; and its interest and power lie in the unfolding of that life rather than in the end imposed upon it.

◆§ V ◆

THE WAY OF SAMUEL BUTLER

Though central to her intellectual development, George Eliot's loss of religious orthodoxy and her search for a secular alternative scarcely touch *The Mill on the Floss*. Samuel Butler's deconversion and its consequences, on the other hand, provide a major theme in *The Way of All Flesh*, and Edmund Gosse's faith or unfaith is the dominant, indeed virtually the single, concern of *Father and Son*. The principal action of both these books is laid in the few years immediately before and after 1860, the date of publication of *The Mill on the Floss*; but both were written at a much later time, and neither appeared till the first decade of the twentieth century; both belong in tone and spirit to a generation as skeptical of George Eliot's moral imperatives as of the religion she rejected.

Father and Son, Gosse told a friend, was designed to make men "face the fact that the old faith is now impossible to sincere and intelligent minds, and that we must courageously face the difficulty of following entirely different ideals in moving towards the higher life." But what, he asked in a moment of unusual diffidence, "what ideals, or (what is more important) what discipline can we substitute for the splendid metallic rigour of an earlier age?"[1] His portrait of his father, however, suggests only a qualified respect for the man and very little love of the rigorous

116

religion to which he was committed. The first sentence of the personal history (Gosse considers it too selective in range to be called an autobiography) announces "the record of a struggle between two temperaments, two consciences and almost two epochs," and the narrator from the beginning is clearly on the side of the son and his relaxed modern sensibility.[2] He undercuts with irony the father's assumption of infallibility, his austere self-denials, his severe but consistent sense of justice, his puritanical distrust of imaginative literature, and even his apparent satisfaction with the sound of his own praying voice. Nonetheless, the bright metallic integrity of the elder Gosse shines through. Here is a man willing to stand or fall by his faith, a distinguished scientist prepared to sacrifice his professional reputation to an essentially quixotic defense of his religious conviction. He is far above self-interest, indifferent to acclaim, careless of money. There is no trace of hypocrisy or equivocation in his belief or conduct. Despite—perhaps because of—its restrictions, his life achieves an extraordinary intensity.

In the end the difference between father and son is one less of temperament than of character. By comparison, the son seems morally timid, evasive, less than candid.[3] He insists that his narrative is "scrupulously true," but he does not hesitate to read his father's motives to his own advantage or to slant his materials in the direction of a personal apologia. He quickly learns to value truth-to-the-self above any more objective principle. "Through thick and thin," he insists, "I clung to a hard nut of individuality, deep down in my childish nature."[4] As a young man he has promised his father that he will meditate each morning on a portion of the Greek Testament, but the great city to which he moves offers many distractions from the task, and he readily rationalizes the breaking of his promise: "the dilemma was now before me that I must either deceive my Father in such things or paralyse my own character."[5] The possibility of frankly confessing to his father his changed attitude apparently never crosses his mind. All that matters, as he completes his initiation, is that he be allowed to exercise what he calls "a human being's privilege to fashion his inner life for himself." Unfortunately, *Father and Son* gives us no real clue to the quality of the inner life that the son will succeed in shaping.

At school shortly before his departure for London, Gosse reaches the climax of his religious experience, a moment of ecstasy:

> Over my soul there swept an immense wave of emotion. Now, surely, now the great final change must be approaching. I gazed up into the faintly-coloured sky, and I broke irresistibly into speech. "Come now, Lord Jesus," I cried, "come now and take me to be for ever with Thee in Thy Paradise. I am ready to come. My heart is purged from sin, there is nothing that keeps me rooted to this wicked world. Oh, come now, now, and take me before I have known the temptations of life, before I have to go to London and all the dreadful things that happen there!" And I raised myself on the sofa, and leaned upon the window-sill, and waited for the glorious apparition.

But when he is not transported heavenwards, he comes back, having lost his gesture, to the mundane reality:

> Sounds began to rise from the road beneath me. Presently the colour deepened, the evening came on. From far below there rose to me the chatter of the boys returning home. The tea-bell rang,—the last word of prose to shatter my mystical poetry. "The Lord has not come, the Lord will never come," I muttered, and in my heart the artificial edifice of extravagant faith began to totter and crumble. From that moment forth my Father and I, though the fact was long concealed from him and even from

myself, walked in opposite hemispheres of the soul, with "the thick o' the world between us."[6]

Whether or not the description of the positive epiphany, if such it may be called, is scrupulously true, it exists here simply for its ironic reduction, the wry anti-epiphany. Placed conspicuously at the end of the last chapter before the Epilogue, the scene strikes the reader as self-consciously literary, contrived and calculated. Whatever its origin in experience, its presentation, like much else in *Father and Son*, suggests its affinity—and possibly its direct indebtedness—to *The Way of All Flesh*,[7] which was published four years earlier and was already the classic exemplar of a skeptical son's liberation.

The Way of All Flesh, said Gosse, shows us that Butler "disliked excessively the middle-class Evangelicism in which he had been brought up, and we must dislike it too, but we need not dislike the persons involved so bitterly as Butler did."[8] Unlike Gosse, Butler is clearly more hostile to the one person most involved, his father, than to the faith itself, which he assumes his father does not really believe. But the role of Evangelical religion in Butler's book is, nonetheless, considerable. More explicitly than any other Bildungsroman, the novel is grounded in the intellectual history of the Victorian period, and the fortunes of nineteenth-century Anglicanism are directly related to the action and the characters. During Theobald Pontifex's Cambridge career in the 1820's, "the great evangelical movement" led by Charles Simeon is "at its height." Like most young men taking orders at the time, Theobald, though no disciple of Simeon's, is a strict fundamentalist; yet he is enough of a "liberal" to examine the claims of geology, in

one of his first sermons, before concluding that all that is
worth anything at all in the science confirms "the absolutely
historical character of the Mosaic account of the Creation
as given in Genesis." In 1858, in his last term at Cambridge,
Ernest Pontifex encounters the Simeonites, or "Sims," who
represent "the remains of the Evangelical awakening of
more than a generation earlier." The University as a whole
is distracted by political events of the fifties, largely indifferent to theological controversy, and for the most part
ignorant of the new free thought of H. T. Buckle and
J. S. Mill.[9] In general, a complacent silence about religion
prevails. The Simeonites, however, holding themselves to
have received "a very loud call to the ministry," are a most
articulate and noisy minority. They enlist the aid of the
Reverend Gideon Hawke, "a well-known London Evangelical preacher," and Mr. Hawke's sermon, given in full,
moves the impressionable Ernest, just as a sermon on Hell,
likewise reproduced at length, will one day touch Stephen
Dedalus. Soon afterwards, during his curacy in London,
Ernest meets Pryer, an Oxonian and a specious spokesman
for the Oxford Movement, and he swings immediately from
Low Church to High. Next he dabbles rather amateurishly
in the Higher Criticism and comes to reject orthodoxy altogether. Later still when he goes home to Battersby to see
his dying mother, he notes that "the ever-receding tide of
Evangelicalism" is ebbing more and more rapidly: Theobald
has become sufficiently "high-church" to preach in a sur-
plice and to conduct a sung service. But in the end Ernest
decides with Butler that the Church, High or Low, is no
serious threat to his soul, since "the spirit behind the Church
is true, though her letter—true once—is now true no longer."
The real menace to the late Victorian is to be sought elsewhere, indeed among the scientists to whom Butler once

looked for salvation, for Ernest is finally convinced that "the spirit behind the Huxleys and Tyndalls is as lying as its letter."[10]

But despite Butler's disillusion with Victorian science, *The Way of All Flesh* remains a "scientific" Bildungsroman, by design a sort of evolutionary case history.[11] The evolution, to be sure, is decidedly Butlerian, a scheme as quirky almost as the elder Gosse's geology, and one prompted by a similar moral and even religious need. After an early enthusiasm for *The Origin of Species* Butler grew increasingly dissatisfied that Darwinism left no place for mind or will in the course of organic evolution but instead posited some unexplained genetic accident as the single cause of variations conducive to survival. During the seventies and early eighties when he was engaged in the writing of his novel, he developed his own anti-Darwinian theory in several monographs, *Life and Habit, Evolution Old and New, Unconscious Memory,* and *Luck, or Cunning?* and defended his stand in incensed letters to Darwin himself and to the public press. Drawing support from Lamarck's biology and other sources, he argued for the inheritance of acquired characteristics and the force of conscious desire, as well as lucky accident, in the process. As a vitalist he speculated on the persistence of thought and emotion through the generations. Heredity was memory; each man had many past existences, prenatal selves, and each must work out his past propensities for joy or pain. Knowledge of whatever kind, when thoroughly assimilated, became unconscious, a property of the self; and that man was in a state of perfect grace whose responses to every social situation were instinctive and immediate, the product of inherited strength and a once conscious self-education.

Much of this theorizing enters *The Way of All Flesh,*

either directly through the digressions of Overton the narrator, who even on one occasion quotes a passage from *Life and Habit*, or indirectly in Butler's proportioning of his fiction. Ernest, though the protagonist, does not appear until we have been introduced to his great-grandfather, John Pontifex (who dies thirty-three years before Ernest's birth), his grandfather, George, and his father, Theobald, and have come to know the character of each with some intimacy. But he has been nonetheless present from the beginning as his prenatal selves and has been molded for better and for worse by his past existences. His purpose in living, which he takes a long time to learn, is to recover something of the grace of old John, a creative spontaneity obscured by the calculations and aggressions of George and Theobald. Heredity thus assumes an importance in Butler's novel even beyond its role in *The Mill on the Floss*. But the development of the theme in such complex terms leads to contradictions and inconsistencies absent from George Eliot's lucid analysis of Dodson and Tulliver attributes. Overton, for example, speaking for the author, blames Theobald and his wife, Christina, for their cruelty to Ernest, but then at once suggests that, given their inheritance, they cannot be held accountable:

> As it was, the case was hopeless; it would be no use their even entering into their mothers' wombs and being born again. They must not only be born again but they must be born again each one of them of a new father and of a new mother and of a different line of ancestry for many generations before their minds could become supple enough to learn anew. The only thing to do with them was to humour them, and to make the best of them till they died—and be thankful when they did so.[12]

Overton seems to have forgotten that Alethea Pontifex, whom he greatly admired, was Theobald's sister and therefore must have shared his lineage, and, more alarmingly still, he ignores the fact that Ernest, sprung from such odious parents and ancestors, must somehow be redeemed. When the latter need does occur to him, he reflects that Ernest's blunders may be "due to postnatal rather than congenital misfortunes." But in admitting as much, he calls into question his own concept of heredity.

Some of the confusion arises from the fact that the scientific premises, though often personal to the point of eccentricity, accord ill with an even more subjective intention. Butler sets out not only to illustrate his evolutionary theory but also to write an apologia for his own life. And the two objectives do not always coincide, for the first involves the relation of the individual to his inheritance, and the second defends the hero's right to assert his complete independence of his father and mother and of all the traditions and pieties, natural or not, they represent. *The Way of All Flesh* is the most directly autobiographical Bildungsroman in English before *Sons and Lovers* and Joyce's *Portrait*. As a novelist Butler is most effective when closest to his own limited experience and least convincing—as in his description of Ernest's imprisonment and his unequal marriage—when imagining himself as his hero in situations beyond his ken. The lonely egoist in life,[13] he is not disposed, whatever his notions of inherited characteristics, to acknowledge in fiction a debt to his immediate forebears.

For most of the novel the autobiography wears little disguise. With a few striking departures, Ernest's career follows the author's even in many minute particulars. Like Butler, Ernest is born in 1835 and baptized in water brought from the River Jordan, passes several unhappy years at boarding school, then attends Cambridge, falls under the influence of the Simeonites, and graduates with some distinction in 1858. Taking orders, as Butler did not, he works, as Butler did, for some months among the London poor. He serves a prison sentence, as Butler did not, and breaks with his parents on the day of his release, September 30, 1859,[14] the precise date of Butler's sailing off from his family to the freedom of New Zealand. After a brief period as tradesman and husband, which Butler considered himself fortunate to have escaped, he settles into a comfortable life as essayist and critic and eventually writes a number of Butlerian books, only the first of which, like the first of Butler's,[15] enjoys any semblance of popularity. In the end he comes to value money as much as Butler did, but he here has one great advantage, a Butlerian wish-fulfillment: he is able to enjoy a much larger fortune at a much earlier age.

Butler's self-portrait is, of course, highly selective. Excluded from it, for instance, are memories of pleasant early visits to Italy, for Ernest's childhood and adolescence must be unrelieved by the joys of travel—even though the mature man, late in his story, lets slip a reference to an agreeable excursion to Normandy which he made as a boy with his parents, a holiday unmentioned before and scarcely in keeping with the grim regime of Battersby.[16] The secondary characters drawn from life are likewise simplified and manipulated, sometimes even exploited, usually to satiric ends. George Pontifex is a biting caricature of Butler's own grandfather, but Butler later felt that he had been so unfair that he prepared at great cost to himself his long, dull, reverential *Life and Letters of Dr. Samuel Butler*. Ernest's sister Charlotte is an unkindly composite of Butler's two sisters, for one of whom in fact he had some real affection. The poised Towneley and the prurient Pryer, on the other hand, are the two halves of Butler's handsome parasitic friend Charles Paine Pauli. Christina represents one aspect of Butler's own mother, and Butler did not hesitate in Chapter XXV to transcribe an actual letter she left to be read by her sons after her death. Aunt Alethea in turn embodies Mrs. Butler's good humor, as well as the wit and sophistication of Butler's confidante Miss Savage, who did more than anyone else to encourage the writing of the novel. And above all these looms Theobald, the father whom Butler can neither forgive nor forget.

As his family letters over many years attest,[17] Thomas Butler like Theobald had a strong self-will and a large measure of self-righteousness. Like Theobald he talked much of money and of the final disposition of his estate. Like Theobald he was disappointed in his son's choice of career and refused steadfastly to read his son's books, of which—he gathered quite correctly—he could only have disapproved. But unlike Theobald, who is described as "indolent in mind and body," Canon Butler was energetic, alert, and far from stupid. Though he did not read *Erewhon* and its successors, he thought enough of the reports "Sam" sent from New Zealand to have them published as *A First Year in Canterbury Settlement*. Near the end of his life he was pleased to see "Sam" stand as a candidate for the Slade Professorship of Fine Arts at Cambridge. He was often generous with money. He was, as far as we can judge, neither hypocritical in his religion nor insincere in his affection for his wife. He seems, in short, to have been no Theobaldian monster, but simply a strict and rather unimaginative father dealing with a son a good deal more cautious, evasive, and disingenuous than Ernest Pontifex. Yet the son's animus against him became the real motive force behind *The Way of All Flesh*.

Between 1873 when he began the novel and 1884 when he made his last revisions, Butler was beset by failure and frustration—neglect, indifferent health, lack of money, anxiety over his false friend Pauli. His concern with evolution inclined him to look to his unhappy childhood for the sources of his adult misery, and his fierce need of self-justification led him to blame his father for all his maladjustments.[18] To his friends he spoke of his home life in terms he would never have dared use at home, and when new irritations arose from correspondence or conversation with Canon Butler he added fresh detail to the portrait of Theobald. Miss Savage urged him to reduce the element of caricature in the interests of realism. But with every revision the bitterness increased: it is, for example, a late and unfortunate addition that allows Theobald as a small child to beat and tease his nurse and sadistically threaten her, "You shan't go away—I'll keep you on purpose to torment you."[19] Nonetheless, each quarrel with his father passed, and Butler remained sufficiently dependent to seek peace. Before he had finished the first draft of the first volume, he told Miss Savage of the difficulty of continuing: "Yes my novel will at last go ahead; but it must be quite innocent, for I am now reconciled to my father, and must be careful not to go beyond scepticism of the mildest kind. I shall have to change the scheme, but shall try to keep the earlier chapters."[20] The writing did not in fact go ahead for four years until another unpleasant exchange with his father gave Butler the necessary impetus, which carried him through to the end of the second volume. Then after further delays the last part, in which Theobald plays a minimal role, was written without the same impulsion and without much spirit; Ernest, as V. S. Pritchett remarks, "seems lost without his enemy"[21]—Butler, we might add, likewise seems half-hearted and perfunctory.

Variation in the degree of personal engagement clearly

did not make for unity of tone or perfect coherence of design. Butler himself, completing the second part, recognized the unevenness of his manuscript and complained to Miss Savage, "It is so much less readable than I yet see my way to making it—and it is full of little contradictions—I having intended at one time to turn the thing in one way, and having then turned it in another. . . ."[22] Though never polished to Butler's satisfaction, the final text clearly demonstrates that the right turning was nearly always in the direction of comedy. A fine dry wit shapes the most memorable scenes and situations: Theobald's dismal honeymoon, George Pontifex's spilling of the Jordan water on his wine-cellar floor, the dinner eaten by Dr. Skinner when he claims no appetite, Christina's many daydreams of acclaim from the high and mighty of the land. Here in each instance Butler develops a controlled satire, slyly amused rather than vindictive, taking off from personal observation of the characters involved, yet sublimating any initial animosity. In all the best passages of the novel his style is quickened by a characteristic irreverence, measured and even-tempered, essentially a kind of intellectual play. He delights in the misplaced epithet and the unexpected negative: Dr. Skinner has "the harmlessness of the serpent and the wisdom of the dove"; Theobald knows that "his father might be trusted not to help him"; and at Christina's funeral Theobald buries his face in his handkerchief "to conceal his want of emotion." He is adept at apposite misquotation: " 'Tis better to have loved and lost / Than never to have lost at all," or "The greatest nuisance to mankind is man." He warmly approves of Ernest's "odious habit of turning proverbs upside down" and gleefully cites an example: "A country is sometimes not without honour save from its own prophet."[23] In his exercise of reductive epigram and paradox for the calculated upsetting of convention, he is Wildean before Wilde, and a master in his own right.

But when his feelings, positive or hostile, are engaged, he writes with far less assurance. He had a lifelong affection for Cambridge and the sense of freedom it had given him. Yet when he comes to describe Ernest's happiness at college, he retreats from the task on the pretext that "the life of a quiet steady-going undergraduate has been told in a score of novels better than I can tell it."[24] Ernest's essay brashly deflating the claims of the Greek dramatists substitutes for all but the most summary account of his first three years at Emmanuel. Not until Ernest meets the Simeonites, who "gloried in the fact that in the flesh they had not much to glory," does the college narrative become circumstantial and alive, sharply defined in a satiric purpose.

And Butler's anger is even less effective than his sentiment, for it is more direct and obtrusive. When he drops the mask of irony to arraign the antagonists, his voice shrills with recrimination:

When I thought of the little sallow-faced lad whom I had remembered years before, of the long and savage cruelty with which he had been treated in childhood—cruelty none the less real for having been due to ignorance and stupidity rather than to deliberate malice; of the atmosphere of lying and self-laudatory hallucination in which he had been brought up; of the readiness the boy had shown to love anything that would be good enough to let him, and of how affection for his parents, unless I was much mistaken, had only died in him because it had been killed anew, again and again and again, each time that it had tried to spring; when I thought of all this I felt as though, if the matter had rested with me, I would have sentenced Theobald and Christina to mental suffering even more severe than that which was about to fall upon them.[25]

The speaker throughout the novel, to be sure, is ostensibly Edward Overton, but Overton's style and ideas are indistinguishable from Butler's, and his review of the child Ernest's suffering may properly be taken as a demonstration of Butler's self-pity. Yet there were distinct advantages in inventing a narrator with some personal stake in the story, but somewhat apart from the hero, a man contemporary with Theobald rather than with Ernest or Butler himself. Removed a generation in time, Overton can know and appraise Ernest's ancestors and so describe his "prenatal selves." Removed some distance in space as a resident of London during most of Ernest's childhood and adolescence, he can ignore such aspects of Ernest's experience as Butler does not choose to discuss. In his detachment he can be, whenever he wishes, as ironical about Ernest's naiveté and indecision as about Theobald's blustering. And, above all, being a worldly-wise older man, he can digress, far more freely than an objective novelist should, on all sorts of matters important to him and to Butler the essayist: family life, heredity, religion, music, schools and scholarship, health and criminality, money and money-making. But there were also problems in the creation of a persona, which Butler failed to solve. Overton must take a jaundiced, Butlerian view of clergymen and fathers; yet Overton's own father, as we meet him briefly in the first chapter, is a country vicar of great good sense and moral intelligence. Overton is a writer of stage burlesques, but he apparently knows less about the Victorian theater than about nineteenth-century evolutionary science. As narrator he violates the single point of view he must be expected to maintain; he reproduces conversations he could not possibly have heard and scenes, like the spilling of the baptismal water, he could

not have witnessed; he enters Ernest's mind, floats away on
Christina's stream of consciousness, and records precisely
what Theobald "exclaimed to himself" in the privacy of his
study. Usually he does not trouble to explain his omnisci-
ence. But when he does wish to account for some portions
of his narrative, he cites Ernest as his informant (though
Ernest's knowledge must, of course, be limited, too):
" 'And then, you know,' said Ernest to me, when I asked
him not long since to give me more of his childish reminiscences for the benefit of my story, 'we used to learn Mrs.
Barbauld's hymns. . . .' " Sometimes Ernest seems to be
almost a collaborating author, or at least the one called upon
to approve the manuscript as it unfolds. Overton, for example, at one point writes that Theobald without much
effort could have placed more trust in his son, and Ernest
immediately remonstrates: " 'Call that not much indeed,'
laughed Ernest, as I read him what I have just written.
'Why it is the whole duty of a father. . . .' " Overton represents the mature Ernest, the direction the young
man's development is to take. Eventually the two are
virtually one, in opinions, attitudes, and manner. Late in
the story, Overton, commenting on the hazards of fortune,
remarks, "I could see that Ernest felt much as I had felt
myself."[26] When such identification is possible, the hero is
ready to become his own narrator; Butler no longer needs
a persona.

In her letters Miss Savage usually refers to *The Way of
All Flesh* as "The Pontifexes," as if the novel were by
design a family saga. Butler himself, however, called his
final manuscript "Ernest Pontifex," a title suggesting that
the family matters were simply incidental to the portrait of
the hero, or, as we might say, to the purposes of a Bildungs-

roman. He was certainly aware of his predecessors in the genre, though he found little he could admire in any work of prose fiction and made no specific comment on the form. On completing the first volume of "Ernest Pontifex," he read *Wilhelm Meister* (possibly because he may have suspected that he was attempting something similar) and promptly damned it as "perhaps the very worst book" he had ever encountered.[27] He probably knew *The Mill on the Floss*, for he was interested enough in George Eliot to read *Middlemarch* on its first appearance and to decry it—ironically, in view of his own novel—as lacking in "sweetness" and "stuffed full of epigrams." He declared Meredith's work repulsive but may nonetheless have learned something of satiric characterization from *Richard Feverel*. And he professed to despise Dickens but was clearly not above imitating Dickensian sentiment as well as comedy.[28]

Whatever his sources apart from personal experience, Butler, consciously or not, invokes most of the conventions of the Bildungsroman. The theme of childhood is, as we should expect, once again important to the pattern of the whole, but it is not developed with anything like the dramatic immediacy of the early chapters of *David Copperfield* or *The Mill on the Floss*. Despite the vivid chronicle of his "prenatal selves," Ernest makes a colorless entrance, and he later seems to have very few clear-cut memories of his boyhood to brighten the impression the narrator has given us. Overton has no great fondness for children as such; nor indeed has the mature Ernest, who is glad to dispose rapidly of his own son and daughter. On the other hand, the motif of the hero's relation to his father receives almost as much emphasis in Butler's novel as in *Richard*

Feverel, and the intensity of alienated feeling is unparalleled anywhere in Meredith's fiction:

> Ernest made no reply to his father's letter, but his desire for a total break developed into something like a passion. "There are orphanages," he explained to himself, "for children who have lost their parents—oh why, why, why, are there no harbours of refuge for grown men who have not yet lost them?"—and he brooded over the bliss of Melchisedec who had been born an orphan—without father, without mother, and without descent.[29]

Like other heroes, Ernest does make the break and leaves behind the narrow provinciality of his parents for the freedom of the city, where eventually, after many trials and errors, he establishes himself as a sophisticated citizen of the world.

Butler insists that Ernest's "apprenticeship to life among the poor" in the slums of London is of more use to him than all his years of schooling, and the trade learned in prison worth the whole classical curriculum. Nonetheless, formal education, both at public school and at Cambridge, has a more precise role to play in *The Way of All Flesh* than in most other English Bildungsromane, for Butler thoroughly knew the discipline of Roughborough (which is Shrewsbury with some touches of Rugby), and he had observed at first hand the Simeonites of St. John's. Yet one sort of education usually of decisive importance in such novels is conspicuously missing. Neither in the provinces nor in the city does Ernest experience the educative power of love. He is virtually untouched by sexuality; he scarcely knows the object of his absurd encounter with Miss Maitland; he has no notion what the homosexual innuendoes of Pryer can mean; he brings no real passion to his marriage of convenience with Ellen and feels no deprivation when it is dissolved. Though only Aunt Alethea has given the child

Ernest a truly disinterested affection, it is still disconcerting to see the unloved boy become the loveless man with no sense of his deficiency.

Like Pip and Tom Tulliver and Julien Sorel, Ernest is concerned with both the gentlemanly ideal and the need of money, and with the possible conflict between the two. After more or less strenuous commitments to religion and irreligion, he decides that practically the man of faith and the freethinker "have the same ideal standard and meet in the gentleman; for he is the most perfect saint who is the most perfect gentleman," and a "charitable inconsistency," a Laodicean tolerance, is prerequisite to such perfection.[30] In his notebook Butler defined Butlerian saintliness: "To love God is to have good health, good looks, good sense, experience, a kindly nature and a fair balance of cash in hand."[31] In the novel Ernest's friend Towneley alone enjoys such attributes; yet godliness, except perhaps in the Olympian sense, is scarcely his most conspicuous quality. Big, handsome, genial, worldly-wise, orphaned from infancy, affluent beyond dreaming, Towneley is Ernest's complete hero, a man touched by special grace, above work and above reproach. "Towneley," he tells Overton, "is not only a good fellow, but he is without exception the very best man I ever saw in my life—except . . . yourself. Towneley is my notion of everything which I should most like to be."[32] Overton apparently shares Ernest's opinion, and to keep the friendship alive he snobbishly confides in Towneley that Ernest, though in disgrace and bound for prison, is, after all, a gentleman—"one of his own class"[33]— and will one day inherit a good deal of money. Towneley apparently needs the reassurance, for he dislikes thinking about the poor or about any other problem that might interfere with his effort "to get on comfortably in the world,

and to look, and be, as nice as possible."[34] Ernest never
loses his respect for Towneley, but he himself, on his
release from prison, prefers "to drop the gentleman and go
down into the ranks" rather than to clutch at a shabby
gentility and refrain from manual labor, which may bring
a living wage.[35] He therefore informs Ellen that he is "no
longer a gentleman" and allows her to instruct him in the
art of money-making as a tailor and small shopkeeper,
though Overton sees to it that he does not abandon his
more gentlemanly interest in books and music. By the
time that Ellen and the shop both fail him, he is almost
old enough to receive his inheritance and presumably to
reassume his role as gentleman. At this point, however, he
surprises Overton by insisting that he must give up Towneley, for he feels that he himself has not the gentlemanly
grace or habit to compete with his friend on equal terms,
and he knows that as an essayist he will now want to say a
great many ungentlemanly things to ruffle the composure of
polite society. He then sharply defends his decision:
"What," he asks, "has being a gentleman ever done for me
except to make me less able to prey and more able to be
preyed upon? . . . Will being a gentleman bring me
money at the last, and will anything bring me as much
peace at the last as money will?"[36] If he has to choose between money and the status of the gentleman as agents of
personal satisfaction, he is at the last emphatically on the
side of money, and, thanks to Overton's skillful speculation,
he is richer than any other young man in all the novels of
youth.

Money being bliss, Ernest finally reaches his Celestial
City. Butler, at any rate, may have thought of his arrival in
some such terms, for the novel was possibly conceived as a
modern satiric *Pilgrim's Progress*, and some clearly allegori-

cal elements mingle with its more realistic details. In early drafts Ernest is called Christian, and his elders in all versions, with appropriate theological or ecclesiastical names—Theobald, Alethea, Christina, and Pontifex itself—enjoy playing God and contending for the possession of his soul.[37] Overton, who is author of a burlesque of Bunyan, "oversees" his godson's progress from a godlike distance, perhaps reminiscent of that maintained by the members of the secret society who superintend Wilhelm Meister's initiation. Miss Savage warned Butler not to make Ernest merely a peg on which to hang his theories and fancies.[38] Butler, however, could not easily conceal the allegorist's will to see his characters as embodiments of the vices and virtues. As a result he has difficulty in sustaining our belief in the physical reality of his hero.

In his innocence and ineptitude Ernest, until quite late in his career, is the *ingénu* like Candide and Don Juan, though he is far less vigorous and gamesome than either of these. At school, where he proves physically frail and timid to the point of cowardice, he admires more robust boys, who scorn his weakness. He has consequently a well-developed sense of his own inferiority and no stability of judgment. In London, as curate, he remains credulous and unsuspecting, readily duped by Pryer's false analogies, naively excited by the news that a handsome income may be obtained simply "by buying things at a place they call the Stock Exchange."[39] He is easily swayed, wavers in what he thinks is his firm conviction, and is at any moment subject to "snipelike change of flight."

On several occasions, however, he is redeemed from delusion by a sudden insight, a brief epiphany. As he rides gloomily away from Roughborough School, the sun itself provides the "illumination"; he has been filled with self-reproach until, looking at the clouded sun, he realizes that his sins and sorrows are temporary shadows—whereupon the clouds part and he is "brought back to *terra firma* by the breaking forth of the sunshine." When he unexpectedly meets Towneley in the London slum and asks him, half-apologetically, half-self-righteously, whether he too does not like poor people very much, Towneley's firm "No, no, no" makes him at once aware of the hollowness of his commitment: "as though scales had fallen suddenly from his eyes, he saw that no one was nicer for being poor, and that between the upper and lower classes there was a gulf which amounted practically to an impassable barrier." Again, when Ellen reproaches him with having married her, "the scales [fall] from Ernest's eyes," and he knows immediately the mistake he has made.[40] In each instance the epiphany reveals personal error rather than timeless truth; it is designed to restore Ernest's common sense and not to provide, as in *The Prelude*, a transcendental vision. At Roughborough Ernest is troubled for the first time by a conflict between his "conscious self" and some darkly intuited "true self" or "inner self," that is, in later terms, between the ego (guided by the superego) and the id. His epiphanies are, in effect, awakeners of the id, his real character, resisting with a sense of perspective and the comic spirit the conventions that the ego has meekly accepted. And from time to time, even without a special signal, the id, or "true self," takes over. At his confirmation Ernest is consciously resolved to feel and be a better boy; but within two hours, to the narrator's great approval, he is ready to join spontaneously in the Guy Fawkes festivities and to see his father burned in effigy. Such episodes are the happy guarantee that he will not always be the amorphous *ingénu*.

Overton explains Ernest's delayed adolescence by insisting that "in mind as in body, like most of those who in the end come to think for themselves, he was a slow grower."[41] As long as he is growing and stumbling in the process, Ernest can be viewed with some measure of irony; when he reaches Overton's maturity, he is beyond Overton's censure. His initiation is completed only after two major crises, the first in prison, the second several years later, both of which Overton describes with all due sympathy and no trace of malice. Ernest learns nothing of the true horrors of prison life, nor does he achieve in his solitude, as the incarcerated Julien Sorel does, a real depth of self-knowledge. Confined to the infirmary for about half of his six-month sentence, he suffers a long delirium—in effect, a little death— from which he arises with a newborn sense of freedom. The illness thus proves an ultimate benefit, and the imprisonment a liberation. Not only does prison release him from bondage to his parents, his greatest obstacle to independence; it also encourages him to cast aside what is left of his religious faith and to substitute a wholly secular optimism, in which there is no commandment to honor father and mother. Regaining his health, he contentedly becomes an apprentice-tailor and, with cheerful inconsistency, serves as organist in the prison chapel.

At the second crisis, the happy ending of his foolish marriage, he is again stricken with brain fever, just as he is beginning "the honeymoon, as it were, of his renewed unmarried life." Neither attack involves present remorse or affliction; each results from reaction to an experience of suffering and responsibility now suddenly and joyfully terminated; each sickness marks a sharp break with the past, and each recovery assures the facing of the future without old encumbrance. The remedy on the second occasion is the sure prescription of Overton's London doctor: "time, prosperity, and rest"[42]—and the strongest of these is prosperity. Ernest is at last ready to enjoy the permanent satisfaction of managing his own inheritance.

In terms of plot the resolution of *The Way of All Flesh* is even less convincing than that of *The Mill on the Floss*. There is little suspense concerning the main issues of the narrative; we know almost from the beginning, since Overton frequently quotes the mature Ernest, that the naive protagonist will one day acquire a sophistication remarkably like Overton's, and we know also that Aunt Alethea's legacy, splendidly accumulating, lies in wait to end all problems. But three impediments, a wife and two children, must be removed before Ernest can achieve his bliss, and Butler, who never adequately revised the final volume of his novel, can hardly have been satisfied with the mode of their removal. The riddance of Ellen is particularly sudden, convenient, and improbable: John the coachman appears from nowhere to tell the astounded Ernest that he once married Ellen:

> "John," said my hero, gasping for breath—"are you sure of what you say—are you quite sure you—you really married her?"
> "Of course I am," said John, "I married her before the registrar at Letchbury on the 15th of August 1851."
> "Give me your arm," said Ernest, "take me into Piccadilly, put me into a cab, and come with me at once, if you can spare time, to Mr. Overton's at the Temple."[43]

The fact that the style seems an intentional burlesque of popular melodrama hardly makes the passage more acceptable or appropriate as the ending to a sketch of alcoholism potentially as grim as a story by Zola. Though less theatrical, the abandoning of the children to the care of the jolly bargeman is no less facile, and a sentimental description crudely glosses over what Dickens or George Eliot would have portrayed as at best a difficult adjustment. Still the children and Ellen are, after all, mere shadows; we are asked in the end to give our undivided attention to Ernest.

In his affluent maturity Ernest tells Overton, "I will live as I like living, not as other people would like me to live; thanks to my aunt and you, I can afford the luxury of a quiet unobtrusive life of self-indulgence, . . . and I mean to have it." Overton, who began his narrative with speculation on the relative success of old John Pontifex and his son George, has no doubt that Ernest at the last is a completely successful man—"those who know him intimately do not know that they wish him greatly different from what he actually is."[44] But the intimates are apparently few and far between, since Ernest has deliberately cut himself off from society; and if the few are complacent hedonists like Overton, they must be rather limited as judges of his character. At all events, insofar as his opinions coincide with Overton's, Ernest is not only approved but self-approving, perhaps the most self-satisfied hero in the history of the English Bildungsroman. Even so, we must suspect that some of his self-possession is ironic and defensive, for Ernest like Butler is more than the idle dilettante; he is the dedicated writer, without audience in his own time, but half-hopeful that he may one day be discovered by a posterity in which he does not wholly believe.

❦ VI ❧

WALTER PATER:
THE DISTANCE OF MARIUS

I n the "Conclusion" to *The Renaissance* of 1873
Walter Pater argued that, since all impressions were relative
to the individual, each man's knowledge was necessarily
subjective: each of us, he said, is isolated by "that thick wall
of personality through which no real voice has ever pierced
on its way to us, or from us to that which we can only con-
jecture to be without, . . . each mind keeping as a solitary
prisoner its own dream of a world." Twelve years later in
Marius the Epicurean he ascribed the same notions in precisely the same imagery to his hero: "so Marius continued
the sceptical argument he had condensed, as the matter to
hold by, from his various philosophical reading:—given,
that we are never to get beyond the walls of the closely shut
cell of one's own personality; that the ideas we are somehow
impelled to form of an outer world, and of other minds akin
to our own, are, it may be, but a day-dream, . . . then, he,
at least, in whom those fleeting impressions—faces, voices,
material sunshine—were very real and imperious, might
well set himself to the consideration, how such actual moments as they passed might be made to yield their utmost,
by the most dexterous training of capacity."[1]
The "Conclusion" to *The Renaissance*, suppressed in 1877
for fear that "it might possibly mislead some of those young

140

men into whose hands it might fall,"[2] was restored in the third edition with a footnote explaining that "the thoughts suggested by it" had been developed more fully in *Marius*. Indeed one of Pater's central purposes in writing the fiction was to clarify the misunderstood counsels of the essay. The Epicureanism of Marius is so patently circumspect, laborious, and discriminating that it is difficult to see how "some among his acquaintance" could regard it as the sanction for a vulgar pleasure-seeking, a life of impressions without values or distinctions. But Pater himself, the object too often of suspicion and ridicule, dreaded to have his views so mistaken. The defense of the young Roman must be read as the apologia of the middle-aged Oxonian.

The resemblances between Marius and Pater are parallels of sensibility and temper rather than action, for Marius acts scarcely at all. The novel is subtitled "His Sensations and Ideas," and the self presented is simply the aggregate of those elements. The self has almost no physical dimension; the sensations pass into the mind where they become ideas, but in passage they bring no appreciable joy or discomfort to the body. Of a climactic moment of vision, we are told: "Himself—his sensations and ideas—never fell again precisely into focus as on that day"; and the experience of that privileged day, apart from the appreciation of a lovely landscape, is entirely mental. From the beginning Marius consciously assumes the role of the spectator, not just observing keenly as David Copperfield does in the course of a more active career, but savoring his impressions and appraising their aesthetic pattern. And at the end we are assured that he has always set the *seeing* "above the *having*, or even the *doing*, of anything," for seeing at its most intense has been his mode of *being*. Pater—with his bare rooms at Brasenose, the bleakest of the Oxford colleges, to bear witness—prac-

ticed a similar austerity, likewise cultivated a wise passive-
ness, also discounted the having and the doing of things, and
imposed a comparable discipline upon his imperious sensations. If there are occasional suggestions of a latent homo-
sexuality in his biography as there may be in the accounts of
Marius's devotion to his friends Flavian and Cornelius,
there is little evidence in the life story or the fiction of any
overt passion for either men or women; human beings apparently kindled less response than congenial ideas or
comely artifacts. It is an unusual sort of hero of whom a
novelist can write as Pater writes of nineteen-year-old
Marius: "And now, in revolt against that pre-occupation
with other persons, which had so often perturbed his spirit,
his wistful speculations as to what the real, the greater, experience might be, determined in him, not as the longing
for love—to be with Cynthia, or Aspasia—but as a thirst for
existence in exquisite places." If Cynthia or Aspasia ever
existed except as types of feminine frivolity (neither has
been previously mentioned in the novel), each might have
expected some personal attention or commitment. The
exquisite place, on the other hand, may more safely engage
the capacities of the aloof spectator; and Pater clearly endorses Marius's preference. Besides, Marius, again like Pater,
has learned from literature a fastidiousness of taste which
gross reality can seldom satisfy; he has found in Apuleius's
tale of Cupid and Psyche "the ideal of a perfect imaginative love," beside which, forever afterwards, "men's actual
loves . . . might appear . . . to be somewhat mean and
sordid."[3]

At twenty-one Pater self-consciously abandoned an early
ambition to be a poet, destroyed his verse manuscripts, and
turned deliberately to the craft of prose. As a schoolboy at
Pisa Marius conceives for himself "the fame . . . of a poet

perhaps," but by the time he is summoned to Rome at
nineteen to serve as amanuensis to Marcus Aurelius, he too
has moved from poetry to prose and resolved to become
a systematic student of rhetoric. As a Roman *rhetor* he may
aspire to become "the eloquent and effective interpreter
. . . of the beautiful house of art and thought," or virtually,
in Victorian terms, a Paterian critic of aesthetic and intellectual culture. Yet whatever his medium, he remains always
"of the poetic temper"—that is, he lives much in reminiscence and asks of each intense impression of the present,
"How will it look to me, at what shall I value it, this day
next year?"[4] If he never proves himself an artist, he is still
essentially the aesthete, the first of his kind in an English
Bildungsroman. Though David Copperfield is a novelist and
Ernest Pontifex an essayist, neither professes a dominant
concern with aesthetic perception or expression. Marius's
response to the harmonious gesture and his regard—reflecting Pater's—for the "science" of words and the magic
of style, his imagining a refined religion of art[5] and his
notion that the insight of the artist may at times supersede
merely conventional morality, all anticipate the attitudes of
Stephen Dedalus and, to a lesser extent, of Paul Morel.
Marius's self—his sensations and ideas—looks forward to a
time when the aesthetic sensibility will claim to be its own
all-sufficient criterion of values.

Throughout the undramatic narrative Pater keeps us
aware of the "modernity" of his second-century hero. "Let
the reader pardon me," he begs, "if here and there I seem
to be passing from Marius to his modern representatives—
from Rome, to Paris or London."[6] The English counterparts are presumably Wildean aesthetes and academic intellectuals of the eighties. The French may well be young
men in fiction from the Romantics through Flaubert and the

Goncourts, for *Marius* derives no less from literature than from observation. Pater was familiar with the Bildungsroman in both France and Germany. He "never tired" of *The Red and the Black,* and he apparently found *Wilhelm Meister* as attractive as Butler found it repulsive.[7] Wilhelm's discovery that his "America is here and now—here, or nowhere" is cited in *Marius* as sanction for an Epicureanism properly heedful of the present. Though less calculating than Wilhelm in his search for self-culture, Marius is almost as conscious of a need to educate the sensibility. From his visit as a boy to the temple of Aesculapius he takes away "a lesson in the skilled cultivation of life, of experience, of opportunity." After Flavian's death he attempts to reorient himself, "to determine his bearings, as by compass, in the world of thought," and he seriously ponders "the aim of the right education of one's self." For a few years he demands the Cyrenaic ideal of *paideia,* "a wide, a complete, education, . . . directed especially to the expansion and refinement of the power of reception, . . . an 'aesthetic' education, as it might now be termed." Finally his development at its end is summed up as "that elaborate and lifelong education of his receptive powers."[8]

Marius's acute awareness of his mental progress, like his aestheticism, distinguishes him from earlier heroes of the English Bildrungsroman. Nonetheless, he shares with them a number of concerns characteristic of the genre. He, too, feels estranged from his father—but by death rather than clash of temperament, though like other fatherless youths he somehow resents the dimly remembered "tall grave figure" simply for dying and leaving him to find a substitute. Like David Copperfield he is devoted to his widowed mother until abruptly bereft of her affection. Like Pip and others he moves from the provinces and provincial simplicities to the city and urban sophistication. But unlike most nineteenth-century heroes he has no economic struggle; despite a spendthrift ancestor, he may assume a considerable affluence as his birthright—a slave to carry his school books, servants to attend him on his travels, and a many-balconied town-house in Rome. The familiar problem of gentlemanly status is here but lightly touched on, for Marius with all the patrician graces is immediately and naturally "the Roman gentleman" and, far more readily than Pip, can also be something of an intellectual dandy, finding himself suddenly "the fashion," remarkable for his reserve and a self-possession "perceptible in voice, in expression, and even in his dress."[9] Since as the surrogate for Pater he is denied passionate attachments, Marius escapes the two love affairs that are usually a part of the hero's initiation—unless the friendships with the worldly Flavian and the spiritual Cornelius may be so regarded. Flavian, before we meet him, has already evidently experimented with sensuality and the "lower" love, has dallied with the Cynthias and Aspasias Marius will coolly pass by, or, as Pater puts it with inimitable discretion, has "yielded himself, though still with untouched health, in a world where manhood comes early, to the seductions of that luxurious town," until Marius wonders sometimes, "in the freer revelation of himself by conversation, at the extent of his early corruption."[10] Marius for his part may possibly be contemplating the "higher," less debasing love when he speculates quite calmly that in marriage to the widowed Cecilia, if indeed the Christians did not oppose second marriages and if he himself did not suspect it might be wrong "to mix together the spirit and the flesh," he might find "such a sister, at least, as he had always longed for."[11] But such half-hearted sentiment, recorded without conviction almost as a parenthetic afterthought, hardly qualifies as experience of even the most rarefied of exalting loves. Cecilia does not emerge with half the vitality of the too-ideal Agnes Wickfield, nor is her presence nearly so important to Marius as that of Agnes to David.

Comparison with *David Copperfield*, which Pater must have read soon after its appearance, helps define the method of *Marius*. There is one striking parallel between the two books, Flavian's resemblance to Steerforth: each is a sort of Byronic hero, satanically self-willed yet charming, able to make the younger boy—Marius or David—feel grateful for his attention and glad to accept his dictates.[12] But Steerforth lives in his restless activity, his speech and gesture, his relationship to his proud mother and the strange Rosa Dartle. Flavian exists only as the sketch of a temperament, an attitude, an ambition, like a Theophrastian character. He comes dramatically to life only when he is dying: in the single snatch of real talk in the whole work, Marius asks, "Is it a comfort that I shall often come and weep over you?" and Flavian replies with appropriate cynicism, "Not unless I be aware, and hear you weeping!"[13] Pater attended the King's School at Canterbury, the model for Dr. Strong's establishment in Dickens's novel. But neither the school nor its fictional counterpart bears any similarity to the shadowy Pisan place where Marius is educated. Pater shows no concern for the precise descriptive detail or any of the other properties of realism that Dickens could manipulate to ends greater than reality. He avoids action as far as possible, dispenses with plot and incident, refuses to traffic in suspense or melodramatic contrivance. By the time of *Marius* he has repudiated the fiction that delighted his boyhood. "Dickens," he told a friend, "is a monument of wasted energy, but then he wrote for the unlettered."[14] *Marius*, on the other hand, is apparently written for the few discriminating enough to appreciate a Paterian sensibility.

Conscious of its difference, Pater chose to regard his book not as a novel at all but as the longest and most elaborate of his several "imaginary portraits." The first of these had appeared in *Macmillan's Magazine* in 1878 as "The Child in the House," the autobiographical memory of a boy as nervous, sensitive, and impressionable as the young Proust, in a style that Proust could have admired. Whether or not the sketch was intended as the opening of a modern Bildungsroman which was abandoned as too circumstantially personal,[15] it is assuredly close in tone and manner to the first two chapters of *Marius*, begun within the next two years. Pater's imaginary portraits are introspective narratives analyzing currents of thought and feeling in a particular ambiance of ideas, against a physical background suggested rather than described. The technique is not that of the omniscient novelist illuminating action but rather that of the historian recording past events, interpreting motives from a distance, and assessing after-effects. The narrator of *Marius*, presumably Pater himself, is distinctly a man of the nineteenth century, and he constantly relates the Roman world of his hero to his own time and to all the centuries between.[16] But since Marius's attitudes and perceptions are largely indistinguishable from his own, he presents a great deal from Marius's point of view. Marius is present as each spectacle rolls past, for the Rome of Marcus Aurelius exists only as Marius the spectator perceives it. Despite the violence of the setting, the roaring parades and the noisy amphitheater, the portrait is consistently quiet, as if Marius must calmly sort and classify his impressions. We are told the import of a few conversations, but we do not hear the words; even at a critical moment, Marius's introduction to a Christian household, talk is translated into gesture as in a silent film: Cornelius "held the door open for his companion to enter also, if he would; *with an expression,* as he lifted the latch, *which seemed to ask* Marius, apparently shrinking from a possible intrusion: 'Would you like to see it?' "[17] Though the sensations are sometimes sharp, the details are frequently blurred, as if too many specifics would distract from the mental life. Thus while Marius muses portentously in the olive-garden, "a bird" sings, "an animal" draws near, and the "child" who keeps it gazes quietly; but we never know what kind of bird or animal it is, or the sex or age of the child; we are but dimly aware, as Marius is, of presences in an objective landscape, outside the mind, on the edges of consciousness. And the vagueness extends to the principal characters. Marius's mother sickens and dies abruptly, without explanation—in a single sentence—and her death is significant only insofar as it propels Marius into a new phase of his development, though we never learn, as we should in Dickens, how the orphaned youth copes with his bereavement. Similarly, later, we are not sure precisely what work Marius does for Marcus Aurelius or how frequently he is granted private audience. We have no idea what Cecilia thinks of Marius or if she considers him at all. And we can only guess the difficulties Cornelius must have in concealing his faith from his fellow-legionnaires or reconciling it to a stern military code. But such matters, though they would be of great moment in a conventional novel, are clearly of little consequence in a "portrait," where a philosophical or spiritual quest is to dominate all else.

As the historian might introduce documentary evidence, the narrator of *Marius* from time to time interrupts his ordered analysis with interpolated materials intended to advance or simply to illustrate his central themes. When he describes his hero's diary as "a register of the movements of his own private thoughts and humours," we expect direct, "dramatic" self-revelation as in Clare's diary in *Richard Feverel* or Stephen's in Joyce's *Portrait* (which, in other respects, is indebted to Pater's "portrait"). The journal, however, proves little more than a commonplace book in which Marius enters his detached, rather impersonal impressions of the world's pain and vignettes of persons in distress whom he has seen on the streets but has had to pass by "on the other side."[18] Yet it serves to suggest Marius's yearning for a wider and deeper charity than the emperor can legislate. The letter from the Christian community in Gaul, quoted at length in the chapter that follows, rings with the commitment of a Pauline epistle and so provides such testimony of fortitude in the face of brutality as the aloof narrator could scarcely offer in his own words. The inclusion of a discourse by Marcus Aurelius and the paraphrase of an address by Cornelius Fronto seems a reasonable way of acquainting the reader with the principles of Stoicism, which Marius, present at both lectures, must carefully ponder. On the other hand, the interpolation of "The Story of Cupid and Psyche," almost as long as the Man of the Hill's tale in *Tom Jones*, may strike us an overindulgence in the niceties of style, for the myth has little direct relation to Marius's development, except as an example of his aesthetic idealism and the measured prose in which he delights.[19] And the Socratic dialogue between Lucian and Hermotimus, a long witty chapter in an exceptionally sober book, may seem to exceed its purpose, which, I take it, is the demonstration to Marius of the indefensible arrogance of the Stoics. Each of these departures or digressions from the central narrative tends to make what is already indirect all the more oblique.

The main source of obliquity in *Marius* is, of course, the remote historical setting, unusual in any autobiographical Bildungsroman. By removing himself altogether in time and place from a hero with a temperament very like his own, Pater is able to present highly personal views of art and life with an air of objectivity. Though we are given few precise dates, references to public events in the reign of Marcus Aurelius suggest that Marius is born about A.D. 149, comes to Rome in 168, and dies about 177.[20] He is fixed so firmly in a specific past that we must consider his sensations and ideas first of all in that distant context. Then reading if we will between the lines, we may discover a Victorian relevance where we might not have expected to find it. Sometimes Pater makes the parallel quite explicit: "That age and our own have much in common—many difficulties and hopes."[21] Sometimes he clearly implies it, as when he discusses the vicarious experience of horror: "For the long shows of the amphitheatre were, so to speak, the novel-reading of that age—a current help provided for sluggish imaginations, in regard, for instance, to grisly accidents, such as might happen to one's self; but with every facility for comfortable inspection."[22] Occasionally he merely insinuates a similarity: "During fifty years of public quiet, a sober brown and gray had grown apace on things"— "fifty years of peace, broken only by that conflict in the East"[23]—phrases which suggest the condition of England as Victoria approached her golden jubilee, and the long peace that had been interrupted briefly by the Crimean War and the Indian Mutiny. One typical judgment of the era might almost have been borrowed from Matthew

Arnold's indictment of the nineteenth-century Philistines:
Marius hopes that "the precept of 'culture,' as it is called,
or of a complete education—might at least save him from
the vulgarity and heaviness of a generation, certainly of
no general fineness of temper, though with a material well-
being abundant enough."[24] Whatever his place in ancient
Rome, Marius from the age of nineteen feels a thoroughly
"modern" alienation from an insensitive affluent society.

By birth and good fortune, Marius belongs to a cultural
elite. He mingles freely with the leading writers and
philosophers of his time, and he duly appreciates their wit,
wisdom, and rhetoric. Yet he senses serious threats to the
intellectual life, both inside Rome and on the far frontiers,
where the barbarians are rapidly gathering strength. Much
as he admires the emperor's Stoic discourse to the Senate,
he feels it remote and irrelevant, powerless to forestall
a grim future. We share his uneasiness as we grasp the
symbolic import of the setting: Aurelius concludes the
address in the failing light of a snowy evening, the first
night, we are told, of an unusually severe winter when the
wolves will descend from the hills to carry off the dead
bodies of plague victims and many citizens will suffer cold
and darkness while the happier few pay high prices for fur
garments and the lustrous red and yellow roses imported
from Carthage.

Marius finds the Roman multitude "a coarse, a vulgar
people," but he sees no moral leadership in his own ruling
class. The indifference of even the emperor to human suffering amounts to an acquiescence in wrong, a tolerance
of evil not unfamiliar, Pater intimates, to later generations
only too ready to rationalize the slave-trade or a religious
persecution or to profit, without twinge of conscience, from
the injustice of innumerable "legal crimes." Acted upon

rather than acting, Marius is saved from despair only by
the unaccountable confidence of Cornelius; otherwise, he
would feel "alternately suffocated and exhausted by an existence, at once so gaudy and overdone, and yet so intolerably empty, in which people, even at their best, seemed
only to be brooding, like the wise emperor himself, over a
world's disillusion."[25] Marius observes corruption in high
places—the crassness of Lucius Verus, voluptuary and co-
emperor, the flagrant infidelities of the empress Faustina.
He helplessly witnesses the sadism of the amphitheater,
the taunting of prisoners of war, the torture of animals, a
courtesan bathed in blood carried through the streets in an
orgy of religious superstition. In short, despite its great
philosopher-king, the age of Marcus Aurelius is, as Pater
judges it, "decadent," and Marius is the first Bildungsroman
hero consciously living in a dying culture.

The aesthete's usual response to social decadence is a
deliberate art for art's sake, the adoption of a self-sustained
style. Even before coming to Rome, when he has only a
dim notion of the unaesthetic world he must eventually encounter, Marius considers such a solution—art as escape and
refuge—or rather is allowed to consider it through Flavian,
who is, as it were, his alter ego or surrogate, a more aggressive self, standing at the center of the Pisan chapters, while
Marius recedes into the background. Flavian discovers his
"golden book," *The Golden Ass* of Apuleius, and carefully
appraises the quality of its mannered prose, itself the product
of a ripe or overripe civilization, an erudite, eclectic style
"full of the archaisms and curious felicities in which that generation delighted, quaint terms and images picked fresh from
the early dramatists, the life-like phrases of some lost poet
preserved by an old grammarian, racy morsels of the ver-
nacular and studied prettinesses." Oscar Wilde's Dorian

Gray, clearly indebted to Flavian's example, seizes upon Huysmans' *A Rebours* and strives to reproduce its decadent sensations. Flavian, however, is more intelligent and sophisticated in using his golden book. From his reading of Apuleius he derives a new semantics; he has learned something of the integrity of words and the mystery of root meanings. Like Stephen Dedalus, he expects to realize himself through language, to control reality by naming it. "Others," we are told, "might brutalise or neglect the native speech, that true 'open field' for charm and sway over men. He would make of it a serious study, weighing the precise power of every phrase and word, as though it were precious metal, disentangling the later associations and going back to the original and native sense of each,—restoring to full significance all its wealth of latent figurative expression, reviving or replacing its outworn or tarnished images."[26] Denying all other religion, Flavian makes a faith of style. Yet style, the art he reveres, does not really exist independently, for art's sake; it is personal and not absolute, not an end, but a means of self-expression, a weapon of self-advancement. Marius for a time presumably accepts Flavian's creed; but Flavian soon dies, and his fierce aestheticism proves to have been but a passing stage in his friend's development. Marius, who will carry no weapon, needs a stronger shield than style to withstand the world's decadence.

Pater does indeed declare Marius's acquisition of a firm prose style a mark of his coming of age—surely a most aesthetic gauge of a young man's majority.[27] The intellectual quest, however, has only begun. Passing beyond Flavian's position, Marius ponders a more and more refined Epicureanism, dedicated to the key principle "Be perfect in regard to what is here and now." But the precept allows him no adequate understanding of what is less than perfect in the present, the inescapable pain and heartbreak of each day's life; and it does not provide for his visions of the future, the extensions of present hopes and fears that repeatedly widen his range. Despite the epithet, Marius in truth is not for long "the Epicurean" at all. Shortly Stoicism, with its recognition of what is to be endured, seems to offer an attractive and viable alternative, especially as the austere ethic is propounded by the philosopher-king. Marius is prepared to see in Marcus Aurelius both the father he has lost and a high heroic ideal, and he is in fact immediately impressed by the emperor's kindliness, courtesy, intelligence, and natural simplicity of manner. He respects his dignity and self-possession, the severe self-control that may cover a personal sorrow or hide a weariness of spirit; and in the journals and diaries that he must copy he finds a congenial inwardness, the same compulsion toward self-portraiture that he himself has felt. The emperor is to him the very incarnation of Stoic reason and self-knowledge. Yet soon after his first visit to the imperial palace, he is distressed to observe Aurelius's deportment in the amphitheater, his bland aloofness from the vulgarity and violence, as if the bloody contests in the arena could be no concern of his. However high his regard for the emperor's intellect, Marius now sees a decisive and abiding limitation: "There was something in a tolerance such as this, in the bare fact that he could sit patiently through a scene like this, which seemed to Marius to mark Aurelius as his inferior now and for ever on the question of righteousness; to set them on opposite sides, in some great conflict, of which that difference was but a single presentment." The negative impression deepens until Marius witnesses the triumph in which Aurelius complacently leads his hapless captives; it is clear then that the man who once represented the golden mean of discipline and temperance has been debased to the level of his public, "in a mediocrity no longer golden."[28] The emperor thus fails in sympathy; as humanist he lacks true humanity: he discerns evil only to ignore it or appease it, never to oppose it. Marius finds the Stoic way scarcely more satisfactory than the Epicurean.

No philosophy of his time answers Marius's discontent with an unstable present, his will to look before and after, his need to discover a continuity of hope and affection. No purely intellectual argument speaks to his essentially poetic sensibility. Significantly, the first "modern" writer Pater mentions in *Marius* is Wordsworth, who is praised for his understanding of the role of tradition among rural men and his awesome sense of a moral life in or behind everyday places and objects. If Marius outgrows the simple religion of his childhood, he must nonetheless recover a Wordsworthian respect for his personal past; like Maggie Tulliver, he requires a "natural piety" to bind his days together. He achieves a mature selfhood only when he is willing to return to White-nights, the home he has loved as a boy. There he repairs the neglected mortuary and dutifully reburies his parents, and in that filial act he is reconciled to his father and brought to a new understanding of compassion:

> That hard feeling, again, which had always lingered in his mind with the thought of the father he had scarcely known, melted wholly away, as he read the precise number of his years, and reflected suddenly—He was of my own present age; no hard old man, but with interests, as he looked round him on the world for the last time, even as mine to-day! And with that came a blinding rush of kindness, as if two alienated friends had come to understand each other at last.[29]

Throughout his short life Marius finds his most vivid
and decisive experience, as here, in sudden accesses of emotion, sharp insights, impressions that linger to elate or alarm
but always to place the self in a new dimension of time.
Like the child Wordsworth he has known the ministry
of fear. As a boy he is troubled for many days by the ugly
sight of snakes breeding by a narrow road, and he remembers his sickened reaction several years later when he sees
an African showman with a serpent in Pisa: "once more, as
the reptile writhed, the former painful impression revived:
it was like a peep into the lower side of the real world, and
again for many days took all sweetness from food and
sleep."[30] Later still, in Rome, he is reminded of his fear by
another exhibition of serpents, and he reflects, like the mature Wordsworth, on the importance of a child's distresses,
which the adult too often underestimates. He values the
force of memory: he attempts to stamp every detail of
Flavian's death on his mind so that he will never forget his
feeling of outrage and resentment, and, remembering some
years later,[31] he views his own imminent death with the same
emotions. But his intuitions of meaning frequently look to
the future rather than the remembered past. At the temple
of Aesculapius he is shown a vista, through a sliding panel,
of distant towers and a dome, and the sight of the far city
becomes at once the promise of what is to ensue, "the vision
of a new world, . . . the very presentment of a land of
hope."[32] In Rome as he listens to the emperor's public
address, his imagination carries him forward to a time when
the Capitol will be in ruins and the Forum overgrown with
grass. This habit of prescience, which Pater describes as the
inverse of the familiar *déjà vu* experience,[33] carries with it
a sense of physical or spiritual renewal, the assertion of a
new vitality on a larger scale.

Marius's most intense epiphany, combining remembrance
and prescience, is his meditation in the olive-garden of a
country inn. There with strange detachment, "lost"—in the
Wordsworthian way—to present things, he sees himself
traveling "through a dreamy land, as if in another life, and
like another person, through all his fortunes and misfortunes, passing from point to point, weeping, delighted,
escaping from various dangers," and he muses on the notion that in his solitude there may always have been some
companion by his side, a secret sharer in all his experience.
The concept of a sacred double, a sort of personal guardian
angel, leads to a contemplation of ideal modes of being, and
so to the Great Ideal that is God. Then by a flash of insight
Marius has a brief glimpse of the mind of God as the infinite
continuum in which all things, even his helpless human self,
move and act and where, as in a fathomless reservoir of
memory, no fleeting impression is ever forgotten. The
mystical vision of "this peculiar and privileged hour" never
returns, but it has given the young man a memorable sense
of integration and, more important, a sanction for the gratitude he has always felt "when he [has] been at his best" (a
phrase close in meaning to Wordsworth's conditional "if
but once we have been strong"). And it has defined his true
object in living, the demands he must make upon the world
as he seeks manifestations of the Ideal "among so-called
actual things."[34]

Though a Roman soldier exposed to the actualities of a
rough age, Cornelius is too highly idealized to seem more—
or less—than a paragon of true knightly virtue. But as he appears at the beginning of their friendship, long before Marius
has discerned his goal in life, he stands transfixed for a moment in a "spot of time," altogether dazzling and prescient
of a new order: he has been fastening on his armor—as if

it were "the whole armor of God"[35]—in an abandoned villa, where the sun falls in bars through the shutters, "and as he gleamed there, amid that odd interchange of light and shade, with the staff of a silken standard firm in his hand, Marius felt as if he were face to face, for the first time, with some new knighthood or chivalry, just then coming into the world." Ever afterwards Marius remembers the moment and the pattern of light in which every object "seemed to be but sign or symbol of some other thing far beyond it,"[36] and he looks to Cornelius as an unfailing source of strength and serenity. He is relatively slow in guessing his friend's religion, but he is brought by his example to a respect for Christian conduct, long before he is actually led to the Christian household of Cecilia.

Whether or not it can be construed as a reasoned defense of Christianity, *Marius the Epicurean* is clearly an attack on the pagan philosophies that Marius explores. "I *did* mean it," Pater told William Sharp, "to be more anti-Epicurean than it has struck you as being."[37] To Marius the real failure of the Epicureans—and the Stoics, too—lies in their skepticism and complete lack of sympathy with all life outside a narrowly circumscribed range, "in the sacrifice of a thousand possible sympathies, of things only to be enjoyed through sympathy, from which they detached themselves, in intellectual pride, in loyalty to a mere theory that would take nothing for granted, and assent to no approximate or hypothetical truths."[38] Marius himself seeks a religion of compassion in an age ready to rationalize its brutality and indifference, and his standard of judgment is implicitly "Christian" before he knows the meaning of that label. Christianity, as he ultimately comes to understand it, is committed to "the maintenance of a kind of candid discontent, in the face of the very highest achievement, . . . the con-

sciousness of some profound enigma in things, as but a
pledge of something further to come, . . . a permanent
protest established in the world, a plea, a perpetual afterthought, which humanity henceforth would ever possess
in reserve, against any wholly mechanical and disheaten-
ing theory of life itself and its conditions."[39] He is attracted
to the new faith by the aesthetic appeal of its ritual, but he
finds that it answers his moral need no less than his sense of
beauty. No doubt he simplifies and possibly distorts, shows
little interest in doctrine or dogma, knows nothing of controversy or heresy within the Church. Mrs. Humphry
Ward, reviewing *Marius*, objected that Pater had not done
justice to the complexity of second-century Christianity or
to the conflicts and divisions among the early Christians,
but her complaint confuses historical fiction with the objective data of history. T. S. Eliot repeated the charge, insisted that Pater knew "almost nothing" of the essence
of the Christian faith, and added that the book was important chiefly as evidence of the inadequacy of Victorian
religion, for to the end the hero "remains only a half-awak-
ened soul."[40] Yet Marius is not presented as a Christian con-
vert; at the end he is still relatively young, still developing
his view of life, slowly moving toward greater and greater
sympathy with the Christian dispensation. Pater is concerned not with apologetics but with the depiction of a
temperament, admittedly very like his own, to whom some
sort of religion is both a necessity and a possibility. Marius's
vision in the olive grove may be as valid as Eliot's moment
in the rose-garden. Religious experience is not limited to a
single orthodoxy.

The ending of *Marius*, however, does give problems,
not because the passive protagonist remains "a half-awak-
ened soul" but because he springs precipitantly into action.

In the first paragraph of the last chapter Pater awkwardly prepares for an unexpected conclusion. Marius, he says, would have welcomed a life of adventure, had not the whole movement of his temper been so inward; now death must provide some final excitement: "Death, . . . as he reflected, must be for every one nothing less than the fifth or last act of a drama, and, as such, was likely to have something of the stirring character of a *dénouement*." The circumstances of the dying are indeed dramatically contrived. Cornelius joins Marius at White-nights and sets out with him for Rome. In a small town on the way Cornelius slips off at day-break for a service at the tomb of a Christian martyr. Just as Marius finds him, an earthquake shakes the town, and almost immediately the townsmen descend upon the worshippers with the superstitious conviction that the Christian rites have offended the old gods and so provoked the disturbance. Marius is mistakenly seized along with the Christians but declines to reveal his identity. Instead, "under a sudden, uncontrollable impulse, hardly weighing what he did" (until now he has always been painfully deliberate), he arranges by a bribe for Cornelius's release in the hope that his friend may solicit aid in Rome and also be free to marry Cecilia. (He has forgotten the obstacle to his own union with Cecilia, the rule forbidding second marriages, and of course he cannot know that Cecilia, if indeed she is the Cecilia of history, will shortly be martyred in the Aurelian persecutions.) The action is soon over, as if Pater were impatient with the narration. Marius remains behind, knowing full well that he is "no hero, no heroic martyr," with no reverence for martyrdom as such, oppressed only by "deep fatigue" of spirit. Too ill to be marched with the Christians over the hills in the autumn rains, he is left in the charge of villagers, who, oddly enough, are also Christians

and who tend Marius as one of their own. Marius is grateful
for their affection but dies before he can either affirm or
deny their faith and, in dying, is given the last rites of the
Church and the respect properly accorded a martyr.

One of the possible sources of *Marius the Epicurean*
treats a mistaken martyrdom with mocking irony,[41] but
there is little that is ironic either in Pater's depiction of
Marius or in Marius's view of Christian faith. The villagers
err only in the generosity of their regard, and their error is
not considerable, for Marius, as the title of the last chapter
suggests, is a "naturally" Christian soul. A degree of final
ambiguity, however, remains. Marius has been able to act
briefly, somewhat furtively, to save Cornelius, but he
scarcely knows how to declare a commitment to the new
faith; he has been the passive spectator too long suddenly
to become the zealous participant. In any case, Pater prefers to indicate the direction of Marius's growth rather than
to describe a religious and philosophical destination. As the
author of a discreetly personal Bildungsroman, he is reluctant, knowing something of himself, to imagine his
hero's life and death as the successful accomplishment of a
complete heroic ideal.

THOMAS HARDY:
THE OBSCURITY OF *JUDE*

WALTER PATER was a resident of Brasenose during all the adult years Hardy allots to the hero of *Jude the Obscure*. Oxford, with a few thin disguises, appears in the novel as Christminster, and Brasenose enters as Rubric College,[1] the outlines of which are visible from the dreary lodgings where little Father Time, in a terrifying gesture against Christminster and the world, hangs himself and Jude Fawley's other two children. Twelve months later Jude himself, frustrated forever in his desire to attend the university, dies in another lonely room, within earshot of cheering undergraduates who are quite unaware of his existence. Hardy was less unfortunate: if he too once wished in vain to be a university man, he concealed his disappointment and eventually made himself acceptable on his own terms to the academic hierarchy; he came to know a good many dons and deans and fellows, including Pater ("whose manner," he said, "is that of one carrying weighty ideas without spilling them"),[2] and in due time received honorary degrees from several institutions with the ceremonial ritual that Jude even in his disenchantment never ceases to admire.

Though he can never reach anyone at Christminster remotely like Pater, Jude is in one respect closer to Pater's Marius than to the heroes of Dickens, Meredith, or Butler:

he is sensitive beyond most men to "Creation's groan," the presence everywhere of undeserved pain, the inhumanities of living. Marius confides in his diary, "But still the feeling returns to me, that no charity of ours can get at a certain natural unkindness which I find in things themselves." From the beginning Jude is haunted by a similar insight into an essential discord in nature: "That mercy towards one set of creatures was cruelty towards another sickened his sense of harmony."[3] Marius grieves for abused animals; Jude suffers with a snared rabbit and as a child can scarcely bear to see the bleeding of pruned trees. Marius is the often distressed but always controlled observer of brutality and violence; Jude is introduced as "the sort of man who was born to ache a good deal before the fall of the curtain upon his unnecessary life should signify that all was well with him again."[4] Both are in search of ethical or philosophic sanction; but Jude grows increasingly alienated from the religion to which Marius looks more and more expectantly for ultimate explanation. Both would agree that without a sense of God's benevolence there can be little joy or even purpose in human lives; for each the alternative to faith must be a tragic despair.[5]

The differences between *Jude the Obscure* and *Marius* are of course more striking than any possible similarity. But like *Marius* and *Great Expectations* and *Richard Feverel*, none of which it resembles in style or method, *Jude* is the chronicle of its hero's growth from childhood to early maturity and a description of the forces, within and without, that advance or impede his progress. In short, it is a Bildungsroman, whether or not Hardy ever used that label, the only such book in the Hardy canon; and it may perhaps best be approached as an example of that genre, rather than as the polemic or thesis-novel that some readers have judged it to be. The earliest extant reference to plans for *Jude*, a notebook entry of 1888, suggests a familiar theme, education and the rougher schooling by experience, given a bitter twist and developed with some personal intensity:

> A short story of a young man—"who could not go to Oxford" —His struggles and ultimate failure. Suicide. There is something [in this] the world ought to be shown, and I am the one to show it to them—though I was not altogether hindered going, at least to Cambridge, and could have gone up easily at five-and-twenty.[6]

As the preface tells us, "the death of a woman" in 1890 provided further stimulus, presumably the will to depict the object of the young man's love, which introduced a second and immediately complicating theme. The proposed short story eventually became a longer narrative, mercilessly cut and bowdlerized for serialization in America, but restored to its full grim integrity when published in book form in November 1895.[7] Whatever other literary type it may suggest, the completed novel has all the salient characteristics of the Victorian Bildungsroman.

Replying in 1919 to a correspondent who asked if *Jude* were autobiographical, Hardy insisted that the book had less to do with his own life than any of his other works and that there was in fact "not a scrap of personal detail in it."[8] Jude is not to be mistaken for a literal portrait of the author as a young man, and Hardy's claim that some circumstances of Jude's career are drawn from observation of another youth rather than from his own experience is scarcely to be disputed. Nonetheless, the novel more than any other reflects Hardy's interests, intellectual concerns, and philosophical misgivings, and from time to time glints of something even more subjective break through its dark surface. The original note about the short story both affirms and denies some sort of personal equation: "I am the one to show" the world the meaning of the young man's failure, "though I was not altogether hindered going, at least to Cambridge. . . ." Jude has been construed as "a heart-breaking caricature" of what Hardy might have been without his great creative gifts or the encouragement of wise teachers.[9] The names themselves of the hero and the first setting of the story establish an identification: Hardy's paternal grandmother was Mary Head of Fawley in Berkshire; "Jude Fawley" appears in manuscripts as "Jack Head," and the village is at first "Shawley," then "Fawn Green," and finally "Marygreen."[10] Despite the refusal to acknowledge any personal detail in the novel, one passage invites immediate comparison with a memory recorded in the life:

Jude went out, and, feeling more than ever his existence to be an undemanded one, he lay down upon his back on a heap of litter near the pig-sty. . . . He pulled his straw hat over his face, and peered through the interstices of the plaiting at the white brightness, vaguely reflecting. Growing up brought responsibilities, he found. Events did not rhyme quite as he had thought. . . . If he could only prevent himself growing up! He did not want to be a man.

Hardy remembered a like incident from his own boyhood, in the same terms, though without the litter and the pig-sty:

He was lying on his back in the sun, thinking how useless he was, and covered his face with his straw hat. The sun's rays streamed through the interstices of the straw, the lining having disappeared. Reflecting on his experiences of the world so far as he had got, he came to the conclusion that he did not wish to grow up.

"Childhood among the Ferns," a poem from Hardy's last volume, presents the early impression yet again, this time with a Wordsworthian nostalgia, set amid odoriferous plants at a far remove from the sty of *Jude*:

> The sun then burst, and brought forth a sweet breath
> From the limp ferns as they dried underneath:
> I said: "I could live on here thus till death";
>
> And queried in the green rays as I sate:
> "Why should I have to grow to man's estate,
> And this afar-noised World perambulate?"[11]

The similarities between the three versions suggest a common autobiographical origin; the differences indicate the ways in which personal detail may be adapted to fictional or poetic ends.

Other parallels between author and hero demonstrate the kind of subjective involvement we associate with the typical Bildungsroman. Jude shares Hardy's interest in church architecture and old music. Like Hardy he works over Griesbach's text of the Greek Testament; he reads widely, as Hardy did, in English literature; he studies precisely the same passages of Homer that Hardy marked in his own edition of the *Iliad*. He ponders like Hardy the gravest questions of theology.[12] And beyond all this, his love of his cousin Sue Bridehead, which is at the very core of the novel, may reflect a love-affair Hardy was too reticent to discuss but ready enough to relive through fiction. The enigmatic reference in the preface to "the death of a woman" in 1890 may apparently be related to a notebook

entry under that year which tells of Hardy's beginning a
poem about a cousin who, though Hardy did not know it,
was actually dying at the time she presented herself to his
imagination. The poem, finished after her death and published as "Thoughts of Phena," memorializes a girl forever
radiant in the poet's memory, but pauses curiously to ask
if her bright gifts dimmed in her last days when the author
had long since lost touch with her:

> did life-light decline from her years,
>   And mischances control
> Her full day-star; unease, or regret, or forebodings, or fears
>   Disennoble her soul?[13]

Phena was Tryphena Sparks, to whom, recent biographers
argue, the young Hardy may have been engaged before
he married Emma Gifford in 1874. Tryphena was almost
certainly the original—or at least one of the originals—of
Sue, who, like Tryphena, attends training school and serves
as a schoolmistress, does illuminated lettering, behaves
coquettishly when young, and eventually is "disennobled"
by regret and fear. That Hardy felt for Tryphena anything
of the passion with which Jude yearns for Sue is purely
conjectural.[14] Yet it is perhaps significant that he remembers
her affectionately in the poem as "my lost prize," at a time
of great unhappiness in his own marriage, which was
shortly to color his view of Jude's marital difficulties.

Whatever then may be the degree of direct autobiography (and in terms of action it seems relatively slight),
Hardy has clearly a strong personal stake in the misadventures of his hero. Yet like other masters of the Bildungsroman, he relies on the conventions of the genre to objectify
what he wishes to conceal, yet feels bound to express. Self-
consciously well informed, he was apparently familiar with

the work of his predecessors, though his style and tone remain as individual as theirs. He placed *Wilhelm Meister* among the supreme examples of candor in world literature as he sought precedents for his own effort at a new frankness in Victorian fiction.[15] He was interested in *Richard Feverel* and in Meredith's courage in the face of hostile reviewers.[16] He considered George Eliot a "great thinker, . . . though not a born storyteller by any means,"[17] and he probably learned from her how to relate books and ideas to the development of his doomed protagonist. Of Dickens's narrative skill he could have had no doubt. He must have known *David Copperfield* and *Great Expectations,* and he cared enough about the author to attend his readings at the Hanover Square Rooms. There is of course little of Dickens's color or humor or sense of place and property in *Jude.* But the fraudulent physician Vilbert with his long quick stride and ready-made sales-talk is rather like a Dickensian grotesque; and the curious scene in which itinerant troupers at Shaston defend the schoolmaster Phillotson against the townsmen, break a few windows, blacken some eyes, overturn an inkbottle on a councillor's shirtfront, and poke the churchwarden's head through the map of Palestine has a good deal of Dickens's delight in the spontaneity of circus people as opposed to the respectabilities of the Philistines.

Jude the Obscure carries the hero from the age of eleven to his death at about thirty sometime in the late eighteen seventies.[18] Like Pip, Jude is an orphan, a superfluous creature, told by his guardian that he is useless and unwanted. But unlike Pip, he becomes, as he matures, increasingly aware of his dead parents, or at least of their maladjustments to life and of what Hardy calls "a doom or curse of hereditary temperament peculiar to the family,"[19] an inheritance more alarming than anything Ernest Pontifex must reckon with. From the beginning Jude is both too old and too young for his years, prematurely burdened by a crushing sense of the world's wrong, yet naively ignorant of the concerns of other boys his own age; he neither enjoys nor suffers the fully engaged energies of childhood that animate Maggie Tulliver or David Copperfield. Like these two, however, and others—Julien Sorel, for example—he is, as his aunt describes him, "crazy for books," though he reads less to stimulate an already quick imagination than to feed an insatiable appetite for knowledge.

As a novel of education, *Jude* pays far more than usual attention to the hero's "private study" and almost none to formal schooling. Indeed Jude receives no instruction at all after the departure, at the very beginning of his story, of Phillotson, with whom he has read for a short while as a "night scholar." A university education, however, is his great objective, and Christminster (though actually less than twenty miles from Marygreen) gleams as if from afar upon his ambitious boyhood. "It is a city of light," Jude tells himself. "It is what you may call a castle, manned by scholarship and religion. . . . It would just suit me."[20] To earn enough to enter this new Jerusalem, he becomes an apprentice to a stonemason near Marygreen; but all the while he keeps up his strenuous study, and he cuts his resolve into a milestone: the inscription "THITHER/J. F." and a hand pointing to his destination. At a moment of exalted daydreaming when he is picturing himself as the beloved son of the Alma Mater Christminster, he is smacked smartly in the ear by a pig's pizzle propelled by the voluptuous Arabella Donn—or by a too sardonic Hardy intent on destroying the illusion.

Henceforth the lure of learning must fight unequal battle with the appeals of sex. When Arabella begins to exert her charms, Jude tries to persuade himself that it is "better to love a woman than to be a graduate, or a parson; ay, or a pope!"[21] But the attraction to Arabella cannot survive her contempt for his books. Sue Bridehead, refined, intelligent, and learned within limits, proves a stronger, if less obvious antagonist to the university tradition and to every orthodox establishment. Eventually Jude confesses, "Under your teaching, I hate convention."[22] And his real education ultimately involves a shedding of his ideals and ambitions, his respect for theology and his delight in classical learning. Yet he can never altogether forget or deny Christminster. When he first sees the unfortunate little Father Time, he at once transfers to the child all his own faded hopes: "Sue, darling," he declares, "I have an idea! We'll educate and train him with a view to the University. What I couldn't accomplish in my own person perhaps I can carry out through him?"[23] At the Great Wessex Agricultural Show Jude and Sue exhibit a model of Cardinal College, Christminster. Three years later Jude makes Christminster cakes to sell at the spring fair at Kennetbridge, and Arabella, stopping at the stall, comments with brutal justice: "Still harping on Christminster—even in his cakes! Just like Jude. A ruling passion. What a queer fellow he is, and always will be!" Though reluctant to agree with Arabella, Sue concedes Jude's obsession: "Of course Christminister is a sort of fixed vision with him, which I suppose he'll never be cured of believing in. He still thinks it a great centre of high and fearless thought, instead of what it is, a nest of commonplace schoolmasters whose characteristic is timid obsequiousness to tradition."[24] Jude for his part professes at last to know the truth about Christminster but determines, nonetheless, "to go back to live there—perhaps to die there!" On his return on Remembrance Day he is excluded from the Theatre and left standing in the rain; only then does he fully recognize his "infatuation" and come to admit its utter hopelessness: "Well—I'm an outsider to the end of my days!"[25]

For all his effort at self-improvement, Jude cannot be accepted either as a scholar or a gentleman. Christminster, he learns, will neither credit nor amend the knowledge of "the so-called Self-taught."[26] When he recites the Nicene creed in a tavern, two undergraduates are amused by his liquored aplomb and perhaps a bit embarrassed that he knows more Latin than they do; but his bravado is self-conscious and pedantic, a sad attempt to prove himself. Later, in a last effort at self-justification, he harangues the bystanders at the Remembrance Day ceremonies with an ill-considered self-pitying eloquence. He has earned but one title in his short life, Tutor of St. Slums, a sobriquet once given him, half in respect, half in derision, by his fellow stonemasons. And there is no possibility at any time that education will raise him, as it promises to raise Pip, to the status of a gentleman. Jude remains to the end the working-class intellectual, earnest, embittered at the establishment, uneasily proud of his painfully acquired erudition. As such he straightway won the sympathy of the young H. G. Wells, who claimed to hear in his dying words "the voice of the educated proletarian, speaking more distinctly than it has ever spoken before in English literature."[27]

Like other young men from the provinces, Jude discovers the cruelty and indifference of the city. Christminster is a place of contrasts, dark alleys as well as open quads, stately colleges and dingy rooming houses for workingmen, a city deeply touched—despite its medieval grandeurs—with urban blight and modern squalor. Yet the countryside he leaves behind has offered him no alternatives of light or joy. There is none of the encompassing mystery, the natural magic, that relates characters in other Hardy novels to a living, breathing universe. At the beginning, as a child alone in Farmer Troutham's field, Jude muses, "How ugly it is here!" As he matures, he learns to take the bleakness of the landscape for granted; when he wanders with Sue along a barren path, the pair, we are told, are "so absorbed in their own situation that their surroundings [are] little in their consciousness."[28] Apart from Sue and possibly Arabella, who engage his love and passion, Jude has no one for whom he can care or who cares for him. Nearly all the other heroes of the English Bildungsroman have at least one close friend or confidant: Steerforth, Herbert Pocket, Ripton Thompson, Towneley and Overton, Flavian and Cornelius. Jude stands distinctly alone, the self-schooled intellectual in a disjunctive world. Though he attacks society in general, he knows little of it in particular; it remains always an indefinite hostile otherness, a Mrs. Grundy or an abstract Public Opinion. The shared values and individual relationships of a rural culture no longer obtain. The atomistic city is the appropriate symbol and setting of Jude's perpetual alienation.

When Jude and Sue reflect on the injustice of Christminster and the inadequacies of the educational system, the novel becomes tendentious, hortatory, and more didactic than a Bildungsroman need be. When they argue at length about marriage and the narrator adds his own jaundiced commentary, *Jude* approaches the condition of the "problem novel," a type popular in the 1890's. Annoyed at reviewers who construed it as such, Hardy insisted that "no more than half a dozen pages" of dialogue in the whole long book could be said "to bear on the *general* marriage question."[29] Certainly *Jude* has but little of the dated topicality of *The Woman Who Did* by Grant Allen, a best-seller on the marriage question which appeared in the same year and has long since been forgotten. Yet even a few pages may suffice to suggest a direction, and any evidence of thesis or bias detracts from objectivity. The tones in *Jude* of the reforming lay preacher may possibly be ascribed to Hardy's recent interest in Ibsen[30] and his desire to present issues with a similar bold anger. The title-page epigraph, "The letter killeth," may suggest, as it would in Ibsen, a plea for the spirit rather than the letter of the law. But the law itself is scarcely the culprit; it dissolves Sue's marriage to Phillotson and Jude's to Arabella without much difficulty or delay, and Jude explains how accommodating to simple souls it can be: "There is this advantage in being poor obscure people like us—that these things are done for us in a rough and ready fashion."[31] When Jude and Sue, free to marry, refuse to do so, they are persecuted not by the law but by their respectable neighbors. Sue claims that she could not love so spontaneously if she were contractually bound to her lover; but it is Sue who in the end invokes the killing letter when she denies that the law ever had the power to cancel her sacred, though mistaken, vow to Phillotson. The novel assails marriage as an institution rather than the marriage laws of Victorian England. The sensible Mrs. Edlin declares that marriage was easier in her day, but in fact it was neither easy nor right for Jude's parents or for Sue's. The narrator, who to all intents and purposes is Hardy himself, obtrudes his own bitter generalizations. He describes Arabella and her second husband, the potbellied publican, as being in "the antipathetic, recriminatory mood of the average husband and wife of Christendom";[32] and he reports —with what might pass for vulgar music-hall humor—that a landlord refuses to believe Jude and Arabella properly married until he hears Arabella haranguing Jude and flinging a shoe at his head, whereupon he recognizes "the note of genuine wedlock"[33] and concludes that the couple must be respectable. As the story moves toward its unhappy ending, Hardy warps his secondary characters to subserve his theme. Phillotson, scarcely the Philistine some readers have considered him, has been more charitable than conventional in his treatment of Sue; it is surely a mistake to show him craftily dissembling in order to win her back, pretending to accept her narrowed views, "carefully hiding his heterodox feelings."[34] Arabella, too, is distorted; at first she appears as "a complete and substantial female animal";[35] by the end, when she seduces Jude into remarriage and abandons him to a lonely death, she has become a gross caricature of cruel self-interest. As long as the iniquity of marriage is the dominant theme, characterization and plotting may be manipulated, sometimes melodramatically, to illustrate the thesis.

In 1926 when a playwright sought to dramatize *Jude*, Hardy asked, "Would not Arabella be the villain of the piece?—or Jude's personal constitution?—so far as there is any villain more than blind Chance."[36] The question points to an uncertainty in the novel itself. The alternative to Arabella is the stronger conception; and the better part of the fiction is distinctly Jude's story—that is, the Bildungsroman. If the conflict, as the preface indicates, is "a deadly war waged between flesh and spirit," the defeat should be ascribed more to Jude's failings than to Arabella's villainous power, and more to misfortune than to evil institutions. "You know what a weak fellow I am," Jude tells Sue. "My two Arch Enemies you know—my weakness for womankind and my impulse to strong liquor."[37] Hardy himself seems to have shared Sue's aversion to sexual passion and

intemperance. At least he brings the two together again in
a macabre poem, "Her Second Husband Hears Her Story,"
where a wife confesses to sewing her husband, "liquored
deep," into the bed sheets—she did not necessarily mean to
kill him, but she had to do something to stop him "When
he should wake up and attempt embracing." There is nothing, however, very remarkable about Jude's drinking bouts,
which are in fact quite infrequent; and the novel is in no
sense a study of alcoholism comparable to Zola's *L'Assom-
moir*. Nor is Jude notably passionate. He is sexually attracted to Arabella, seized suddenly by a sensual power
which cares "little for his reason and his will, nothing for
his so-called elevated intentions,"[38] and tricked into marriage; but sexuality does not consolidate the union, and he
and Arabella are soon tired of each other, though she is
able to seduce him again years later when she finds him
lonely and despondent. His only other love is far greater
and more complex; he desires Sue physically more than she
desires him, but he respects her reserve, commands her affection, and reaches his only real happiness, brief as it is, in
their nomadic life together. Jude is neither the drunkard
nor the amorist; he is betrayed by ordinary appetites and
feelings, by his own temperament, and perhaps most of all
by the disparity between flesh and spirit in the world itself,
the distance between the real and the ideal. Sue calls him
"a tragic Don Quixote,"[39] a man destined to be destroyed
by his dreams. Yet without his illusions he could scarcely
have existed at all, and he could certainly not have dedicated
himself, for better and for worse, to Sue.

On her first appearance, in the ecclesiastical art shop, Sue
is already a young woman in her twenties; thereafter she
supplies but few details of her life before coming to Christminster, and we know very little of her childhood apart

from Aunt Drusilla's report that she was "a pert little thing, . . . with her tight-strained nerves."[40] Otherwise, *Jude the Obscure*, like *The Mill on the Floss*, might be a double Bildungsroman; for from the time of her introduction Sue's development is inseparable from Jude's and quite as important. The earlier titles, *The Simpletons* and *Hearts Insurgent*, under which the narrative ran as a serial, and *The Recalcitrants*, suggested as an alternative to these, all clearly imply at least two protagonists, somehow related by attitude or feeling or misdirected action. Jude and Sue are in fact complementary characters, wholly dependent on each other, bound by strong affinities almost as closely as Heathcliff and Cathy. When he first discovers Sue, at work with her lettering, Jude is startled to recognize in her speech the qualities of his own voice. When Sue escapes from training school by wading the river and comes, thoroughly drenched, to Jude, he reflects happily that they are true "counterparts" and dresses her, like another self or a double, in his own best Sunday clothes. In the schoolroom at Shaston where "by an unpremeditated instinct" they clasp hands, Jude tells Sue that they are "both alike," though Sue insists that the identity is of emotion rather than thought.[41] Phillotson, abandoned by Sue, acknowledges "the extraordinary sympathy, or similarity, between the pair," and sadly concludes: "They seem to be one person split in two."[42] Finally the narrator invokes almost the same figure to describe their appearance at the Stoke-Barehills fair: "That complete mutual understanding, in which every glance and movement was as effectual as speech for conveying intelligence between them, made them almost the two parts of a single whole."[43] Despite many correspondences of feeling, however, Sue is right to emphasize a difference at almost any given time between her thinking and Jude's. The two travel intellectually from one side to the other, as if on crossing diagonals, where the point of intersection is the completely shared moment at the fair. Sue, when introduced, is the advanced freethinker, skeptical of revealed religion and scornful of middle-class proprieties; by the end she has moved from reason as well as rationalism to superstitious self-immolation and misconceived orthodoxy. Jude begins as a devout idealist and ends questioning all the values he has lived by, and his course is plotted with reference to Sue's: as he sheds his faith, he is, we are told, "mentally approaching the position which Sue . . . occupied when he first met her."[44] Dismayed by what is happening to Sue, Jude himself observes, "How we are changing places!"[45] Sue agrees, but asks Jude's forbearance: "I was strongest once, I know, and perhaps I treated you cruelly. But Jude, return good for evil! I am the weaker now."[46] Jude, however, finds no joy in the strength from which Sue has turned away; he suffers miserably in her suffering.

Though livelier intellectually in the beginning than her counterpart, Sue is never a match for Jude in moral fiber or in honesty and directness of response. Many readers have found her self-protective attitudes distasteful and her sexual equivocations altogether repulsive.[47] In a letter attempting to defend Sue, Hardy himself makes a formidable case against her:

You are quite right; there is nothing perverted or depraved in Sue's nature. The abnormalism consists in disproportion, not in inversion, her sexual instinct being healthy as far as it goes, but unusually weak and fastidious. Her sensibilities remain painfully alert notwithstanding, as they do in nature with such women. One point . . . I could not dwell upon: . . . her intimacies with Jude have never been more than occasional, . . . and one of her reasons for fearing the marriage ceremony is that she fears it would be breaking faith with Jude to withhold herself at pleasure, or altogether, after it; though while uncontracted she feels at liberty to yield herself as seldom as she chooses. This has tended to keep his passion as hot at the end as at the beginning, and helps to break his heart. He has never really possessed her as freely as he desired. [48]

Nonetheless, Hardy concluded, "Sue is a type of woman which has always had an attraction for me," and it is more than likely that Sue's evasions reflect Hardy's own aloofness, his reticence, his dislike of touching another person or having another person touch him.

Yet Sue is less "a type" than an individual of mixed attributes, both attractive and unpleasant. In the English Bildungsroman she is variously foreshadowed: like Dora Copperfield she enjoys playing the coquette, acts like a child when reprimanded, and proves a woefully inept housekeeper; like Estella she demands attention and cruelly abuses the men who give it to her; like Maggie, though with less philosophic reason, she eventually practices self-renunciation. And in turn she herself anticipates D. H. Lawrence's Miriam in her general high-strung nervousness and in her particular love of flowers as a surrogate perhaps for more dangerous passions.[49] But she has her own peculiar vibrancy and real, though often exasperating, charm. She is quick, elusive, birdlike in her movements, sensitive as well as selfish, intensely self-conscious, bold in her opinions, half-afraid of her feelings. She can be gentle and considerate, as in her welcoming of Jude's sad-faced child, but she can also be incredibly unkind, as when she forces Jude to go through a sort of mock wedding with her at the church where two hours later she is to force herself to marry Phillotson. She justifies her impercipience by posing as "an epicure in emotions," a hedonist of the kind Pater could not have admired: "My curiosity to hunt up a new sensation always leads me into these scrapes." Jude, however, suspects a more complex psychology at work and seriously wonders whether Sue is not "simply so perverse that she wilfully [gives] herself and him pain for the odd and mournful luxury of practising long-suffering in her own person, and of being touched with tender pity for him at having made him practise it."[50] But Sue is far less and much more than a sadist or masochist. She remains an enigma even to the narrator, who speaks of "her curious double nature" and "her strange ways and curious unconsciousness of gender." Jude thinks of her as "uncarnate," scarcely more earth-bound than Shelley's skylark, and in spite of himself he admires her relative lack of physicality. In her final turmoil of spirit, he reassures her of her goodness and purity as "absolutely the most ethereal, least sensual woman [he] ever knew to exist without inhuman sexlessness"; and at a less troubled time when she has rebuffed him, he salutes her tenderly as a "dear, sweet tantalizing phantom—hardly flesh at all."[51] This last, we may suppose, represents Hardy's own opinion of Sue and possibly also his remembered judgment of Phena or of whoever else was Sue's original.

Together Jude and Sue, the narrator concedes, are "happy —between their times of sadness";[52] but we are allowed no glimpse of their happiness, except the scene at the Agricultural Show, which appears as a spot of light to deepen the gloom that follows. Some of their suffering is related to their conduct and its consequences; some of it is entirely gratuitous. When Jude abandons his academic ambition and gives up his struggle for a career in the church and is driven from his home and his work as a mason by malicious gossip, he must still be stricken by a grave illness and plagued by the misfortunes that culminate in the innocent murders by

Father Time. An immitigable darkness broods over the whole novel. Jude's moments of insight or spots of time are bleak and negative or else merely delusive. When as a child he catches a message in the breeze blowing from Christminster, he imagines a city of perfect joy and, like Wordsworth, is briefly but completely "lost to his bodily situation during this mental leap";[53] but the vision is of course simply a cheat engendered by his fierce will to believe. Jude's most decisive epiphany may be contrasted with Marius's hour in the olive-garden which establishes an unforgettable sense of purpose and integration. Jude climbs to the octagonal top of the university Theatre (suggested by the cupola of the Sheldonian at Oxford) and surveys Christminster from every side with the sudden sickening realization that the life of the colleges will never be his. Years later he remembers the experience, "the afternoon of his great meditation" when he awoke with pain from his dream of happiness.[54]

Even without the bitter revelation, however, Jude has little reason to expect success in his undertakings or indeed any real measure of contentment or self-satisfaction. From the beginning he is again and again made aware of his sad inheritance. Aunt Drusilla reminds him that "there never was any sprawl"—which is to say, any luck—among the Fawleys, and Arabella taunts him with the charge that his people always were "a queer lot." Told that his mother drowned herself, Jude vainly attempts to take his own life by jumping on the ice of a frozen pond. Later he learns that a common ancestor of his and Sue's was gibbeted for a crime he did not commit and that the man's wife went mad with grief. Sue, hearing the story, feels "as if a tragic doom overhung [the] family, as it did the house of Atreus," and she shrinks from remarriage, while Jude reflects, perhaps not for the first time, that he and Sue "ought never to have been born."[55]

When he first sets aside his Greek Testament and rushes off to meet Arabella, Jude is described as "predestinate," and his immediate future seems inevitable. Thereafter through all "his years of struggle against malignant stars," we may wonder how much of Jude's career may be ascribed to his own free choice and how much is determined by the hereditary doom or some other hostile force utterly beyond his control. In the ambiance of the novel nature is cruel and scornful of man's values and aspirations.[56] The doctor explains Father Time's desperate act as "the beginning of the coming universal wish not to live," as if the thrust of human evolution were against life itself. Sue in her days as a Hardyesque intellectual has postulated a First Cause moving "automatically like a somnambulist," indifferent to mankind and unable to imagine the emergence of human sensibilities; but in her final remorse and defeat she pictures Jude and herself as fleeing from a wrathful God intent upon conscious persecution of the guilty. Jude insists that they are not "fighting against God" but "only against man and senseless circumstance."[57] The logic of the novel never makes clear which of the three is the great antagonist, society or blind chance or malevolent destiny; and the novelist himself, pointing first to one, then to the others, seems deeply confused.

Reluctant to accept a complete determinism, Jude at the end of his unhappy pilgrimage struggles to indict society and the temper of the times for his misfortunes. "I was, perhaps, after all," he tells the Remembrance Day crowd at Christminster, "but a paltry victim of mental and social restlessness, that makes so many unhappy in these days! . . . I perceive there is something wrong somewhere in our social formulas: what it is can only be discovered by men and women with greater insight than mine,—if, indeed, they ever discover it—at least in our time."[58] If man-made rules and formulas are wrong or inadequate, they may eventually be changed, whereas the laws of nature, the conditions of a cruel universe, are fixed and unalterable. Sue has once suggested that a future age will consider the nineteenth century "barbarous" in its customs and superstitions. Jude now tries to persuade her that he and she have been moral pioneers living before their time: "Perhaps the world is not illuminated enough for such experiments as ours!"[59] On his deathbed he speaks in the same vein to the widow Edlin: "As for Sue and me when we were at our own best, long ago, . . . the time was not ripe for us! Our ideas were fifty years too soon to be any good to us." Moreover, he at last has some slight evidence to support his wishful thinking; he has just heard that some plans may soon be laid to help working-class students attend the university.

Yet it is difficult to argue convincingly, as one critic has attempted to do, on the basis of such possibilities and extrapolations, that "Hardy's hopefulness for the future . . . was in large measure responsible for the writing of the book."[60] Hardy is essentially no reformer of education or society, and neither he nor his hero is really confident that the years to come will bring vast improvements. Both, we suspect, may in characteristic moods share the doctor's fear that the human race before long may will its extinction. "Obscure" in its primary meaning connotes darkness and gloom, and *Jude the Obscure* is assuredly not a hopeful novel, bright with the promise of the future. Its sporadic attacks on Victorian society accord ill with its arraignment of the great inexorable scheme of life itself.

Aware of the contradictions in *Jude*, Hardy sought to disarm criticism by a prefatory disclaimer. He was concerned, he wrote, simply "to give shape and coherence to a series of seemings, or personal impressions," and he regarded "the question of their consistency or their discordance, of their permanence or their transitoriness, . . . as not of first moment." At the time of publication, however, he confessed privately that he was somewhat less than satisfied with the final form of the novel; the adaptation of manuscript to magazine serial and the shift from serial to book had been a tedious labor: "I have lost energy for revising and improving the original as I meant to do."[61] Presumably further revision would have made for greater clarity. As the suffering protagonist, Jude may be understandably uncertain about the source of his troubles; the novelist, on the other hand, should have valued some "consistency" of interpretation if he really wished to establish the "coherence" of his work. But it is unlikely that any amount of editing would have removed a confusion in technique and a consequent serious lapse in taste. *Jude* is starker in texture than any of Hardy's earlier novels, more matter-of-fact, less poetic, and accordingly less able to accommodate symbolic action. Into the bleak narrative intrudes fanciful allegory; little Father Time, difficult to accept on any terms, strains all credibility in a context of prosaic realism, and his single atrocious act of assertion threatens to turn Jude's already too grim life-history into a sensational melodrama.

Yet Jude somehow survives both Father Time and Hardy's distortions; he lives his span as a character and succumbs only to the agony of his own being. When planning the novel, Hardy jotted down a definition, perhaps for his own guidance: "The best tragedy—highest tragedy in short—is that of the WORTHY encompassed by the IN-

EVITABLE."[62] The worth of the traditional tragic hero is represented in part by his status, the greatness he has achieved and must relinquish: the prosperity of Job, the majesty of Oedipus or Lear, even the local prominence of the mayor of Casterbridge. Jude, like Tess, has no place to lose; he does not rise and fall; he begins near the bottom of the scale, and again and again, each time he aspires to a more elevated position, he is driven back down. His worthiness is entirely a matter of mind and spirit. We must recognize his struggle to learn as heroic, his patience as exemplary, his love for Sue as almost infinite. And from the outset we must see his virtues rebuffed and doomed to final and utter defeat. Unlike Richard Feverel's tragic end, which almost until the last minute seems unnecessary, Jude's tragedy is from the first inevitable; the hero is fully encompassed by the forces of his destruction. Despite his appetites and early ambitions, he is essentially innocent of all worldliness; he is always, and not only with regard to Christminster, the "outsider." His history, whether the "world" involves the human condition or society or both, reads like a secular meditation on some verses from the Gospel appointed for St. Jude's Day in the Book of Common Prayer:

> These things I command you, that ye love one another. If the world hate you, ye know that it hated me before it hated you. If ye were of the world, the world would love his own: but because ye are not of the world, but I have chosen you out of the world, therefore the world hateth you.[63]

Jude dies alone in Christminster, which was to have been his holy city; and his desertion by Arabella, who goes off to the Remembrance games, is but an index of the calloused world's cruel indifference. On his deathbed he quotes passages not from the Gospel but from the Book of Job, which has been familiar to him since childhood,[64] and his recitation is punctuated by hurrahs from the river:

> "Let the day perish wherein I was born, and the night in which it was said, There is a man child conceived."
> ("Hurrah!")
> "Let the day be darkness; let not God regard it from above, neither let the light shine upon it. Lo, let that night be solitary, let no joyful voice come therein."
> ("Hurrah!") . . .

The irony is heavily calculated yet singularly effective, earned, absorbed by the gravity and pathos of the situation. Darkness closes on Jude when he has nothing left to live for; yet his obscure death has for the moment more meaning than all the distant shouting in the garish sunshine, and the pity it evokes admonishes our too complacent acceptance of less profound emotions. By the conclusion of *Jude* Hardy for the first time in English fiction has successfully adapted the form of the Bildungsroman to the true and proper ends of tragedy.

ᴈ§ V I I I §ᴖ

H. G. WELLS:
THE HERO AS SCIENTIST

Uɴʟɪᴋᴇ Hardy, who focuses attention relentlessly on Jude and his narrow circle, H. G. Wells in *Tono-Bungay* often ranges far from his hero-narrator, George Ponderevo, to more amusing characters and to the machinations of a vast empire of commerce and high finance. Halfway through his narrative, after a circumstantial description of his mismarriage, George announces that he will now resume "the main line" of his story—as if the account of his private life were merely a long digression. He will now return, he says, to his Uncle Teddy (with whom he has served part of his apprenticeship), to the patent medicine Tono-Bungay and his uncle's other promotions, and to "the vision of the world these things have given me."[1] Uncle Teddy, "the Napoleon of domestic conveniences," who zooms like a rocket across the financial skies, is indeed so dynamic and peremptory that in his presence George, though conscious of greater strength, often seems listless and ineffectual. And in the same way Teddy's speculations, his inventions and combines and cartels and advertising campaigns, reach imaginatively far beyond George's painstaking experiments with gliders and balloons. Yet George is nonetheless the "hero" of *Tono-Bungay;* and the uncle and all his promotions exist, in the logic of the book as a whole, only for what

186

they contribute to George's developing and darkening "vision of the world."

As narrator George is a middle-aged engineer, proud enough of his scientific accomplishments but immensely self-conscious and apologetic about his literary resources. *Tono-Bungay*, he tells us at the outset, is to be his first and last novel. "I like to write," he confesses, "I am keenly interested in writing, but it is not my technic. . . . Most of whatever artist there is in me has been given to turbine machines and boat-building and the problem of flying, and do what I will I fail to see how I can be other than a lax, undisciplined story-teller."[2] He has tried his hand at fiction before now, but he has always been driven from the effort by "the restraints and rules" of the novelist's art, the necessity of selection and formal design. His present novel will be "comprehensive rather than austere," or—as Wells later described it—"extensive rather than intensive," deliberately indifferent to ideals of Henry James.[3] We may think the result a curious mélange of genres: adventure story, science fiction, comedy of manners, social satire, and realistic Bildungsroman. But George's prologue, seeking to disarm our criticism, warns us to expect "something of an agglomeration," and the shifts in tone and mode prove no great liability once we discover that George, despite his literary diffidence, is as adroit a stylist as Wells at his best could be—for *Tono-Bungay* is in fact Wells's most ambitious and most carefully planned and executed novel.[4]

It is not clear, however, why George himself must imperil the illusion of verisimilitude by reminding us, in the actual telling, that his story *is* a "novel"—unless he understands by the term simply a narrative with dialogue and description, not necessarily in any way fictional. In spite of the label, he strives constantly to preserve the air of complete fidelity to the facts of his experience. He does not avail himself of the privileges of the omniscient novelist; he presents all from his own point of view and in the first person; unlike Butler's Overton, he never enters the minds of other characters or reports what he himself could not have witnessed. He casually mentions his uncle's most daring advertising strategies as if they were common knowledge, notorious landmarks in current business history: "You must," he tells the reader, "unless you are very young, remember some of them." He refers to formal documents outside the present narrative as evidence of Teddy's devious manipulation of the market. "That sort of development," he says, "is not to be told in detail in a novel. I have, indeed, told much of it elsewhere. It is to be found set out at length, painfully at length, in my uncle's examination and mine in the bankruptcy proceedings, and in my own various statements after his death." He speaks of Ponderevo's Principle, one of his own formulations, as a now accepted scientific law, and he cites the learned journals in which he has published his researches.[5] His effort, in short, is to mirror a real world and not, like a novelist, to create another more or less like it; his aim is to present persons he has known rather than to call imaginary characters into being. His "novel" then is essentially his autobiography, written expressly to trace his "social trajectory" (the rocket imagery throughout the book comes of course from his real profession) and to record inconsistencies of conduct and feeling that he will be "the clearer-headed" for acknowledging. "I suppose," he sums up his intention, "what I'm really trying to render is nothing more nor less than Life—as one man has found it. I want to tell—*myself*, and my impressions of the thing as a whole, to say things I have come to feel intensely of the laws, traditions, usages, and ideas we call society."[6]

However he may describe his retrospect, it is first of all and by design the true story of his growth and initiation.

As a Bildungsroman, *Tono-Bungay* has most of the earmarks of the genre. It follows the career of a fatherless boy, alienated from an unsympathetic mother, through a period at school (where he finds a friend and confidant) and an apprenticeship (during which he discovers substitute parents, Uncle Teddy and the warm, vivacious Aunt Susan), to his arrival at his mental and physical maturity. In the course of his development the young man moves from the provinces to the city, learns something of the joys and trials of love, faces the problem of what it means not to be a gentleman, and is sorely tempted by the lure of money and the prospects of worldly success. Dickens, especially as in *Great Expectations*, is quite apparently the major influence throughout on both characterization and incident. But Wells was also impressed, as we have seen, by *Jude the Obscure*, and he admired the works of Meredith and must indeed have been familiar with most of the novels and novelists we have been considering. At any rate, *Tono-Bungay*, apart from any possible direct derivation, recalls its predecessors in many of its themes and even in some details. The great house Bladesover where George's mother serves as housekeeper is as impressive in its proportions and setting as Raynham Abbey in *Richard Feverel*. Uncle Teddy bears some resemblance to Wilkins Micawber and even more to the volatile, scheming Richmond Roy. George's friend Ewart is a less generous but no less honest Herbert Pocket. The imperious Beatrice Normandy is another cruel Estella, prepared to compel George's affection and to sneer at his working-class status. As a child Beatrice watches impartially as George thrashes her effete half-brother Archie, just as Estella secretly watches Pip's sparring with frail Herbert; and as an adult she leaves George against her own better judgment for the decadent Lord Carnaby, much as Estella turns coldly from Pip to the brutal Bentley Drummle.[7] Like David Copperfield, George finds imaginative escape in old books hidden away in an attic room. Like Ernest Pontifex, he suffers the intolerance of self-righteous piety; though his uncle Nicodemus Frapp is far less cultivated than Ernest's father, George speaks of him as Overton might of Theobald, "After supper my uncle, in a few ill-chosen words, prayed me to repent before I slept."[8] And like both David and Ernest, and Jude, too, he plunges into a regrettable early marriage with a woman who can share nothing of his intellectual life.

Nonetheless, for all its parallels, *Tono-Bungay* achieves its own distinct accent. As in most other first-person Bildungsromane, the narrator is close to the author and reflects his essential values and often his actual experience. Like Wells, George is restless and rootless, unable to give himself for long to any one person or object, yet self-approving in his detachment. He belongs neither to the country nor the town. The provinces seem to him torpid, dull, unimaginative, void of all culture, courage, spiritual stimulus and "valiant sin"; the city, on the other hand, though far more dynamic, strikes him as purposeless and irresponsible, seductive in its diversity, a distraction from his research and a painful waste of his ambitious energies. And wherever he may find himself physically, he is socially displaced or placeless. Like Wells, he is more conscious of class distinction than even Pip or Jude and from the beginning far more distrustful of rank. He vows never to be a servant and scorns his mother's regard for the gentry and their putative gentility. He confesses to having no real acquaintance with the lives of vagrants and day-laborers and "all such as sit in

1834 beer-houses," and he dispatches the aristocracy with a breezy Cockney raffishness: "My intercourse with the ducal rank too has been negligible; I once went shooting with a duke, and in an outburst of what was no doubt snobbishness, did my best to get him in the legs."[9] From the moment that Beatrice betrays him to Lady Drew for pummeling Archie, he considers himself "one against the world." Not long afterwards when, still in disgrace, he returns to Bladesover and from ambush surprises his mother on her way home from church, he has "a queer feeling of brigandage," as if he were intruding upon an immutable sacred order. It was, he writes, "the first time I remember having that outlaw feeling distinctly, a feeling that has played a large part in my subsequent life. I felt that there was no place for me—that I had to drive myself in."[10] Some earlier heroes suffer the sense of exclusion, but unlike these, George prides himself on standing alone. If he cannot be a "gentleman" in any accepted sense of the word, he will be a success in his own way, a disciplined and efficient engineer, a man of science wholly indifferent to the sentiments of the middle class and the manners of a polite establishment. By the end his alienation is virtually—and in his own estimate, virtuously—complete.

Like much else in the novel, the loneliness of George derives from autobiographical sources. *Tono-Bungay* is the most personal of a number of fictions which to some degree reflect Wells's own career and seek to justify his choices.[11] Even the bumptious Uncle Teddy, depicted with some irony, reveals something of the essence of a man who in other spheres was also a promoter and practical visionary; Teddy's first London home accurately mirrors the young Wells's seedy lodgings; and Teddy's experiments, when he comes up in the world, with unfamiliar delicate foods and rare wines clearly image the rising author's systematic effort to educate his palate.[12] But Wells's real representative is of course George, who bears his middle name, is almost his exact contemporary,[13] comes from a similar background, and moves across much of the same terrain. Wells's mother like George's was a housekeeper, and Bladesover is clearly Uppark, the handsome Restoration house at the edge of the South Downs where she was employed and where Wells like George did much of his early reading and made his first silent, wry appraisals of the landed gentry.[14] George's return as an "outlaw" to Bladesover precisely parallels the retreat of Wells to Uppark after a dismal apprenticeship to a draper at Southsea. George's happier days at school in Wimblehurst recall Wells's experience of a Latin class in Midhurst, and Uncle Teddy's shop in the same town is drawn from memories of the establishment of Mr. Cowap, who concocted a cough syrup almost as exhilarating as Tono-Bungay, though considerably less remunerative. Like George, Wells won a scholarship to the Normal School of Science in South Kensington, where, again like George, after a good beginning, he eventually proved an indifferent student, distracted by unscientific concerns. Finally, like George, he ended his adolescence in a miserable marriage, which George's narrative of Marion describes in painful detail.

George's career and Wells's, of course, sharply diverge until the one becomes a master designer of gliders and rockets and the other a master of science fiction and shaper of imaginary flights through outer space. But similarities in thought and temper remain. George has marked opinions about a wide range of social and intellectual concerns; he digresses frequently from his particular story to generalize, to present his views of science and commerce, Fabian socialism, art, sex, morals, religion, and family life. So close are his ideas to those we know to be Wells's own, and so expository is his presentation of them, that he sometimes seems to be simply Wells's mouthpiece. He is, in fact, much more: a partial self-portrait even more revealing perhaps than Wells intended to make him. He has several unattractive attributes, vanity, aggressiveness, coarseness of sensibility, which the otherwise quick-witted Wells recognized but imperfectly in himself. George arrogantly rationalizes his "failure" at science school:

> After all, those other fellows who took high places in the College examinations and were the professor's model boys, haven't done so amazingly. Some are professors themselves, some technical experts; not one can show things done such as I, following my own interest, have achieved. . . . Could I have done as much if I had had a turn for obeying those rather mediocre professors at the college who proposed to train my mind?[15]

With a similar sense of his own superiority, Wells spoke of winning a scholarship prize; it gave him, he is reported to have said, "satisfaction to beat the regular University teachers in their own examinations; he saw himself at war with the world, and these were intimations of victory."[16] Defiant self-confidence—perhaps with the young Wells the invalid's protest against threats of prolonged physical debility—was no doubt the necessary sanction for many an ambitious intellectual enterprise, but it was scarcely conducive to equable judgment or patient understanding.

By all accounts Wells was especially crude and imperceptive in the conduct of his frequent amorous affairs—on one occasion, for example, his friend Arnold Bennett was embarrassed to notice photographs of "three of his lady-loves" on the mantelpiece beside that of Mrs. Wells.[17] George, in turn, is a singularly insensitive lover, a man with appetite rather than affection, a primary self-regard and a strong penchant for rhetoric: "I had extraordinarily limited, extraordinarily painful, desires. I longed intolerably to kiss her lips. . . . There can be no doubt of my passion for her. In her I had discovered woman desired. The nights I have lain awake on account of her, writhing, biting my wrists in a fever of longing!" He condemns Marion's "commonplace mind" and readily demonstrates her conventional gestures, but he is quite unable to imagine her feelings and responses. Years later he declares himself prepared at last to "take her part against the equally stupid, drivingly energetic, sensuous, intellectual sprawl I used to be," but he is still far less interested in Marion than in himself as her dynamic adversary. The "infidelity" with Effie Rink that ends his marriage is nothing more than a tawdry liaison, not to be dignified by George's description of it as a reciprocated "sudden fierce hot-blooded passion." And the contrived romance with Beatrice remains a sentimental dream, a cheap wish-fulfillment, made no more credible by clichés or the claim that words have failed: "We made love. There is no prose of mine that can tell of hours transfigured. The facts are nothing. Everything we touched, the meanest things, became glorious. How can I render bare tenderness and delight and mutual possession?" Nor is the attempt to reproduce the talk of love more convincing: "I want you to marry me," entreats the lover; "I want you to play the game of life with me as an honest woman should. Come and live with me. Be my wife and squaw. Bear me children." George seeks to excuse his clumsiness in describing his love for Beatrice on the ground that he is "a very objective-minded person," forgetful of his moods, "and this was so much an affair of moods," elusive and subjective. But his love story, nonetheless, is marked by a crudity difficult to excuse or ignore in assessing his character.[18]

Fortunately, when he turns his narrative to other objects, George proves himself capable of a warmer understanding and responsive to a rarer selfhood. He shares with Wells not only the assurance of the aggressive amorist but also something of the sense of wonder and momentary insight, the tender yearning for a lost or never lived childhood, that animates Wells's most suggestive short story, "The Door in the Wall." He sees his whole life as a search for some hidden principle of linkage or cohesion, which forever eludes his skeptical intellect, something "beautiful, worshipful, enduring"[19] and redemptive. He is contemptuous of Uncle Teddy's vague belief that "God comes in on the off-chance" and that men, even when most self-willed, are unwittingly "being led";[20] yet he confesses that he himself has found no stronger faith. His "novel" is designed as a summing up or retrospect, and like David Copperfield he is fascinated by the processes of remembering, which allow him now to rush over considerable stretches of time, now to prolong a short interval. He speaks with an almost Wordsworthian reverence of "these rarely visited and lonely tarns of memory" and is troubled by the sudden awareness of "how inconsecutive and irrational a thing the memory can be."[21] Like Wordsworth and most of the Bildungsroman heroes, he can recall privileged moments, "spots of time" which have enriched or at least complicated his vision. At his mother's funeral he is seized by the sharp realization that the stern, unapproachable woman he never much cared for loved him more than anyone or anything else in her constrained and thwarted life. As a restless student in London he is surprised by a blaze of asters and sunflowers set against red bricks, a burst of color in which he senses a vitality and wholeness quite at odds with his own drab routine. Finally another rapid impression becomes a shattering "epiphany"; looking upon the abandoned waste of Crest Hill, the last and most pretentious of Uncle Teddy's houses, he sees a true image of the delusions of his world: "This was our fruit, this was what we had done, I and my uncle, in the fashion of our time. . . . It came to me like a revelation, a revelation at once incredible and indisputable of the abysmal folly of our being."[22] Again and again a sudden intuition of value adds new depth to his expression.

In one of his moods of "pellucid and impartial clairvoyance" George grasps the sorry truth of Tono-Bungay: "Well," he tells his uncle, "in the first place—it's a damned swindle!"[23] But, despite his knowledge that the nostrum is a dangerous fraud, he is willing to set aside his scruples, to become a manager of the Tono-Bungay company and eventually a director of its no more ethical subsidiaries, and so to share freely in Uncle Teddy's handsome profits. If at first dissatisfied with his compromise of principle, he has little difficulty in rationalizing a choice which provides the ample wherewithal for his marriage. Later, when he has disposed of Marion, he finds it convenient to ignore the probability of increasingly vast peculation and to remain "wilfully incurious" about his investments. Having withdrawn from an active part in the Ponderevo enterprises, he welcomes substantial subsidy, whatever its source, for his expensive aeronautical experiments. When his income is threatened by the trembling of Teddy's business empire, he offers at once to lead a desperate expedition to Africa in search of the mysterious radioactive "quap." Away from England and English restraints, he has no reluctance to play the ruthless imperialist; in his greed and terror, he "quite coolly" shoots and kills a harmless native—and feels no serious remorse for his deed. Wells no doubt intended the murder as the symbol of colonial exploitation or simply of mercantile inhumanity, and George's moral bankruptcy at this point neatly foreshadows his uncle's ruin. But the realistic narrative that precedes the theft of the quap presents George not as a grim figure in an allegory but as a relatively personable young man who, even if sometimes insensitive, is expected to engage our sympathies. The act of gratuitous violence is not easily reconciled with any more positive notion we may have formed of his strength and understanding.

Long before the African venture, however, George himself warns us not to expect too much of his moral capacity, which he sees at odds with his yearning for great and beautiful things. "I'm a spiritual guttersnipe in love with unimaginable goddesses," he declares as if half-proud of his deficiency; "I've never seen the goddesses nor ever shall—but it takes all the fun out of the mud—and at times I fear all the kindliness too. . . . I am a hard and morally limited cad with a mind beyond my merits." In the only real crisis of his life he seeks an intellectual rather than a moral resolution of his problems. Like the despondency of Richard Feverel when the "apple-disease" strikes him, George's depression when his marriage fails and he finds no joy in the promotion of Tono-Bungay recalls the nervous breakdown of J. S. Mill. He, too, suffers "a sort of *ennui* of the imagination," and like Mill he questions the purposes of living, finds no one to confide in, ponders suicide, and for the first time experiences "what the old theologians call a 'conviction of sin.' "[24] But whereas Mill recovered by broadening his vision, by admitting the necessity of an emotional component in his strenuously intellectual philosophy, George relies on the intellect alone, on the mind beyond his moral merits: "I decided that in power and knowledge lay the salvation of my life." George resolves to become the scientist; and Science, idealized, in effect deified, "with her order, her inhuman distance, her steely certainties," saves him from despair.

As scientist, George finds, he tells us, a peculiar satisfaction in the pursuit of truth when unhampered in any way by the lack of money; he is apparently untroubled by the fact that his true research is lavishly supported by the lie that is Tono-Bungay. Scientific truth, he claims, is the one reality he has discovered in a confused world, and the truth, as he conceives it, involves a kind of beauty and even a measure of goodness. Science teaches him to admire the austere aesthetic form and to strive in his designing for the clean economical line and the clear-cut graceful pattern. And if it gives him no social ethic or any reason to view his neighbors with love and compassion, it nonetheless imposes on him a self-control and a disinterested objectivity, which may approximate personal moral attributes. After a long period of research he can boast that he has been "self-forgetful and scientific," as if the terms were almost synonymous. From his first coming to London he is proud of his ability to discipline both body and mind in the service of science, to renounce bad habits, to resist physical flabbiness and mental quiescence. He recognizes the pursuit of Marion as an unfortunate distraction, a sort of apostasy ("Such supplies of moral energy as I still had at command shaped now in the direction of serving Marion rather than science"), and he confesses that his desire to impress Beatrice with his gliders leads him to take short cuts in research and to shirk the longer harder road of science. Fortunately after each defeat he can reinstate the redeeming self-discipline. Until the end he can remember the early advice of his good angel, Aunt Susan: "Stick to your old science and things, George, and write and tell me when they make you a Professor." By his own account his "growing scientific reputation" carries him far beyond mere academic distinction; he resolutely affirms his "special aptitude" and refuses, he says, to be "either conceited or modest" about his achievement.[25]

But once he has established his professional credentials, George intimates that his research is too abstruse, too technical, to describe in his "novel." His scientific mind turns accordingly to the realm of the social rather than the natural sciences, and he becomes like Wells the analyst of the sort of world that a new technology has made and that in turn has helped determine the direction or misdirection of technological enterprise. Again and again throughout his narrative he moves from the specific details of his private life to generalizations about the condition of England, denunciations of its improvidence, and diagnoses of its sickness and decline.[26] For all its antique charm, the Bladesover of his childhood seems to him moribund, symbol of the waste and inequity of an outmoded system, and London, the capital of a kingdom of Bladesovers, proves but "a foolish community," squalid, unjust, impermanent. With Wells's shrewdness and journalistic vigor, George examines and exposes modern advertising, fraudulent promotion, monopolies, the manipulation of the market, and indeed the whole mood and manner of a late Victorian and Edwardian plutocracy. In his Uncle Teddy (whose name, Edward, must have some relation to the new era), he finds a phenomenon for scientific study, a representative case history; for he perceives "that all this present commercial civilization is no more than [his] poor uncle's career writ large, a swelling, thinning bubble of assurances; that its arithmetic is just as unsound, its dividends as ill-advised, its ultimate aim as vague and forgotten; that it all drifts on perhaps to some tremendous parallel to his individual disaster." Uncle Teddy in defeat rightly compares himself to Whitaker Wright, a notoriously venturesome Edwardian financier, who built an empire of shares and, for himself, Witley Park, known as Whitaker's Folly, an enormous house in Surrey with great arcades and pinnacles and a six-mile stone wall to guard the property. Following Wright's example, Teddy has set out to raise at Crest Hill a many-towered monument to his power of acquisition. But George, as we have remarked, is able to see the never-finished structure for what it is, a sign of the times, "the compactest image and sample of all that passes for Progress, of all the advertisement-inflated spending, the aimless building up and pulling down, the enterprise and promise of [the] age."[27]

Virginia Woolf complained—though without specific mention of *Tono-Bungay*—that Wells and the Edwardian novelists generally, inept at characterization, depicted houses to the neglect of the people who lived in them.[28] But Uncle Teddy is defined rather than blotted out by the description of his residences; the dismal Camden Town lodging, the carpeted suite in the Hardingham Hotel, Beckenham, Chislehurst with its grounds and gatekeeper, beautiful antique Lady Grove, all mark stages in his restless ascent; each in the adjustment it demands of him reveals something of the quality of the man, his ambition, his vanity, his final unworthiness. As social analyst George looking back on Teddy's career relates the houses to the class structure of the Bladesover system. As hero of the Bildungsroman he himself develops against the background of the houses, in each of which he is given his own room; for despite his intellectual endowment, his rise in the social and economic world is bound all too intimately to his uncle's, and his growth is partly determined by the settings he can later review with some ironic detachment.

In Africa, when the discovery of quap has made him fearful, cruel, and greedy, George three times dreams of Uncle Teddy, the face "ghastly white like a clown's" and the throat slit from ear to ear—a grotesque symbol of his own abasement. Though he has hitherto been severe in his judgments of Teddy, on his return to England he feels only "pity and affection" for the man in his melancholy ruin, and he resolves, like Pip hoping to save Magwitch, to take any risk to help him elude the law. When flight—melodramatically, by balloon across the Channel to the west coast of France—carries Teddy to his deathbed in a remote Basque village, George attentively nurses him till the end and then shares, at least emotionally, in his death: "It seemed to me almost as though I had died too." But unlike Pip, George does not recover from his half-death a wiser person with a deepened love of humanity. He is simply left with the empty conviction that he must forever walk alone, that "there was no reality except this solitary road, this quite solitary road, along which one went rather puzzled, rather tired."[29] And when, back home once again, he looks to Beatrice for a more positive faith, he finds brief intense passion but no lasting reassurance, no final escape from his lonely self.

George's mature "vision of the world," then, is as disillusioned, bleak, and bitter as the true view of the apparently optimistic Wells.[30] From the time that he recognizes the radioactivity of quap as a contagious, cancerous disease of matter, he is obsessed by the notion that atomic decay may eventually destroy the whole earth, and by rapid analogy he extends his idea of the disintegration of nature to himself and to a declining society. By the end of his story he confesses, "It may be I see decay all about me because I am, in a sense, decay," and he reflects that he might far better have called his book *Waste* than *Tono-Bungay*.[31] No protagonist in the English Bildungsroman, not even Marius or Mackenzie's Michael Fane, is more oppressed by the sense of cultural decadence.

George closes his "novel" with a description of a trip down the Thames on his new destroyer and of the panorama of England spread out along the river banks, tangible evidence, he believes, of past dignity and present sacrilege, "a feudal scheme overtaken by fatty degeneration and stupendous accidents of hypertrophy." He has offered the destroyer to his own countrymen first, but they, he says, "would have nothing to do with me." This, in one of the last sentences, is the first indication he has given us that, because of his involvement with Uncle Teddy, he has suffered social ostracism, and it may possibly help explain his final alienation. But for the most part his rejection of the society that rejects him is less self-interested and rests upon a more objective analysis. So trenchant is his repudiation of the new capitalism that a Marxist critic has hailed him as a socialist hero and interpreted the destroyer as the logic of socialism turning its guns against the system.[32] Yet George has already summarily dismissed the Fabian Socialists and their many meetings and endless gritty discussions, and we cannot imagine his showing much patience with Marxian dialectics and party organization or working happily toward the perfect Communist state. He is essentially not the socialist at all, but the scientist as social observer; he has no political idealism and little or no confidence in the future of mankind.

Aware till the end that he is writing a "novel," George

himself elucidates the meaning of the destroyer in the context of his narrative. Against all the decadence, decay, and death of nature and society, he discerns some ongoing thrust of life, an inviolate reality which he will call sometimes Science, sometimes Truth. "I have figured it in my last section," he explains, "by the symbol of my destroyer, stark and swift, irrelevant to most human interests." Apparently indifferent to the more alarming connotations of the symbol, he has no final concern with a social ethic and the hopes and fears of common men. His scientific truth is specialized, narrow, and exclusive, an intellectual defense against all emotional demand. At the last he is more or less content henceforth to be the dedicated scientist, or at least resigned to that role, and virtually unconscious of the fact that as such he may be less than the complete human being.

◄§ IX §►

D. H. LAWRENCE:
THE BURDEN OF APOLOGY

"You *must, must* read *Tono-Bungay*," D. H. Lawrence excitedly told his friends when Wells's novel first
appeared; ". . . read, *read Tono-Bungay*, it is a great
book."[1] Yet to Jessie Chambers, his closest confidante, he
admitted a sense of discouragement as much as delight in
the reading. Wells, he said, was obviously writing out of
a large personality, whereas he, the young Lawrence, could
not but wonder whether he would ever have so dynamic a
self to express.[2] But despite his misgivings, he was already
beginning his own career as a novelist with the assurance
that the novel, "the one bright book of life," was the most
intensely personal of literary forms; and he was finding
support for his conviction not only in *Tono-Bungay* but in
a number of other novels he admired—among them George
Borrow's *Lavengro*. In the latter, he explained to Jessie,
the author "mingled autobiography and fiction so inextricably . . . that the most astute critics could not be sure
where the one ended and the other began."[3] Jessie suspected
that Lawrence was planning some similar blend of personal
experience and imagination, and before long she was aiding
the effort that eventually (to her dismay) produced *Sons
and Lovers*, a work of probing subjectivity far beyond the
reach of either Wells or Borrow, and perhaps indeed the

204

most passionately autobiographical of all major English novels.

We must not forget, however, the fictional component that mingles "inextricably" with the detail from private life and helps determine the method and pattern, the emphases and exclusions, of *Sons and Lovers*. Lawrence was remarkably conscious of the tradition of the Bildungsroman to which his own story would relate. We do not know precisely when he first encountered *Wilhelm Meister*, but we know that he remembered it in later life, with distaste, as revealing "the perversity of intellectualised sex" and Goethe's "utter incapacity for any *development* of contact with any other human being."[4] He was considerably more sympathetic with *The Red and the Black*,[5] which he read—in French—in 1911, while at work on his own book; he admired Stendhal's sardonic wit and admitted to feeling rather like Julien Sorel, though more metaphysical and far more sentimental and always English. When he and Jessie, early in their reading together, discussed Dickens, he delighted, we are told, to identify himself with David Copperfield.[6] When both began writing, he recommended George Eliot as a model and spoke with particular fondness of *The Mill on the Floss* and of Maggie Tulliver as his favorite heroine.[7] He must have been familiar with Meredith's *Ordeal* before December 1910, when he complained to his fiancée Louie Burrows that he could not offer her "the pristine fervour of a young Feverel."[8] And by that time he surely knew *Jude the Obscure* and may even have begun to plan his long essay on Hardy with its discerning analysis of the character of Sue Bridehead.[9] None of these novels is a "source" of Lawrence's, but all could suggest ways in which highly personal materials might be adapted to the conventions of a genre.

Paul Morel, the earlier working title of *Sons and Lovers*, suggests the intentions of the book as a Bildungsroman, an account of the life and character of the one nominal hero, rather than a narrative of several protagonists or an even broader generalization about all young men in love. The opening chapters, as in other fictions of the kind, describe the boy's troubled relation to his family, though Paul's hostility to his father is even more extreme than Julien's hatred of old Sorel, and his dependence on his mother far surpasses in intensity the considerable filial affection of David Copperfield or Marius. The principal setting, as in most Victorian Bildungsromane, is provincial and indeed semi-rural, for the drab village of Bestwood is open to green hills and farmlands and flowered fields. The drift of the action is typically toward the city, "the faintly humming, glowing town" of the last sentence, where Paul finds his first job and where in the end, if anywhere, he is to make his lonely way. And the theme of money once again is insistent; the Morels must watch every penny and scrimp for small indulgences—a pot of tulips, a new crockery dish, tea in a restaurant, a rare seaside holiday; though never destitute, Paul knows from early adolescence the necessity of long hours' work for little pay and the confinement he must suffer in a warehouse as "a prisoner of industrialism."[10]

A novel of "education" only in the broad sense of the word, *Sons and Lovers* pays little or no heed to formal instruction but, like other Bildungsromane, lays much stress on the educative results of emotional experience. Paul, we must assume, receives at school and from his mother a grounding in the liberal arts, some training in foreign languages, and a taste for good books. At any rate, we know that he gives French lessons to Miriam Leivers, the fictional counterpart of Jessie Chambers, and that he discusses with her a wide range of reading; and we are told that such learning, as Tom Tulliver discovered with much less discomfort, is of no "commercial value" and so of little consequence to practical tradesmen.

Paul's studies are indeed not very different from those that Tom was taught to consider prerequisite to the making of a gentleman. The problem of the gentleman, however, is now no major issue. Paul's brother William naively deceives himself that by adopting citified manners and meeting a few men with money he can achieve gentlemanly status. But Paul has no such illusions. His mother recognizes the fact that he looks "quite a man" in William's evening suit, but "not . . . particularly a gentleman." Still she wants him "to climb into the middle classes" and "in the end to marry a lady," and he feels he must rebuke her genteel ambitions:

> "You know," he said to his mother, "I don't want to belong to the well-to-do middle class. I like my common people best. I belong to the common people."
> "But if anyone else said so, my son, wouldn't you be in a tear. *You* know you consider yourself equal to any gentleman."
> "In myself," he answered, "not in my class or my education or my manners. But in myself I am."
> "Very well, then. Then why talk about the common people?"
> "Because—the difference between people isn't in their class, but in themselves. Only from the middle classes one gets ideas, and from the common people—life itself, warmth. You feel their hates and loves."[11]

Paul's own "loves" are distinct and individual and hardly common, but they, too, fall into a pattern we detect in *Great Expectations, Richard Feverel,* and *Jude the Obscure:* the relatively spiritual or intellectual love, associated here with Miriam, and the fleshly passion, represented by Clara

Dawes. And both are presented—with Lawrencian fervor—
as stages in the development, the conscious *Bildung*, of the
hero. Paul's only complete sexual experience with Miriam
is to be understood as a ritual initiation ("he felt that he was
initiated. He was a youth no longer"), and his hot-blooded
taking of Clara is no less than "a sort of baptism of fire in
passion," "the baptism of life."[12]

Like other Bildungsroman heroes, Paul has a quick aesthetic sensibility. He is not solemnly dedicated to art as
Stephen Dedalus will be, nor does he submit to the strenuous
professional self-discipline of David Copperfield the novelist
or George Ponderevo the designer of beautiful machines.
But he does like to sketch and shows some real talent, wins
several first prizes at Nottingham exhibitions, sells a picture
for twenty guineas, and from time to time talks confidently
if rather vaguely of one day earning both money and reputation as a painter. We learn nothing of his style or technique,
but we can gauge the quality of his vision from his warm
response to natural forms and colors and from what he tells
Miriam of his work. One piece seems especially vivid in its
lack of shadowing: "It's . . . more shimmery," he explains,
"as if I'd painted the shimmering protoplasm in the leaves
and everywhere, and not the stiffness of the shape. That
seems dead to me. Only this shimmeriness is the real living."[13] The horizontals of the level Lincolnshire landscape
he is sketching suggest, he says, his own will to rush
doggedly forward, whereas the Gothic perpendiculars remind him of Miriam's ecstatic yearning for heaven. Nonetheless, though he makes clear his distrust of the Gothic
mode, he looks to Miriam for the inspiration and encouragement he needs as a painter:

> There was for him the most intense pleasure in talking about his
> work to Miriam. All his passion, all his wild blood, went into

this intercourse with her, when he talked and conceived his work. She brought forth to him his imaginations. She did not understand, any more than a woman understands when she conceives a child in her womb. But this was life for her and for him.[14]

Such aesthetic sharing serves Paul, for a time, at any rate, as a sublimation, a safe and happy surrogate for a more troublesome sexuality.

Most of the detail with which the familiar motifs of the Bildungsroman are developed in *Sons and Lovers* derives from a real and specific time and place remembered with an intense but literal vision. Until the end Lawrence wrote his best of the little world in which he grew up; his extraordinarily rich imagination, always less inventive than evocative, worked most effectively with impressions involuntarily absorbed before the years of questioning maturity and restless exile. Abundant evidence makes clear the close correspondence between the data of *Sons and Lovers* and the facts of Lawrence's experience, parallels to the novel in his own letters and poems and a short autobiographical sketch, in the reminiscences of his sister Ada, in the several memoirs by his early friends, and in notes on Nottinghamshire by scholars and pilgrims.[15] Bestwood is unmistakably Eastwood, reproduced in its setting with minute accuracy. The Morel house is to be identified and photographed as the Lawrences', and the Leivers' farm as The Haggs, where the Chambers family lived. Paul resembles the young Lawrence in physique, manner, and sensibility; but Paul is simply a painter, whereas Lawrence was both writer and painter, and Paul works not unhappily for some years at Jordan's surgical-appliance factory, whereas Lawrence spent but three months in misery at such an establishment and several more productive years as a college student and elementary-school teacher. Gertrude Morel, with her rectitude, resourcefulness, and courage, her devotion to her children and her bitterness in marriage, is very like Lawrence's mother as he pictures her in his letters and as his sister remembers her. And Walter Morel is a stronger, warmer portrait of Lawrence's father than Lawrence himself at the time intended; though the novel presents him as shiftless, coarse, and often brutal, Morel emerges as a vibrant man deserving of as much sympathy as censure—and various witnesses testify to Arthur Lawrence's vitality. The contempt that Paul and his mother shower on his father accurately reflects the alienation of the elder Lawrence from his family, which his daughter Ada later regretted and which on the occasion of a visit so distressed May Chambers (Jessie's sister) that she could not swallow her food.[16] Clara Dawes seems to have been suggested, at least in part, by Louie Burrows, though Louie was Lawrence's friend and certainly not his mistress. And Miriam is a complex study of Jessie Chambers, drawn from life (but not without distortion, subtraction, and dramatic heightening), the Jessie whom Mrs. Lawrence feared precisely as Mrs. Morel fears Miriam.

Jessie's own memoir not only authenticates much of the detail of *Sons and Lovers;* it stands in itself as a curiously complementary Bildungsroman. In it Jessie appears rather more robust than Miriam, more like the intelligent dark-eyed Emily of *The White Peacock,* whose portrait she also inspired;[17] and Lawrence has considerably more humor and vigor than Paul, a playfulness and charm as well as great sensitivity, a will to join joyfully in the chores of the farm ("Work goes like fun when Bert's here," says Jessie's father). The course of their love for each other runs closely parallel to the early Miriam chapters, but, unlike the fictional love, it leads to no later sexual relationship. The Lawrence of the memoir, when he must act the lover, creates a frightening atmosphere of "utter negation." Afraid of all demonstrative tenderness, he tells Jessie quite bluntly, "You have no sexual attraction at all, none whatever." Yet he insists that there are two kinds of love, the physical and the spiritual, and he offers her simply the latter as the basis of an engagement: "One man in me loves you," he explains, "but the other never can love you." In retrospect he blames the frustration of his love on family interference, which he describes as "the slaughter of the foetus in the womb." Jessie, however, suspects deeper sources of difficulty; she is dismayed by the split in Lawrence's affections and also, and more thoroughly, by his unnatural dependence on his mother. When Mrs. Lawrence dies, he freely confesses, "I've *loved* her, like a lover. That's why I could never love you." The "strange obsession" remains in his bereavement, and Lawrence, writing his novel, must distort (so the memoir claims) the association with Jessie "so that the martyr's halo might sit becomingly on his mother's brow." When it is at last clear that she has been wronged by both word and act, Jessie knows that her own sad initiation is complete; she looks back with nostalgia to the first coming of love and forward to a disillusioned maturity: "Life without him had a bleak aspect. I had grown up within his orbit, and now that he was definitely gone I had to make a difficult new beginning."[18]

    In all of this Jessie seems honest, inevitably defensive but restrained in self-pity, worshipful of the adolescent Lawrence and eager to be fair to the troubled young man, and always, above all, reluctant to see the facts violated or diluted with fictions. The ultimate irony is that Jessie did more than anyone else to encourage the writing of the novel that in a sense both celebrated her and destroyed her. As a means of therapy, by which Lawrence might see his confusions and fixations in a liberating perspective, she urged that *Paul Morel*, already begun as an imaginative narrative, be revised and brought closer to the author's Eastwood experience; and her plea for a greater realism prompted the inclusion of many fresh vignettes of actual family life and the addition of the character William Morel, modeled on Lawrence's ill-fated elder brother. Though too modest to claim the role of a collaborator, Jessie contributed notes for the Miriam chapters, and such of the notes as survive suggest that Lawrence freely availed himself of her suggestions, reproduced some of her precise phrasing, and drew on many incidents and impressions and snatches of dialogue she had remembered for the occasion. At first, to her delight, he seemed to be affirming the integrity of her recollections, though he alone of course had the skill to select and sharpen detail. As his manuscript advanced, however, the need for self-apology demanded that he invent circumstances and encounters to discredit Miriam in order to rationalize the character and conduct of Paul. He himself recognized the breach of faith, even the cruelty, to which he felt helplessly driven. "I am going through *Paul Morel*," he told Jessie; "I'm sorry it has turned out as it has. You'll have to go on forgiving me."[19] But Jessie considered the finished portrait of Miriam, which seemed so like herself in many ways and yet so very unlike, nothing short of a libel and forever beyond forgiveness.

However literal and inartistic her concept of truth in fiction may have been, Jessie was no doubt aesthetically right in asking of Lawrence a primary concern with the realities of living he himself had personally observed. The first nine chapters of *Sons and Lovers*—that is, the narrative up to Paul's first sharp break with Miriam—represent a triumph of the realistic mode in the English novel,[20] where warmth of sentiment typically makes a stronger claim than clinical analysis in the Flaubertian manner. When not intent on self-apology, Lawrence presents his own past with a remarkable objectivity, an empathic power which respects the integrity of people and settings and relationships. He beautifully renders both the tensions and the loyalties of the family and the peculiar grace of a reunion such as William's homecoming for Christmas: "Everybody was mad with happiness in the family. Home was home, and they loved it with a passion of love, whatever the suffering had been."[21] Between the parents flow waves of sympathy as well as deep mistrust and sad estrangement; when all love seems dead, a sudden show of tenderness may quicken the memory of a lost feeling. The mother, far from being a monster in an oedipal case history, is a woman of courage and compassion, worthy of her children's abiding devotion. And the father, though often sullen and defeated, still from time to time evinces something of the agility, verve, and self-command that once made him a sprightly dancer. The early chapters, especially, are—as Lawrence himself described the whole book—intensely "visualized": every scene is dramatically focused, sensuously alive, abruptly clipped off when complete, sharper in outline than the later Lawrence thought desirable. Yet the definition is seldom so rigid or static as he feared.[22] Here life abundantly satisfies his essential requirement: it is "something that gleams, that has the fourth-dimensional quality,"[23] something that reveals (to repeat Paul's words) its inner "shimmeriness" and not simply "the stiffness of the shape."

When Paul is an infant as yet unchristened, Mrs. Morel

experiences a gleaming spot of time, "one of those still moments when the small frets vanish, and the beauty of things stands out, and she [has] the peace and strength to see herself."[24] Instinctively she lifts the child up against the red sunset and resolves at once, for no reason she knows, to call him Paul. Miriam is subject to similar epiphanies; as she shares with Paul her delight in the radiance of a white rose bush, she feels a mystical communion with him and "the holiness of the night"; and as she comes upon Paul standing in a lane, bent over his dead brother's broken umbrella, she regards her impression of his loneliness as an "annunciation" of love, a "revelation" to be remembered always.[25] Paul, however, is suspicious of such ecstasies and too self-conscious to yield himself completely to any moment of insight. On a seashore walk with Miriam, he is gripped by the sensation that a great orange moon is staring at them, but he is less concerned with the moon as an ultimate presence than with the troubling half-understood sexual impulse it has awakened in him.[26] Unlike the ardent apostle whose name he bears, Paul is struck by no blinding vision that alters his destiny; he travels no purposeful road to Damascus, and his bondage to his childhood conditioning denies him any real conversion or vital new commitment. Nonetheless, he is educated in large part by what he observes with a painter's intensity, by the details he assimilates and recomposes, as if for a canvas, in his imagination; his world is indeed acutely "visualised."

As primarily Paul's story, *Sons and Lovers* is narrated mostly from Paul's point of view. But Paul is often the absorbed spectator rather than the active participant. One of the most effective passages in the novel describes Mrs. Morel's coming home to die:

Mrs. Morel did not change much. She stayed in Sheffield for two months. If anything, at the end she was rather worse. But she wanted to go home. Annie had her children. Mrs. Morel wanted to go home. So they got a motor-car from Nottingham—for she was too ill to go by train—and she was driven through the sunshine. It was just August; everything was bright and warm. Under the blue sky they could all see she was dying. Yet she was jollier than she had been for weeks. They all laughed and talked.

"Annie," she exclaimed, "I saw a lizard dart on that rock!"

Her eyes were so quick; she was still so full of life.

Morel knew she was coming. He had the front door open. Everybody was on tiptoe. Half the street turned out. They heard the sound of the great motor-car. Mrs. Morel, smiling, drove home down the street.

"And just look at them all come out to see me!" she said. "But there, I suppose I should have done the same. How do you do, Mrs. Matthews? How are you, Mrs. Harrison?"

They none of them could hear, but they saw her smile and nod. And they all saw death on her face, they said. It was a great event in the street.

Morel wanted to carry her indoors, but he was too old. Arthur took her as if she were a child. They had set her a big, deep chair by the hearth where her rocking-chair used to stand. When she was unwrapped and seated, and had drunk a little brandy, she looked round the room.

"Don't think I don't like your house, Annie," she said; "but it's nice to be in my own home again."

And Morel answered huskily:

"It is, lass, it is."

And Minnie, the little quaint maid, said:

"An' we glad t' 'ave yer."

There was a lovely ravel of sunflowers in the garden. She looked out of the window.

"There are my sunflowers!" she said.[27]

Presented almost entirely in simple declarative sentences, each like a deftly placed line or stroke of color, this scene has a reality quite independent of the hero and his reactions to it. Every element contributes to its aggregate dramatic force: the tension between implication and setting, the chill of impending death against the bright warmth of August; the vitality of the spirit in the stricken body, Mrs. Morel's pride rising to the dignity of the moment; the great event itself, her ride in triumph down the humble street; the lizard and the sunflowers as gleaming life symbols; the suggestion of Walter Morel's mood in the one adverb "huskily" and his five spoken monosyllables. The whole is as Paul must see it, for we are to imagine his coming from Sheffield with his mother and his sister; and all of it must touch Paul most intimately. Yet Paul is not once mentioned; he remains for the occasion self-effaced, alert in withdrawal, observant but silent about his feelings.

Lawrence was less than fair to *Sons and Lovers* when he wrote of it some months after its publication: "One sheds one's sicknesses in books—repeats and presents again one's emotions, to be master of them."[28] For the novel has for us a power far beyond the therapeutic purpose its writing may have served; at its best it has the strength of distanced autobiography, of subjective insight shaped into objective drama. When most confidently the artist, as in the above scene, Lawrence is able to recreate with resolute detachment what was undoubtedly most painful to remember. Mrs. Morel's return to Bestwood corresponds almost exactly to his own mother's last homecoming. But from the vivid description we learn nothing of the son's response (Paul's or the novelist's). As readers we are concerned for the moment only with Mrs. Morel's illness and her brave gesture, and not at all with Paul's psychological sickness or the shedding of Lawrence's.

This particular passage, however, coming late in the

novel, differs sharply in style from its immediate context; for the narrative has already largely shifted to a more subjective mode. Throughout the second half of the book, analysis tends more and more to displace delineated action. Paul's personal problems become Lawrence's dominant interest—and what Paul suffers unfortunately proves far less engaging and persuasive than his earlier unself-conscious experience. The richly dramatic fiction takes on the aspect of a typical case history, such as the paradigmatic naming of a late chapter "Passion" or the charge of title from the specific *Paul Morel* to the generalized *Sons and Lovers* might suggest.[29] When his revised manuscript was complete, Lawrence spelled out his theme reductively in a letter to Edward Garnett, his editor:

> It follows this idea: a woman of character and refinement goes into the lower class, and has no satisfaction in her own life. She has had a passion for her hsuband, so the children are born of passion, and have heaps of vitality. But as her sons grow up she selects them as lovers—first the eldest, then the second. . . . But when they come to manhood, they can't love, because their mother is the strongest power in their lives, and holds them. . . . As soon as the young men come into contact with women, there's a split. William gives his sex to a fribble, and his mother holds his soul. . . . The next son gets a woman who fights for his soul—fights his mother. . . . The son decides to leave his soul in his mother's hands, and, like his elder brother go for passion. He gets passion. Then the split begins to tell again. . . . The son casts off his mistress, attends to his mother dying. He is left in the end naked of everything, with the drift towards death.[30]

This is of course the same split that Jessie Chambers grieved to find in Lawrence, "that self-division" which first manifested itself, she said, when he was nineteen or twenty.[31] In

the novel Miriam believes Paul torn between "higher" and
"lower" desires and desperately hopes that the higher, the
more spiritual, will bring him surely back to her, even
though the lower, the more physical, turn him for a while to
Clara Dawes. Paul indeed loves Miriam "with his soul," but
he refuses to see that Miriam wants more than "a sort of
soul union" and conveniently blames her spirituality for his
sexual diffidence and frustration. Yet he himself has insisted
repeatedly that their relation is "only friendship," and he has
been for so long a time too timid and ashamed to confess
any physical attraction that we are hardly convinced either
by his eventual aggressive "test on Miriam" or by Lawrence's awkward effort to establish her frigidity. We are
confused by the proposition that Paul is now betrayed by
the object of his affection[32] rather than by the "sickness"
within himself that we have seen developing since his childhood and have come to consider the real source of his
maladjustment. On the other hand, when Paul discards
Miriam, chooses Clara, and "goes for passion," we are assured that he cannot love completely, cannot offer his whole
self even to a woman who suffers from no excess of spirituality. "You know," he tells his mother, "I think there
must be something the matter with me, that I *can't* love. . . .
I even love Clara, and I did Miriam; but to *give* myself to
them in marriage, I couldn't. I couldn't belong to them.
They seem to want *me*, and I can't ever give it them."[33]

Despite much talk of the split, which attempts to shift the
onus onto Miriam and Clara, the novel as a whole makes
the matter with Paul sufficiently clear. From the beginning
dramatic evidence of a mother fixation rapidly accumulates,
and in the late chapters analysis of the complex becomes
explicit and repetitively insistent. "Mrs. Morel's intimacy
with her second son," we learn at the outset, is "more

subtle and fine, perhaps not so passionate as with her eldest."[34] Paul from early childhood is completely devoted to his mother, confides in her, reverences her every opinion, admires her stoic fortitude, and aches with pity for her frailty. When fourteen years old and off to Nottingham with her for a job interview, he regards her as a "sweetheart," and his heart contracts "with pain of love for her."[35] Later he accepts as reasonable her jealousy of Miriam and is relieved to recognize that "the deepest of his love belong[s] to his mother." By comparison, Miriam seems to him vague and unreal—"And nobody else mattered. There was one place in the world that stood solid and did not melt into unreality: the place where his mother was. . . . It was as if the pivot and pole of his life, from which he could not escape, was his mother."[36] And he is infuriated when his drunken father questions a demonstrative embrace of mother and son, "At your mischief again?"[37] But the mischief is greater and more lasting than he will admit; in the end it is almost paralyzing, for his attachment threatens to leave him never really "free to go forward with his own life."[38]

Lawrence himself seems to have been as slow as Paul to foresee the consequences of his fixation. He was in fact rather proud of his devotion and eager to believe that many men of genius were similarly dependent on their mothers' protection and encouragement. Yet of the many confessional verses he wrote on his mother's death, "The Inheritance" alone suggests that her brave example has made possible his final assent to living. The other elegies, often fulsome and embarrassingly erotic in imagery, simply declare his surrender to darkness and despair. Lawrence knew nothing of Freud until he began to revise the final draft of *Sons and Lovers;* and even then, according to Frieda Lawrence, who introduced him to the new psychology, he "quite missed the point," failed to understand the real implications of an excessive commitment to his mother. Frieda for her part grew tired of all of Paul's entanglements and wrote a burlesque, "Paul Morel, or His Mother's Darling," to register her protest;[39] but Lawrence was more annoyed than amused by such levity. Later he was incensed at the attempt of a psychoanalyst, Dr. Alfred Booth Kuttner, to elucidate the novel. "You know," he complained, "I think 'complexes' are vicious half-statements of the Freudians. . . . When you've said *Mutter*-complex, you've said nothing—no more than if you called hysteria a nervous disease. . . . My poor book: it was, as art, a fairly complete truth: so they carve a half lie out of it, and say '*Voilà*.' Swine!"[40] Nonetheless, his work, especially insofar as it veers in the second half toward the case history, invites a Freudian reading; and he himself, in the turgid preface he prepared in 1913 but never used, seems ready enough to appropriate Freudian jargon: "The old son-lover was Oedipus. The name of the new one is legion."[41]

Dr. Kuttner indeed spoke an incomplete truth when he described Paul Morel as thoroughly unpleasant and unhealthy, an abnormal young man with the earmarks of degeneracy, "who is alternately a ruthless egotist and a vicious weakling in his dealings with women, and who in the end stoops to shorten the life of his own mother."[42] Yet there is much evidence in the text to support this reading. For Paul as surely as Maugham's Philip Carey, who appeared two years later, is one of the many sick heroes of modern literature whose psychic wound is not soon healed. His nervous mannerisms are emphatic and disturbing. Hypersensitive to all impressions, he is ready, when crossed or disappointed, to sob aloud or "smash things in fury." His

eyes blaze with anger; he grows "mad with impotence."
Frustrated by Clara's sudden return to the city, he writhes
on his bed in pain and rage and bites his lips until they
bleed. After his mother's death his men friends, quite
understandably, have "a certain mistrust of him" when they
see "him go white to the gills, his eyes dark and glitter-
ing."[43] He is often cruelly impatient with Miriam, and he
becomes "passionate with hate" as he denounces her to
Clara. When he decides to break altogether with the girl,
he sinks his teeth into a pink blossom—symbolically perhaps
but nevertheless histrionically—and spits the chewed petals
into the fire. He fails to perceive (or else Lawrence cau-
tiously dissembles) what seems obviously a deep homosexual
attraction to Clara's sullen husband, Baxter Dawes.[44] He
resorts to the mercy-killing of his mother partly indeed
to shorten her suffering but largely to spare his own
tortured sensibilities. And in all circumstances he habitually talks of himself, "like the simplest egoist," for, though
never simple, he is often self-centered, self-opinionated, self-
satisfied, a true egoist in fact, in the Meredithian sense, seldom touched by the comic spirit.

Unlike Meredith, however, Lawrence apparently regards
his fictional counterpart without irony; he condones most
of Paul's conduct and presents his moodiness, sentimentality, arrogance, and rage as if they were all necessary
concomitants, perhaps even tokens, of the artistic temperament. When Mrs. Morel reflects on her husband's lack of
steadiness and principle, the narrator implicitly endorses
her judgment. But when Miriam in her thoughts charges
Paul with having "no fixity of purpose, no anchor of
righteousness," Miriam herself, we must understand, is to be
judged: while she ponders "his lack of religion, his restless
instability,"[45] she unwittingly exposes her own too narrow

code and too timid character. Again, Lawrence obviously shares Paul's condemnation of the erotic way in which Miriam caresses flowers as if she would possess their very essence; yet Paul escapes censure as he strokes "the fleshy throats" of the purple iris or yearns to drink up the yellowness of fresh cowslips—and Lawrence himself, as Frieda reports, felt no self-consciousness in responding with similar intensity to a blue gentian.[46]

Whether or not the latter part of *Sons and Lovers* was intended to persuade Jessie Chambers of the justice of Lawrence's behavior, Paul, often with the author's sanction, is patently unjust to Miriam. Eager to rationalize his own inadequacies of response, he again and again seizes the opportunity to humiliate, rebuff, and deny her. When, for example, she is provoked into accusing him of always fighting her off, he at once convinces himself that she has never loved him at all but always deceived and secretly despised him; and when, in their last interview, she makes her continued devotion perfectly clear, he remains altogether passive and yet in his heart charges her with being reticent and unaggressive and so failing "to relieve him of the responsibility of himself."[47] Paul's "religion" which Miriam refuses to credit serves as a similar rationalization of his self-interest. Miriam grieves to see him "arguing God on to his own side, because he wanted his own way and his own pleasure."[48] Though the phrasing seems weighted against her, the idea is repeated in a quite objective statement: "He had shovelled away all the beliefs that would hamper him, had cleared the ground, and come more or less to the bedrock of belief that one should feel inside oneself for right and wrong, and should have the patience to gradually realise one's God."[49] Paul's creed may owe something to the ambiance of the Socialist, Suffragette, Unitarian world to which Clara Dawes belongs.[50] But it derives far more from his need for self-justification, and it is turned always to serve his personal convenience. At all events it is close to the Nietzschean individualism, defiantly amoral, that shocked Jessie Chambers. "With *should* and *ought* I have nothing to do," said Lawrence; and Jessie accepted his declaration, for she found him frighteningly "the measure of his own universe, his own god—and also his own hell."[51]

Unfortunately Paul has a more fragile claim than Lawrence to the personal religion of the aesthetic superman, above and beyond the inhibiting demands of society. His creative energies as artist are not sufficient to sustain him after his mother's death. He can no longer paint at all; he cannot shed his sickness in pictures.[52] In the end he stands alone, disconsolate, a child crying in the night:

> "Mother!" he whimpered—"mother!"
> She was the only thing that held him up, himself, amid all this. And she was gone, intermingled herself. He wanted her to touch him, have him alongside with her.[53]

The last chapter of the novel is entitled "Derelict," and Paul is left aimless, as Lawrence told Garnett, "with the drift towards death." Yet he is committed no more to dying than to living. Vacillating between the two, he turns, at the last minute, from the darkness and walks, as the last line puts it, "towards the faintly humming, glowing town, quickly." The final adverb has been construed as an affirmation, connoting the "quickness" of life. But nothing has prepared us for so positive a resolution, and there is little reason to believe that the sudden assent is really decisive and permanent. If we are indeed intended to consider Paul at last free and whole, his victory is not inherent in his story but imposed upon it from without. We know of course that

Lawrence himself did achieve at least a partial adjustment which allowed him to go on living. By intimating even tentatively that Paul, too, somehow ultimately recovers, he is being true to his own experience but nonetheless false to his creation. Any such personal intrusion in the end must contradict the facts against which it has been struggling throughout the latter part of the fiction.

Unlike Paul, Lawrence relied on his art and his religion as artist to carry him through his ordeal. Two and a half weeks after his mother's death he begged Louie Burrows to forgive his frequent almost inhuman detachment and to respect its cause:

> It is the second me, the hard, cruel if need be, me that is the writer which troubles the pleasanter me, the human who belongs to you. Try, will you, when I disappoint you and may grieve you, to think that it is the impersonal part of me—which belongs to nobody, not even to myself—the writer in me, which is for the moment ruling. . . . Remember I love you and am your husband: but that a part of me is exempt from these things, from everything: the impersonal artistic side.[54]

Herein lies an aestheticism scarcely less fierce and determined, self-confident and self-protective, than that of James Joyce. As autobiography *Sons and Lovers* describes the conflicts from which that credo offered escape, and as a work of art in itself it testifies at its best to a power greater than Paul Morel's to transcend the distortions of a personal apology.

❦ X ❧

PORTRAIT OF JAMES JOYCE
AS A YOUNG AESTHETE

UNLIKE Lawrence, who stood painfully close to the events and emotions he describes in *Sons and Lovers*, Joyce was able to look in a longer, more leisurely perspective at the autobiographical materials he was shaping and reshaping into *A Portrait of the Artist as a Young Man*. Thanks to his difficulties in finding a publisher for his early poems and collected stories, his novel was delayed for at least ten years from inception to completion, and the dates he affixed to its last page, "Dublin 1904, Trieste 1914," carefully emphasize the distance in time and space. As aesthetic theorist, Stephen Dedalus, the hero, speculates on the posture of the ideal artist, who must remain apart from his creation, in godlike detachment, "invisible, refined out of existence, indifferent, paring his fingernails."[1] Joyce himself, for all his resources of art and artifice, never achieved, and perhaps never really desired, such complete impersonality. Some deeply subjective impulse underlay all his work from the first sensitive sketches of *Dubliners* to the last lonely cadences of *Finnegans Wake*. But he was fascinated from the beginning by the image of the aloof dispassionate craftsman and until the end was alert, as Lawrence frequently was not, to the problems of involvement and the possibility of self-betrayal. He therefore approached his Bildungsroman with deliberate caution and eventually in the final drafts succeeded in reducing the emotional content of the form and at the same time enlarging its capacities for self-protective ironic statement.

Joyce sums up, even as he transforms, the traditions of the nineteenth-century Bildungsroman. The most literary of major novelists, he was familiar with most if not all of the books and authors we have considered. Though he had no great respect for Goethe,[2] he referred to him directly several times in an early version of the *Portrait* and was apparently fascinated by *Wilhelm Meister* as a study of the artist at odds with a Philistine public and possibly also by Wilhelm's quest for self-culture, comparable as it is to Stephen's self-conscious dedication to his Daedalian destiny. He admired *The Red and the Black*, perhaps for its intellectual texture and for the self-possession of Julien Sorel as a player of roles worthy of Stephen's emulation; and Ezra Pound properly saw in the style of the *Portrait* something of "the hard clarity of a Stendhal."[3] He professed only contempt for Dickens, whom indeed he does not much resemble; yet like Dickens, he identifies his secondary characters—for example, Stephen's college friends Cranly and Lynch—by properties and mannerisms, symbols as it were of their essential quality. *The Mill on the Floss* is mentioned in *Finnegans Wake* (though by that time it has become the John Stuart Mill on the Floss), but there is little of George Eliot in the *Portrait*, apart from a similar awareness of the role of religion in troubled adolescence and the knowledge that a willed rejection of worldliness may induce a dangerous pride in humility. Joyce read Hardy's novel not long after its appearance and was amused by his brother's asking for it at the library as *Jude the Obscene*, but he was clearly less impressed by Hardy's technique than by his defiance of popular taste.[4] And if, as seems likely, he knew *The Way of All Flesh*, which attracted much attention during the years of the writing of the *Portrait*, he must have found in its treatment of a young man's breaks with faith and family a ready precedent for his own story.[5]

Among all the Bildungsromane, however, by far the most conspicuous influences on Joyce's practice were *The Ordeal of Richard Feverel* and *Marius The Epicurean*. Meredith's novel was a particular favorite during his university days, and Meredith's work in general provided the subject of one of his early reviews.[6] The germ of the *Portrait* is an essay-sketch written in January 1904, and already called "A Portrait of the Artist," some of which recalls Meredith's manner so vividly that it reads almost like a parody:

> It was part of that ineradicable egoism which he was afterwards to call redeemer that he imagined converging to him the deeds and thoughts of the microcosm. Is the mind of boyhood medieval that it is so divining of intrigue? Field sports (or their correspondent in the world of mentality) are perhaps the most effective cure, but for the fantastic idealist, eluding the grunting booted apparition with a bound, the mimic hunt was no less ludicrous than unequal in a ground chosen to his disadvantage. But behind the rapidly indurating shield the sensitive answered. Let the pack of enmities come tumbling and sniffing to the highlands after their game—there was his ground: and he flung them disdain from flashing antlers. There was evident self-flattery in the image but a danger of complacence too. Wherefore, neglecting the wheezier bayings in that chorus which leagues of distance could make musical, he began loftily diagnosis of the younglings. His judgment was exquisite, deliberate, sharp; his sentence sculptural.[7]

Here everywhere are abundant marks of Meredith's most intellectual mode, the difficult and laborious prose, allusive, elliptical, the sporting metaphor relentlessly pursued, the epithet ("sensitive") standing oddly as a substantive, the curious diction blending the Latinate with a more sensuous, slightly archaic English, the effort to generalize a specific mood, the will to express the demand of the proud ego and yet to reduce the aspiration to an epigram, the disposition to vindicate and mildly to rebuke, reminiscent of Meredith's view of the Magnetic Youth. Joyce was later less extravagant in the homage of imitation, but his indebtedness was still considerable. Padraic Colum spoke of the earliest draft of *Stephen Hero*, the next and much longer version of the *Portrait*, as "Joyce's Meredithean novel,"[8] perhaps by virtue of a certain arch and erudite exposition, though what survives of the manuscript is quite lacking in Meredith's richness of texture. The finished *Portrait*, in every way a more distinguished work, better recalls the stylistic variation of *Feverel*, the rapid shifts from satire to sentiment, from analysis to poetic impressionism. Stephen's ecstatic vision of the birdlike girl by the seaside, the "epiphany" that ends Chapter IV, has frequently been compared to Richard's entranced discovery of Lucy bending over the riverbank, though Meredith's carefully arranged vignette remains the clearer and more credible. Stephen's diary, which ends the book, may hark back to Clare's diary as a device for dramatic self-revelation. And Stephen's romantic daydreaming, his burnishing of heroic images of the self, seems not far from Richard's reveries, which indeed at times approach a Joycean stream of consciousness. Through intellect, attitude, and method, the one self-conscious novelist, gifted and to a degree arrogant, speaks across the years to the other.

The debt to Pater was also apparent and even more pervasive. "He is a purely literary writer," T. S. Eliot told Virginia Woolf of the author of *Ulysses;* "he is founded

upon Walter Pater with a dash of Newman."⁹ The founda-
tions clearly underlie the *Portrait*. When working on his
manuscript, Joyce, who felt that the best way to study
a prose writer was to transcribe a few representative paragraphs, copied out long passages of *Marius the Epicurean*.¹⁰
From Pater he learned to mold the sentence as a subtly
contoured artifact, to let the language, formal, fastidious,
a bit precious, stand not just as a description of the experience but often also as a substitute for it:

> He longed for the minor sacred offices, to be vested with the
> tunicle of subdeacon at high mass, to stand aloof from the
> altar, forgotten by the people, his shoulders covered with a
> humeral veil, holding the paten within its folds, or, when the
> sacrifice had been accomplished, to stand as deacon in a dalmatic
> cloth of gold on the step below the celebrant, his hands joined
> and his face towards the people, and sing the chant, *Ite, missa est.*
> . . . In vague sacrificial or sacramental acts alone his will seemed
> drawn to go forth to encounter reality; and it was partly the
> absence of an appointed rite which had always constrained him
> to inaction whether he had allowed silence to cover his anger
> or pride or had suffered only an embrace he longed to give. . . .
> His mind, when wearied of its search for the essence of
> beauty amid the spectral words of Aristotle or Aquinas, turned
> often for its pleasure to the dainty songs of the Elizabethans. His
> mind, in the vesture of a doubting monk, stood often in shadow
> under the windows of that age, to hear the grave and mocking
> music of the lutenists or the frank laughter of waistcoaters until
> a laugh too low, a phrase, tarnished by time, of chambering and
> false honour, stung his monkish pride and drove him on from
> his lurkingplace.¹¹

Here the measured quiet falling rhythm, the mingling of the
sensuous and the spiritual, and the suggestion of the passive
young man dreaming of a comelier order recall the style and
content of Pater's "imaginary portraits," of which *Marius*

is simply the most ambitious; and Joyce's essay "Portrait of the Artist" and the title of his novel apparently acknowledge the Paterian genre. Stephen Dedalus, if not Joyce, seems to have taken as his model of aesthetic detachment the scholarly Marius or, more strikingly still, Marius's aggressive friend Flavian, who has a thoroughly Joycean love of words and a delight in a "literary conscience . . . awakened to forgotten duties towards language"[12]—which anticipates Stephen's ultimate concern with quickening an aesthetic "conscience." Stephen's "epiphanies," when they are actually revelations of meaning or value, resemble Marius's privileged insights, and the logic of both is inherent in the "Conclusion" to *The Renaissance,* where Pater reminds us of the importance of discriminating each specific impression and so of isolating the intense and vital moment from the relentless flux of time. Pater, in short, more precisely than any of Joyce's predecessors, defines the aesthetic temper in terms that Stephen as the aspiring young artist can understand and emulate.

Whatever its derivations from particular books or authors, the *Portrait* is developed within the recognizable general framework of the Bildungsroman. It is an autobiographical novel of "education," tracing the growth of the hero from infancy to young manhood, describing his slowly decreased dependence on father and mother, his schooldays, his adolescent fantasies, his choice of a career, and his ultimate approach to his maturity or at least to his legal majority. Stephen is not precisely Joyce in character or mental endowment—we can scarcely imagine his ever writing *Ulysses.* Yet he has much in common with Joyce to the age of twenty and shares many of the young Joyce's experiences: he has an identical political and religious background, attends the same Jesuit schools, is myopic like

Joyce and as a child likewise breaks his glasses and suffers unjust punishment; at twelve he pays a similar visit to Cork with his father (who like John Joyce vainly hopes to recoup his declining fortunes), and at fourteen he encounters, as Joyce did, a Dublin prostitute, who provides his sexual initiation; like Joyce, he practices a strenuous piety for a period at Belvedere College and seriously considers entering the priesthood; he reads the same books at the university, entertains many of the same ideas and prejudices, harangues friends readily identifiable as Joyce's classmates, and in the end prepares like Joyce to exile himself as the dedicated artist from country, church, and kindred. Though not direct autobiography, the novel, as many early readers observed and most later critics are eager to deny, draws at almost every point on the life of the author.

As a Bildungsroman, the *Portrait* is strikingly successful in its depiction of childhood. Stephen as a small boy is as convincing in his way as young Pip or little Maggie, and more vivid than Paul Morel. Joyce, like Wordsworth, whose "genius" he extolled,[13] was apparently convinced that the child was father of the man, that the formative early years forever set the pattern of the personality. At any rate, Stephen's first sensitive impressions, fears, defiances, feelings of guilt and aloneness, all mold the proud self-defensive temper of the adult—though they invest the nervous boy with a vitality, a sort of three-dimensional reality, which the very aesthetic young man hardly preserves.

The hero's parents, on the other hand, absorb little of Joyce's attention; the elder Dedaluses seem mere shadows when we place them beside the full-bodied Morels or the Tullivers or even the Pontifexes. The novel is said to pursue a biological metaphor,[14] to begin with the father and end with severance from the mother; but neither is in fact a substantial being. At the Christmas dinner, the father defending Parnell is a fine clear Irish voice to be admired by his listening son; but before long he becomes a stage Celt full of blarney, and then just a shapeless symbol of embarrassing improvidence. Well into the second half of the book, when Simon Dedalus has receded into the background, Stephen gathers from "her listless silence" that his mother resents his entering the university; he mentally charges her with disloyalty, but soon, ignoring her mistrust, he is "made aware dimly and without regret of a first noiseless sundering of their lives."[15] We have been given, however, no evidence up to this point that there has ever been any particularly close relationship between mother and son, and even now we have no sense of a distinct identity setting itself against another's will. In the end we must deduce as best we can the character of the long-suffering woman who prays that Stephen may learn in his own life "and away from home and friends what the heart is and what it feels."

Formal education plays an unusually large and decisive role in the *Portrait*. Whereas Lawrence virtually ignores Paul Morel's academic career, Joyce associates the main events of Stephen's life with his schooling. The greater part of the novel unfolds against the settings of Clongowes and Belvedere and University College, Dublin, or in peripatetic undergraduate colloquies not far from St. Stephen's Green, and Joyce has a thorough grasp of the principles of Jesuit instruction and a sharp ear for student idiom. Accordingly the freer "education" by experience of work or play, travel, nature, adolescent romance, and imaginative reading receives far less emphasis than in most Bildungsromane. If Stephen is the young man from the provinces insofar as his Dublin is provincial and parochial, the cosmopolitan city to which he turns in the end, the world "away from home and friends," lies wholly outside the narrative. It is unlikely from the evidence of the *Portrait* that he will there learn what the heart is,[16] for learning to love or even learning through love has been no considerable factor in his development. The two loves of the typical hero are perhaps present by implication, but both are drastically reduced. The "higher" love presumably is represented by E— C—, to whom Stephen addresses Byronic verses; yet E— C— as a person is a mere blur on the page, and we must turn back to the discarded *Stephen Hero* to see the girl in any sort of focus or to hear her speak or even to discover that her name is Emma Clery. The "lower," fleshly love may be typified by the prostitute who floats into view under the gas lamps at the end of the second chapter; but she is a momentary delirium less real than the huge doll that sprawls in her easychair. Sexuality in the *Portrait* is illicit, indecent, and vaguely repulsive, important only for the vividly delineated feelings of guilt it inspires in Stephen.

The motif of money common in the genre from Dickens to Wells and Lawrence is once again prominent, and the familiar theme of the gentleman also briefly recurs. The Dedalus family, steadily growing in size until Stephen seems unsure how many brothers and sisters he has, sinks from a relatively genteel respectability into a deeper and deeper indigence, a life of hunger and squalor, lice and dunning creditors. For a short spell Stephen gallantly attempts, by spending all his prize money from school, to restore a lost sense of well-being in the family and to overcome his own sense of alienation from his parents. But the money is soon gone, and he sees the futility of his effort: "How foolish his aim had been! He had tried to build a breakwater of order and elegance against the sordid tide of life without him and

to dam up, by rules of conduct and active interests and new
filial relations, the powerful recurrence of the tides within
him."[17] Stephen is constantly assailed by ugly circumstance
which mocks his love of ritual and his dreams of beauty.
From the beginning he has been taught to respect a gentlemanly ideal. In his first conversation as a small boy at
school he identifies his father as "a gentleman." Later his
father in turn urges him to be a gentleman—that is, a decent
good fellow with easy bearing—and always "to mix with
gentlemen," and he wonders for a while whether it is to be
his gentlemanly duty "to raise up his father's fallen state."[18]
In the end he has not become a gentleman in station or in
manner, but he has found what seems to him a more than
adequate substitute in the role of the artist, conceived as a
sort of Nietzschean hero whose pride of intellect and
sensibility is as assured as a true gentleman's perfect composure.

To accommodate the heroic aesthete, to give the temperament absolute centrality, Joyce dispenses with much of the
objectivity of the less narrowly focused Bildungsroman. If
Stephen's family and friends and E—— C—— often seem
elusive shadows, it is only that they are presented from
Stephen's point of view, and Stephen is so self-absorbed, so
intent on his difference from others, that he refuses to
honor the reality of those who move in the outside world
and make claims upon his affections. All that happens in
the novel exists in Stephen's immediate response to it, and
much takes place only in his trains of mental association.
"My own mind," Stephen insists in the earlier fragment,
"is more interesting to me than the entire country."[19] In the
finished *Portrait* the developing mind clearly has priority
over the setting, and the prose style intended to capture
its processes changes to reflect each stage of Stephen's

growth toward maturity. The objective narrative voice of the author seldom intrudes with judgment or commentary; in its place an indirect narration paraphrases the hero's thought and illustrates by pitch of rhetoric and level of language the quality of his emotion. The "stream of consciousness" technique (or its near-equivalent), highly effective in registering the infant's sensations and the schoolboy's timidity and homesickness, disappears after the first chapter, though it is suggested again in some of the diary entries at the end. But Stephen's impressions, ideas, and reveries, however they are recorded, dominate the entire novel; physical events count for less than images, and episodes crystallize into moments of vision. Defined in *Stephen Hero* as "a sudden spiritual manifestation, whether in the vulgarity of speech or of gesture or in a memorable phase of the mind itself,"[20] the Joycean "epiphany" is more subjective than the Wordsworthian "spot of time," or at any rate less empirical, often more remote from a visual stimulus. The "epiphanies" collected by Joyce for use in his fiction sometimes seem arbitrary, almost meaningless apart from context, dependent less on the perception of an outside timeless order than on the weight that he—or Stephen, to whom they will be assigned—attaches to an idea, a well-turned phrase, or a snatch of dialogue.

From the beginning when "baby tuckoo" hears a story and sings his song and dances to the sailor's hornpipe played by his mother on the piano, Stephen's sharpest impressions are auditory. Sound is everywhere more intense than sight, and when the penitent youth decides to mortify the senses, the punishment of the ear exceeds that of the eye:

> In order to mortify the sense of sight he made it his rule to walk in the street with downcast eyes, glancing neither to right

nor left and never behind him. His eyes shunned every encounter with the eyes of women. From time to time also he
balked them by a sudden effort of the will, as by lifting them
suddenly in the middle of an unfinished sentence and closing the
book. To mortify his hearing, he exerted no control over his
voice which was then breaking, neither sang nor whistled and
made no attempt to flee from noises which caused him painful
nervous irritation such as the sharpening of knives on the knife-
board, the gathering of cinders on the fireshovel and the twig-
ging of the carpet.[21]

Unlike David Copperfield the observer, Stephen learns
most by what he hears, either in short exchanges of speech
or in long heated debates like the quarrel at the Christmas
dinner or in extended harangues like the terrifying sermon
on Hell. Eventually he, too, joins the indefatigable talkers
in his eagerness to expound his aesthetic. But long before
this, talk has surged like the sea about him, and he has had
deliberately to screen out the din of "hollowsounding
voices" clamoring for his attention.[22] Like Joyce, Stephen
is responsive to the ring of words, the texture, the connotation, the ultimate power. As a little boy he is fascinated
by the ambiguity of *belt:* "He kept his hands in the side-
pockets of his belted grey suit. That was a belt round his
pocket. And belt was also to give a fellow a belt." As he
grows up, he listens avidly to political gossip and family
legends; and whenever he encounters new words, he says
them "over and over to himself till he [has] learned them
by heart: and through them he [has] glimpses of the real
world about him."[23] At the climax of his development,
when, wandering on the sea strand, he has decided to
dedicate himself to art, he ponders the magic and mystery
of words and the matchless poise of "a lucid supple periodic
prose." He hears a dim music from within, constantly re-

ceding, and "one longdrawn calling note," and then, from
without, his own name shouted irreverently by sea bathers,
a name to make him think, in defiance of the mocking
voices, of Daedalus the artificer and to set him weaving a
spell of words around himself and finally around the vision
of the girl by the shore until she is not so much seen as
heard, an imagined call to life in an ecstasy of echoing
language.[24]

The Daedalian symphony fades for the reader in the
banal chatter of the Dedalus breakfast table that begins the
last chapter. Stephen moves from one impression to the
next; the talking and the thinking are discontinuous and
inconclusive. Lacking or deliberately breaking up a clear
narrative sequence, the novel is held together by chains of
imagery, repeated symbols, a ingenious superstructure contrived by the author partly perhaps to suggest the unity of
Stephen's sensibility but largely to make of his book a
shapely artifact. The first two pages,[25] brilliant as an evoca-
tion of the infant mind, establish the symbolic texture of
the whole. The moocow, the water in the wet bed, the
color green, the singing of the song, the hiding under the
table, the threatened eyes, the fierce birds, all these may be
seen as portentous of what is to come, as introductions to
the main themes, religion, Ireland, and above all art and
the temper of the aesthetic hero. "The moocow came down
the road where Betty Byrne lived"—even Betty Byrne,
never mentioned again in the entire novel, may have her
place in the ingenious iconography; she is to be construed,
we are told, as St. Elizabeth, insofar as Stephen's friend
Cranly, whose name in real life was John F. Byrne, is
equated in the last chapter with John the Baptist (though,
some say, also with Judas).[26] Recurring symbols help distance the autobiographical materials by imposing upon

them a sort of ritual artifice. But the symbol violates rather than supports the integrity of the art work when it depends for identification on a private world outside the fiction. And even recognizable symbolism exacts a high price when it reduces or distorts character to the purposes of an intricate pattern.

Though the sermon on Hell and Stephen's exposition of his aesthetic theory seem unnecessarily long-winded, the *Portrait* as a whole evinces a remarkable economy. It has evolved from the earlier manuscript by a process of ruthless exclusion and steady narrowing of focus. What remains of *Stephen Hero* is nearly as long as the completed book but it covers only the ground of Chapter V, Stephen's two years at the university. The fragment presents in some detail Stephen's affection for his brother Maurice, the death of his sister Isabel, his quarrel with his mother about making his Easter duty, descriptions of houses and the weather, sketches of Cranly and Lynch and Emma Clery. In the *Portrait* Maurice and Isabel do not appear at all, the quarrel is simply reported to Cranly, most settings exist by implication, and Stephen's friends are scarcely more than his auditors. The pruning indeed has sometimes been excessive, for *Stephen Hero* remains an essential gloss on much that Stephen in the final more cryptic version refers to by innuendo or veiled allusion.[27] Nevertheless, the relatively austere revision dispenses with a great deal not strictly relevant to the central design and disciplines and heightens a frequently awkward, rambling prose. Pages of undigested self-vindicating autobiography have become concentrated paragraphs of a fiction from which the author has attempted to withdraw. Whatever Stephen's status as poet, Joyce himself is now distinctly the artist more concerned with the form of his novel than with his own close involvement in its subject matter. He is able to reshape phrase and sentence as if they were quite impersonal things to be manipulated to aesthetic effect; and his fussing with small points of spelling, punctuation, and typography in the serial publication and again in the book proofs indicates a craftsman's interest in an independent artifact.[28]

Seen in the longer, colder perspective of the *Portrait*, Stephen is clearly a less engaging young man than he seems in *Stephen Hero*. Readers have found him egregiously self-satisfied (less attractive in his egoism than Richard Feverel), "Byronic" (though he lacks Byron's dash and style), pedantic, humorless, inhuman, given to *fin-de-siècle* swoonings and languors, and in the end suffering something very like "messianic delusions."[29] Whereas Yeats and other early admirers of the novel accepted it as "a disguised autobiography,"[30] many later Joyceans have been reluctant to think the unpleasant hero a recognizable image of the author and accordingly have taken the *Portrait* as a detached and richly ironic study of an arrogant aesthete with whom Joyce could have no sympathy. And a few have gone so far as to suggest that Stephen has good reason to dread Hell-fire,[31] for the book, they say, presents the youth's mortal sin and probable damnation, and even the name Dedalus signifies not only the fabulous artificer but also his unfortunate son Icarus, who "falls" in his Satanic pride. Joyce himself, we are told, was far livelier and less sober-sided than Stephen, fonder of fellowship and witty talk, a fine singer and a good mimic. Joyce was less independent of his mother, and he even had some half-amused respect for his father, who was very like the man that Stephen only detests. Moreover, the argument continues, since the *Portrait* combines and sometimes distorts episodes and occasionally violates the precise chronology of the Dublin

years, Joyce must have had other objects than a literal
realism in mind and so could not have intended to present
in Stephen a true transcript of his own life and character.

Nonetheless, the difference between the author and his
protagonist should not be overestimated. If in some respects
Stephen is unlike the young Joyce, in many others he bears
a strong resemblance. The child Stephen seems in most
essentials Joyce as he remembered himself to have been; the
young man, we may assume, represents the serious-minded
young aesthete, the image that Joyce once tried to project,
as he recalled it at a distance of five to twelve years after
the events described. Joyce, who all his life wrote freely
of himself, never denied that there had been a large measure
of identification with Stephen. He published the first stories
of *Dubliners* in 1904 under the pseudonym "Stephen Daedalus." He intended at one time to end *Stephen Hero* with
the painterly signature, *Stephanos Daedalus pinxit*,[32] which
in effect confesses that the "painter" and his subject, though
described in the third person, are one and the same. The
final title, *A Portrait of the Artist as a Young Man*, with
which most critics have curiously failed to reckon, is likewise inspired by painters' practice (as well as by Pater's
verbal sketches) and implies a "self-portrait" just as it
would if attached to a picture by Rembrandt or Degas.
Long after the publication of the novel Joyce made his
intention clear by a query to his Spanish translator, who
was perplexed as to how he should render the title: "What,"
he asked, "is the usual description of self-portraits made in
youth used in the catalogue of your Spanish picture gal-
leries?"[33] If we need evidence, apart from the text itself,
that the "self-portrait" was not designed as a serious study
of sin and damnation, we may cite the limerick addressed

to Ezra Pound a few months after the book's first appearance:

> There once was a lounger named Stephen
> Whose youth was most odd and uneven.
>   He throve on the smell
>   Of a horrible hell
> That a Hottentot wouldn't believe in.[34]

Here we have an amused comment on the guilt-feelings
that Stephen like Joyce sheds before the age of eighteen;
we have no attack on the selfish pride of the twenty-year-
old aesthete. The detachment is that of a man who can smile
at his own naive youth, not that of one eager to dissociate
himself from a vicious person he has known and repudiated.

Joyce in fact was less alarmed by a proud aloof aestheticism than Stephen's detractors have been. For most of his
life he himself remained egocentric, self-protective, withdrawn into a private world where he expected to be observed and reverenced but not followed. The early essay
"Portrait" speaks of the artist's adopting "the enigma of
a manner." During his university days Joyce apparently
struck a similar pose, influenced no doubt by the attitudes
of the European Decadents, especially Gabriele D'Annunzio, whose self-dramatizing fiction he admired.[35] His
natural wit and conviviality he reserved for a few close
friends; in public he played the role of the solitary sensitive Romantic artist, and indeed until the end he seemed to
believe that art necessarily alienated him from other, less
perceptive men. Like Stephen he had a high regard for his
own genius long before his work could validate his estimate.
Though he soon destroyed his Ibsenite play, *A Brilliant*

Career, written when he was eighteen, he never wholly rejected the tone of its solemn dedication: "To / My own Soul I / dedicate the first / true work of my / life."[36] In 1905 near the beginning of his exile, he complained to his brother Stanislaus that residence in Trieste might be stifling his artistic nature, and added menacingly, "If I once convince myself that this kind of life is suicidal to my soul, I will make everything and everybody stand out of my way as I did before now."[37] Later, when the writing of the *Portrait* was well advanced, he described himself frankly but not at all humbly as "a jealous, lonely, dissatisfied, proud man."[38] Whatever his final judgment of Stephen, he must have been readier to defend than to censure the young man's imperious pride.[39]

Our estimate of the relative proportions of satire and sympathy in the novel and our sense of the purpose and effect of both will determine our interpretation of the whole. There is undoubtedly an ironic component, sometimes held in abeyance, sometimes apparent even when Stephen seems most like the young Joyce. The realities of the everyday world mock Stephen's dream of a lover's tryst with Mercedes (from *The Count of Monte Cristo*) and his hope to be transfigured in a moment of supreme tenderness toward her: "Weakness and timidity and inexperience would fall from him in that magic moment."[40] The rude shouts of the swimmers ironically interrupt his meditation on his legendary name, and the wry commentary of Lynch undercuts his high-flown aesthetic theorizing. Irony also helps determine the general design insofar as each chapter after the first begins with a realistic anti-climax to the ecstatic ending of the preceding chapter, and the opening of *Ulysses*, which presents Stephen returned unheroically to

Dublin, may be said to deflate the brave rhetoric that concludes the *Portrait*.[41]

Not all the irony, however, is directed against Stephen. He, too, is capable of the ironic vision. He is struck by the disparity between the hieratic religious life he has just rejected and the chaotic mundanities to which he descends: "He smiled to think that it was this disorder, the misrule and confusion of his father's house and the stagnation of vegetable life, which was to win the day in his soul."[42] At the university he finds Moynihan's rough humor a wholesome corrective to his own priestly sobriety, and he begins to look with satiric eye on the antics of his professors. There, also, he sees the irony of his friend Davin's petitioning for universal peace and at the same time agitating militantly for Irish nationalism. His diary mingles sentiment and ironic self-regard:

Long talk with Cranly on the subject of my revolt. He had his grand manner on. I supple and suave. . . .

This mentality, Lepidus would say, is indeed bred out of your mud by the operation of your sun. And mine? Is it not too? Then into Nilemud with it! . . .

Read what I wrote last night [i.e., a contrived "poetic" description]. Vague words for a vague emotion. . . .

Yet the last entry but one may be more ironic than Stephen realizes: "Mother is putting my new secondhand clothes in order."[43] Stephen may smile at the "new secondhand" but fail to see the incongruity of the bold rebel's being mothered in his flight from home, like a little boy off on a summer holiday.

But the irony of the *Portrait*, whether Stephen's or the narrator's, is less often corrosive than self-conscious and defensive. It is a "Romantic irony," such as we find in *Don Juan*, intended to disarm criticism and so to re-establish sympathy. A simpler irony would have us invert Stephen's values; in the *Portrait* we are not expected to admire what Stephen rejects, but rather to approve the lonely course he follows. We are to recognize that he is in some respects a callow young man but at the same time to remember that naiveté is the prerogative of youth. Stephen was conceived in Joyce's memory of his own adolescent dread of making a premature public statement; as the Trieste notebook put it, "He shrank from limning the features of his soul for he feared that no everlasting image of beauty could shine through an immature being."[44] In drawing Stephen, Joyce looks back on his own past with sentiment, amusement, and indulgence. The childhood for the most part is too sad to excite a smile; the young manhood, though extravagant in pose and gesture, is to be taken seriously as the artist's necessary deliverance from false claims upon him. The undercutting at the beginning of each chapter qualifies but does not destroy the preceding epiphany; both are real; if his dreams must be ended by repeated returns to the commonplace, Stephen nonetheless grows by his emotional experience, and his moments of insight, ecstatic or dispiriting, are never to be altogether repudiated. Though Romantic irony protects Joyce from the special pleading he did not escape in the earlier version of the novel, the *Portrait* remains to a degree a self-apology; like most Bildungsromane, it demands a considerable sympathy for the hero, who is at least a partial portrait of the author as he was in his immaturity and early promise.

Stephen is not yet the artist; as the full title implies, he is a young man who will eventually become the artist capable of drawing his own portrait, ready to limn "the features of his soul." By the end of the novel we have heard much of his talk of art, but we have no evidence of his creative capacity except his "Villanelle of the Temptress," and this, though we know it to be a product of Joyce's own apprenticeship, hardly warrants the prediction of great things to come. The temptress recalls more menacing late-Victorian *femmes fatales*, especially Pater's Mona Lisa, likewise "weary of ardent ways," and Rossetti's Lilith, whose glance also set the eyes and heart of youth afire; and her alliterative "languorous look and lavish limb" apparently derive, by sad declension, from the more vigorous attributes of Swinburne's "lithe and lascivious" Dolores. Yet the poem, with its further suggestions of Wilde and Dowson and its precious diction and cliché epithets, is no weaker than most of the pieces that Joyce, whose taste in verse was unreliable, thought worthy of saving for publication; and we are probably expected to receive it as a quite adequate example of a skill which in the fullness of time will produce a mature work of art.[45]

What may disturb us more, however, than the fiction of Stephen's talent is the celebration of his aesthetic theology and the ultimate confusion in his mind—and possibly in Joyce's—as to whether he is the minister or the god of his new religion. Composing his villanelle, Stephen thinks of himself as "a priest of eternal imagination, transmuting the daily bread of experience into the radiant body of everlasting life."[46] Whether or not Joyce intended Stephen's breakfast of watery tea and crusts fried in lard, at the beginning of Chapter V, to represent the elements of the eucharist, he clearly took pains to fill the chapter with the language and symbols of priesthood and oblique suggestions that Stephen, a martyr to art (or at least to art theory), is a new Jesus.[47] For his part Stephen himself in the end seems to assume some sort of identification with Christ; when he links Cranly to John the Baptist, he adds complacently, "Then he is the precursor." Though we might well question the sanity of a young man who so exalts himself (and Stephen is not more than half-ironic in his self-esteem), Joyce has prepared the context in the conviction that there must always be about every true artist an air of "profane sanctity,"[48] which proclaims his inviolable difference. However we regard Stephen's other immaturities, we are invited to respect his substitute religion and perhaps even his self-idolatry. And at the last we are not to smile too broadly at his grandiloquently phrased resolve "to forge in the smithy of [his] soul the uncreated conscience of [his] race." For this corresponds almost exactly to the godlike mission of the mature Joyce, as he described it, in all seriousness, shortly before writing the last part of the *Portrait:* "I am one of the writers of this generation who are perhaps creating at last a conscience in the soul of this wretched race."[49] But knowledge of the author's attitudes does not assure our acceptance of his solutions. If the novel is appraised in and for itself, Stephen's apotheosis must strike many readers as contrived and unconvincing, ironic in a way that the often ironical novelist did not intend.

Yet, even apart from the ambiguous pseudo-theology, the ending, like that of many another Bildungsroman, presents problems of indecision and inconclusiveness. Unsure of how to assess his own youth in terms of the fiction and perhaps aware that the sacerdotal symbolism was as much an evasion as an answer, Joyce carried his hero and surrogate over into *Ulysses* where, having a number of characters to identify with, he could look at Stephen, somewhat changed in the transition, with a harder objectivity. There Stephen through abasement, and Joyce through imagining the motives of others, may learn that human relationships are no less important than a resolute aesthetic detachment. But no such wisdom is possible at the end of the *Portrait*, where all is proud alienation. The fifth and last chapter advances hardly at all beyond the epiphany of the girl by the sea that ends the fourth. Despite its tight web of imagery, it is fragmentary and discursive, full of the hero's soliloquy and talk and of remonstrances to which he will not listen. For Stephen as the committed aesthete has no will to change his mind or enlarge his vision, and his renewed search for the "reality of experience" inspires little confidence in us that he will recognize the truth when he finds it.

⊰ XI ⊱

OF BONDAGE AND FREEDOM:
LATER NOVELS OF YOUTH

A T the time of *Sons and Lovers* and before the
book publication of Joyce's *Portrait*, there appeared a number of other autobiographical fictions, the most conspicuous
of which, J. D. Beresford's *Early History of Jacob Stahl*,
Compton Mackenzie's *Sinister Street*,[1] and Somerset
Maugham's *Of Human Bondage*, seemed to place their
authors beside D. H. Lawrence as the most promising of
the new Georgian novelists. Each of these books is indebted
in some sort to the example of *The Way of All Flesh* and
Tono-Bungay and to the realistic method of Arnold Bennett's *Clayhanger*.[2]

Beresford, who studied Butler's notions of heredity and
imitated his philosophizing but not his wit, conscientiously
explores at length (for the narrative spins into a long
trilogy) the accidents of birth and social standing that condition Jacob Stahl's indecision, passivity, and self-absorption. Mackenzie, whose style is as exuberant as Beresford's
is drab, presents a colorful panorama of a self-consciously
liberated pre-war society before he leaves his protagonist,
Michael Fane, after some eleven hundred pages of escapade
and misadventure, at the age of twenty-three, weary of a
mad world's materialism and eager to enter the Catholic
priesthood. For all the effort, however, neither Mackenzie

248

nor Beresford makes of his hero a vital character, distinct and memorable in himself, independent of the author and his attitudes; both Jacob and Michael remain shadowy figures, more or less amorphous, like Ernest Pontifex acted upon by circumstance and, almost to the last, dazed by experience.

Of Human Bondage is also far too long, but it has a greater strength in its amplitude and the reiteration of its central theme, and the hero, Philip Carey, does emerge as a well-defined and wholly credible person. The settings are drawn from a clear unsentimental memory and documented by precise detail: Blackstable, representing the Whitstable in Kent where Maugham spent part of his unhappy orphaned boyhood; Tercanbury, the Canterbury where he found himself a lonely misfit in the school that Pater once attended and that Dickens chose as the model for Dr. Strong's benevolent academy; Heidelberg, where he enjoyed a release from English constraints; the Paris of artists, which he knew from frequent visits; the London hospital where he received his medical training, and its dreary wards where he observed the ailing poor. Philip himself, as Maugham explained, is not a literal self-portrait. Philip suffers the burden of a club foot, whereas Maugham was afflicted with a painful stammer (here the awareness of handicap matters far more than its nature). Philip rejects painting for medicine; Maugham turned from medicine to literature. In the end, having qualified as a doctor, Philip chooses to practice in Dorset and so renounces his dear ambition to travel; Maugham, on the other hand, having completed his studies, set out to realize his dreams of foreign adventure and spent years abroad in France and Spain. Yet Philip is very like the young Maugham in temperament and aspiration; the writing of the novel was a personal act and, like

the composition of *Sons and Lovers,* served a frankly therapeutic need, and the author in later life could not reread it
without breaking into tears.[3]

Nonetheless, close as he was to his unheroic hero, Maugham achieves and sustains a remarkable detachment. Philip
is drawn with the clinical dispassion that the novelist learned
from Maupassant, and his motives are dissected with a piti-
less irony. He is often a thoroughly unpleasant person,
morbidly aware of his deformity and quick to take offense
at fancied slights, snobbish and sometimes cruelly indifferent to the pain of others, pathetic in defeat but inspiring
only contempt when he grovels for sympathy. He is self-
protective and self-destructive and again and again proves
the masochist of his emotions. Having failed an examination
in biology, he returns to the hospital to face the satisfaction
of the students who passed: "because he hated so much to
go just then, he went: he wanted to inflict suffering upon
himself."[4] Insanely devoted to Mildred Rogers and sick
with jealousy as soon as he introduces her to his friend
Griffiths, he perversely encourages the relationship: "Then
a strange desire to torture himself seized him. . . . He
wanted to leave them by themselves. . . . He was throw-
ing them together now to make the pain he suffered more
intolerable."[5] Shortly thereafter he gives Mildred the money
to go away for the weekend with his false friend; abject
self-abasement could scarcely be more complete. Philip is
assuredly not an idealization of Somerset Maugham; and
his story, unlike many other Bildungsromane, is in no real
sense an apologia for the author's life.

As impervious as Philip is vulnerable, Mildred is one of
the least agreeable women in English fiction, vulgar, vain,
cruel, and violent, far less robust and less convincingly

seductive than Jude's scheming Arabella, whom she may sometimes recall. Philip willfully deludes himself about her worth and honesty, suffers her brutal insults, rejects her and repeatedly takes her back, hates and adores her, and more and more curses "the fate which [has] chained him to such a woman."[6] Nevertheless, Mildred contributes to his education, helps him to understand by his own sad experience the terrible bondage of all human desire and so to appreciate the depths of loneliness and frustration that others have plumbed, the misery of Fanny Price, the art student who hangs herself, and the frayed soiled wisdom of Cronshaw, the minor poet drowned in talk and alcohol. For the novel is ultimately concerned with Philip's development and not just with his obsession.

Philip consciously fosters his own intellectual growth. He questions the grounds of his early naive religious faith and quietly sheds his belief, and, among the painters of Paris, he opens his mind to new theories of art at odds with all his aesthetic preconceptions. He reads diligently in the philosophers, especially Hobbes, Hume, and Spinoza, until he discovers in Darwin a liberating new ethic. Good and evil, he deduces from *The Origin of Species*, are simply matters of social convenience: "The free man," he decides, "can do no wrong. He does everything he likes—if he can. His power is the only measure of his morality."[7] Yet such a code—more Nietzschean surely than Darwinian—does not overcome his suspicion that no man is really "free," that free will is simply an illusion one must live by and that every act, once completed, has been "inevitable from all eternity."[8]

Philip is only too ready to rationalize his bondage, to assume that he is fated to suffer and to fail and that all regret or blame is useless. But he is also eager to discover some pattern in his destiny. When he earnestly asks what is the meaning of life, Cronshaw tells him that he will find the answer to his question in the pattern of a Persian carpet. For years of his prolonged adolescence Philip ponders the riddle. Then one day, depressed by the news of his friend Hayward's death, he reviews his own past as he contemplates a group of Greek funerary sculptures in the British Museum, and suddenly, in a flash—an epiphany, as it were, —the answer comes to him: life has no objective meaning at all; the design is in the mind of the individual who seeks it: "As the weaver elaborated his pattern for no end but the pleasure of his aesthetic sense, so might a man live his life, or if one was forced to believe that his actions were outside his choosing, so might a man look at his life, that it made a pattern."[9]

The intuition of meaninglessness brings Philip not despair but joy, a new sense of power and freedom from responsibility; if it is not his role to serve some large remote purpose, then he may trace smaller patterns, or at least the semblance of them in his own immediate experience. By the end of his initiation, when he is nearly thirty, he feels free to choose between lonely travel and marriage to Sally Athelny, and he happily elects the latter, for he is now convinced that "the simplest pattern" to be made out of "the meaningless facts of life" is "likewise the most perfect," a man's ultimate fulfillment in his work, home, and family. Finally he is able to accept even his deformity, which has, he knows, "warped his character" but at the same time has driven him back upon the self and so has conferred upon him the saving "power of introspection."[10] In the strength of self-knowledge he will turn at last from dreams of an unreal future to the demand of a living present. Whatever may lie ahead and beyond, "America," Philip concludes with Wilhelm Meister, is "here and now."[11]

The echo of Goethe is hardly necessary to relate Maugham's novel to the proper genre, for *Of Human Bondage* from beginning to contrived end evinces characteristics of the nineteenth-century Bildungsroman and prompts comparison in substance and method with the books we have examined. Philip's move from Blackstable to Paris and London parallels the progress of many young men from the provinces to the sophisticated and corrupt city. His mad infatuation with Mildred recalls Pip's unreasoning devotion to the proud Estella. His readings in philosophy resemble Marius's program of study and Maggie Tulliver's wrestling with intellectual prose and Jude Fawley's efforts at self-improvement. His concern with money and his bad investments and descent to trade are reminiscent of Ernest Pontifex's economic misadventures, though the depiction of poverty has now gained an uncompromising grimness of circumstantial detail. His final review of his apprenticeship to life may remind us of the spiritual or mental stocktaking of most of the heroes from Wilhelm Meister to George Ponderevo. And the idyllic ending of his story may seem like the author's attempt to imitate the happy and more logical resolution of *David Copperfield*. Within the text itself Hayward refers directly to a passage in *Marius the Epicurean* and talks of *Richard Feverel* and of Pater and Meredith in general; and Philip implicitly compares himself to Feverel when he is forced to admit that the fading Miss Wilkinson is no match for Meredith's Lucy. The familiar motif of the gentleman recurs throughout the novel. Philip at eighteen in Heidelberg assumes his own status, knows that an American or dissenter cannot be a gentleman (Weeks, the erudite young man from

Harvard, is of course disqualified), and naively attempts to define the species: "First of all he's the son of a gentleman, and he's been to a public school, and to Oxford or Cambridge. . . . And he talks English like a gentleman, and he wears the right sort of things, and if he's a gentleman he can always tell if another chap's a gentleman." Later, when his uncle insists that Bohemian Paris is no fit place for a gentleman, Philip questions the gentlemanly ideal. And later still, when Mildred reproaches him for his conduct, he replies, in quite ungentlemanly fashion, "If I were a gentleman, I shouldn't waste my time with a vulgar slut like you."[12] Yet we are to assume that, despite moments of gross caddishness, he retains to the end something of the trueborn gentleman's tact and grace. Finally, though Philip is an artist manqué, the novel, like most English Bildungsromane, describes the unfolding of an aesthetic sensibility, and we are not surprised to learn that Maugham, influenced most perhaps by Pater, called the unpublished first draft, written at least fifteen years before the final manuscript, *The Artistic Temperament of Stephen Carey*.[13]

Of Human Bondage, then, written in full awareness of its precedents, successfully reworks the conventions of the genre and stands as a notable example of the realistic method. But it is retrospective rather than innovative; it contributes little that is new in form or technique. Measured against *Sons and Lovers*, which was published two years earlier, it seems shallow in its psychology and limited in its mode of analysis. Beside Joyce's *Portrait*, it seems uninventive, unable to discover a means of dramatizing the consciousness of the hero. If the Bildungsroman were to renew itself as a type after Joyce and Lawrence, it would have to assimilate their experiments in subjectivity. Yet in doing so, it would lose much of the objective substance that animated its varied course from Dickens to Maugham.

In 1915, the year of Maugham's novel, appeared Dorothy Richardson's *Pointed Roofs*, the first installment of the thirteen-part *Pilgrimage* tracing the uneventful career of Miriam Henderson. In an effort to describe the technique by which Miriam's point of view was captured and followed, May Sinclair, an avid reader of the new fiction and herself already a well-established novelist, hit upon the phrase "stream of consciousness." "In this series," she wrote, "there is no drama, no situation, no set scene. Nothing happens. It is just life going on and on. It is Miriam Henderson's stream of consciousness going on and on." Though Miss Richardson, diving beneath the surfaces of things, "has not plunged deeper than Mr. James Joyce in his *Portrait of the Artist as a Young Man*," she has managed, said Miss Sinclair, by "identifying herself with this life which is Miriam's stream of consciousness," to produce "her effect of being the first, of getting closer to reality than any of our novelists who are trying so desperately to get close."[14] The *Pilgrimage* is hardly a Bildungsroman, for Miriam develops very little in the endless process of savoring impressions from the time we first meet her in her late teens till we leave her, many volumes later, in her solitary, sensitive middle age. But, like Joyce's *Portrait*, it suggested a method by which other novelists might register stages in the growth of their protagonists from childhood to maturity; and the writer most immediately influenced by that method was May Sinclair herself.

In *Mary Olivier* of 1919 May Sinclair, self-consciously indebted to the new psychology, plunges as deep as

Dorothy Richardson or Joyce beneath the surfaces of life and shows herself as concerned as Lawrence with the hidden sources of suffering, unreasoned loyalty, and conditioned action. We first meet Mary, as we met Stephen Dedalus, in a baby's crib, and we follow her sensations and impressions from infancy. By the time she is four years old she has learned to distrust her mother, to fear her father, and to love and envy her brother Mark; we find her then in a garden, trying to think of herself objectively (in the second person), quietly observing others, already sensing the trouble in her little Eden:

> The garden flowers stood still, straight up in the grey earth. They were as tall as you were. You could look at them a long time without being tired. . . .
> The garden flowers wouldn't let you love them. They stood still in their beauty, quiet, arrogant, reproachful. They put you in the wrong. When you stroked them they shook and swayed from you; when you held them tight their heads dropped, their backs broke, they shrivelled up in your hands. All the flowers in the garden were Mamma's; they were sacred and holy.
> You loved best the flowers that you stooped down to look at and the flowers that were not Mamma's; the small crumpled poppy by the edge of the field, and the ears of the wild rye that ran up your sleeve and tickled you, and the speedwell, striped like the blue eyes of Meta, the wax doll.
> When you smelt the mignonette you thought of Mamma.
> It was her birthday. Mark had given her a little sumach tree in a red pot. They took it out of the pot and dug a hole by the front steps outside the pantry window and planted it there.
> Papa came out on the steps and watched them.
> "I suppose," he said, "you think it'll *grow?*"
> Mamma never turned to look at him. She smiled because it was her birthday. She said, "Of course it'll grow."
> She spread out its roots and pressed it down and padded up the earth about it with her hands. It held out its tiny branches, stiffly, like a toy tree, standing no higher than the mignonette.

Papa looked at Mamma and Mark, busy and happy with their heads together, taking no notice of him. He laughed out of his big beard and went back into the house suddenly and slammed the door. You knew that he disliked the sumach tree and that he was angry with Mark for giving it to Mamma.

When you smelt the mignonette you thought of Mamma and Mark and the sumach tree, and Papa standing on the steps, and the queer laugh that came out of his beard.

When it rained you were naughty and unhappy because you couldn't go out of doors. Then Mamma stood at the window and looked into the front garden. She smiled at the rain. She said, "It will be good for my sumach tree."

Every day you went out on the steps to see if the sumach tree had grown.[15]

We have here not only an attempt to capture a child's point of view and to illustrate a psychology of association and memory. We discover also a deliberate dealing in the motives and impulses that the Freudians at the time of the novel were beginning to explore: the child's unanswered craving for affection and her inability to love Mamma's beautiful cold flowers; Mamma's alienation from Papa, her turning to her son, and her alliance with the repressive rain to thwart Mary's desire to escape; brother Mark's excessive regard for his mother, shaping the Oedipus complex that will eventually destroy him. As she moves through her harassed adolescence, Mary sees the tragedy of souls thwarted, unable to articulate their loneliness and pain; her father becomes a hopeless alcoholic; happy Uncle Victor commits suicide; Aunt Charlotte plays with naked dolls and goes mad. Her story, in which there is little physical action, is psychological in substance as well as technique.

Both *Mary Olivier* and *Arnold Waterlow*, which followed five years later, bear the same subtitle, "A Life." Each carries its protagonist into early middle age, but both qualify as essentially novels of youth insofar as they lay heavy stress on the formative years and all the adjustments required for a mature equipoise. Like the typical Bildungs-roman, both apparently are autobiographical; each traces the development of a sensitive intellectual born, as May Sinclair was, in 1863 into an anti-intellectual family in a provincial town. If Mary is the almost literal image of the author, Arnold is to be seen as the male counterpart, or perhaps in Jungian terms the animus, very like her in temperament, but as a man able to take bolder options, to assert at least partial independence of home and even, when past thirty, to marry. Both Mary and Arnold are dominated in youth by a sanctimonious and thoroughly selfish mother. Mamma Olivier deceives, thwarts, and humiliates Mary, jealously discourages her piano-playing, resents her learning Greek, frustrates her love affairs. Mamma Waterlow makes clear her preference for Arnold's elder brother, refuses to credit Arnold's quick intelligence, forces him to leave school far too soon, decries his interest in books, berates his friends, and at every turn challenges his will:

> Again it was her will against his, her intense, small driving will, against all the things he loved and wanted most. Always he would have to fight her, or give in and go under; always his love for her would fight against him, and for the pain he gave her he would get more pain.[16]

Mary and Arnold seem passive victims, committed to self-sacrifice and accordingly exploited, prepared to love when not loved in return. Yet each in fact retains some core of integrity, a mental and spiritual strength never to be wholly conquered by family or outrageous fate.

Despite her mother's disapproval, Mary Olivier reads deeply in the ancient classics and pores over the German idealists. Her metaphysical concern is sufficiently intense to perplex and even to frighten off her few admirers. Maurice Jourdain, to whom she is briefly engaged, asks impatiently, "Do you suppose any man wants to hear what his sweetheart thinks about Space and Time and the Ding-an-sich?"[17] But Mary persists in her philosophic probing, her quest for a substitute religion more satisfying than the narrow fundamentalism her mother invokes against her. Like Maggie Tulliver, she must discover some clue to life's meaning. "I wanted to know things," she tells her skeptical brother, "to know what's real and what isn't, and what's at the back of everything, and whether there *is* anything there or not. And whether you can know it or not. . . . I want *the* thing. Reality, Substance, the Thing-in-itself. Spinoza calls it God. Kant doesn't; but he seems to think it's all the God you'll ever get, and that, even then, you can't know it."[18] In her maturity, after countless rebuffs, she achieves balance and inner peace; she becomes, if not a fine original poet, at least a highly successful translator of Euripides; she accepts an understanding lover and then calmly, though regretfully, renounces passion for duty. In the end she is sustained by a vision of the reality she has strenuously sought. A spot of time, an epiphany, suddenly reveals the essence, the inner truth, of a lime tree in the garden:

> She saw that the beauty of the tree was its real life, and that its real life was in her real self and that her real self was God. The leaves and the light had nothing to do with it; she had seen it before when the tree was a stem and bare branches on a grey sky; and that beauty too was the real life of the tree.[19]

Unlike Paul Morel, Mary wins psychological deliverance by the discovery and affirmation of her real self.

Arnold Waterlow follows a similar path. When his

schooling is cut short, he studies Greek and Latin in the moments he can spare from the drudgery of a warehouse job and teaches himself German in order to read Kant and Hegel. His friend Mr. Godden (a sort of intellectual god-father) introduces him to Spinoza's *Tractatus* and the *Ethics* and to new Victorian books, Spencer's *First Principles*, Huxley's *Lay Sermons*, Arnold's *Literature and Dogma*, substantial fare for a mind as hungry for ideas as that of the self-taught young Jude. From the beginning Arnold, like Mary, has been in search of God or some fortifying philosophy. As a small child he is punished by Mamma for too gleefully announcing, "God is Love," and, on one occasion, chastised for declaring that he has seen God looking at him from the sun, and, on another, sent directly to bed for defending the neglected third member of the Trinity, "If nobody wants the Holy Ghost I'll have him."[20] But the decisive revelation comes only with maturity when, abandoned by his selfish wife, Rosalind, he finds joy in the selfless love of Effie Warner. Yearning for Effie as he stretches out on a grassy hillside, he sees the landscape wondrously transfigured:

> He saw the same hills, the same green fields, the same white river, but as if lifted to another level of reality, and shining with another light; light intensely still, intensely vibrating. They were no longer spread out in space and time, but they stood as if inside his mind, in another space and in another time; his mind held them, and was inseparably one with them. At the same moment he had a sense, overpowering and irrefutable, of Reality, no longer hidden behind them, but apparent in them, the strange secret disclosed; Reality breaking through, shining through all the veils of sense; Reality present before him and in him, and stretching beyond him, out of time and out of space, as it was in eternity.[21]

When Effie dies, Arnold's grief dims his faith in the truth that the epiphany has taught him. Not until he can transcend all personal concern, even the selfishness of his sorrow, does the "mystic vision" return to reassure him. Then at last he recovers "the sense of irrefutable certainty": "In one moment, his will, after a year of bondage, [is] set free." Thus Arnold's religious quest is accomplished; the God he has intuited exists as "the Self of self, the secret, mysterious Will within his will,"[22] the guarantor of a man's ultimate belonging and wholeness.

Few Bildungsromane end so ecstatically. Yet mysticism at best translates awkwardly into prose fiction, and *Arnold Waterlow* is far less effective in its spiritual affirmation that in its probing of darker impulses. The whole idyllic relationship with Effie seems little more than a romantic wish-fulfillment, as if May Sinclair were identifying herself with Effie, as well as with Arnold, in an idealized passion ending in a perfect self-denial. The author throughout the episode seems too engaged with her characters, just as George Eliot at times stands too close to Maggie Tulliver. At any rate, Arnold's love of Effie, spread over the last quarter of the novel, does not compare in cogency with his troubled dreams, described in a single paragraph. When Rosalind after the death of their infant son deserts him and returns to her habitual infidelity, he dreams himself back in the garden of his own childhood, vainly pursuing her and finding her person blur into the images of other women who once have been attracted to him:

> He went through the fields, looking for her; he knew that she waited for him by the stile. But when he came to the stile she was not there. A snake lay along the grey bar of the stile; it

pushed out its head and bit his hand. He passed into his mother's house by the kitchen stair and went up and up to the top story. In the old nursery he found Rosalind. She was sitting on the ottoman with her feet among his tin soldiers, trampling them, and when he put his arm round her she turned to him with an abominable look that woke him. In his dreams she was Eva Baxter and Vera Lister. Once she was Winifred; and once she lay naked, curled up in the cat's cupboard, nursing a dead baby.[23]

Though the sexual symbolism here is almost too deliberate, the passage nonetheless testifies to an intelligent writer's interest in the process of association and the nightmares of the unconscious mind and to her willingness to open her art to the concerns of the new psychology.[24]

By January 1920, Virginia Woolf was also trying to shape "a new form for a new novel," a form apparently influenced by Joyce and Dorothy Richardson but, she hoped, less egotistical than either and less restricted in focus. At work some months later on *Jacob's Room*, she confessed that what she was attempting to do, Joyce could probably do better. But when her new book was at last completed and Leonard Woolf praised its "method," she was reassured about her originality, convinced that she had finally found "how to begin (at 40) to say something in [her] own voice."[25]

Jacob's Room, to be sure, is not entirely new. In broad outline it is another "life," touching, though lightly, on the main themes and conventions of the Bildungsroman. It sketches the career of an unheroic hero, born in 1887, from his childhood through adolescence to his death in his late twenties sometime during the First World War.[26] Though a fatherless and far from affluent young man from the provinces, Jacob Flanders is clearly a "gentleman" by instinct, education, and bearing, and when he playfully questions the gentlemanly ideal he does so with the nonchalance of an insider. We glimpse Jacob briefly—late for a don's luncheon at Cambridge, miserable at a London soirée, happily sailing off the Scilly Isles with a college friend, visiting the Acropolis under a dazzling sun. We learn something of his reading in Greek drama and Elizabethan poetry. We observe his relations, remote or casual, with various women: Clara Durrant, whom he seems to love but whose nervous propriety puts him off; Florinda and Laurette, whose vapid promiscuity bores him; Sandra Williams, the diplomat's wife, with whom presumably he has a clandestine affair in Greece. From time to time we follow Jacob's thought—but only for a moment, for as soon as we enter his mind, we are spirited away and floated off on some other character's stream of consciousness. If *Jacob's Room* is potentially a Bildungsroman, we never really know the young man who is growing into maturity, and the apparent point of the book is that he is essentially unknowable.

On the train bound for Cambridge Mrs. Norman, an "elderly" lady of fifty, sitting opposite Jacob, tries to imagine what sort of person he must be and what he is thinking and feeling. But she has determined only that he is distinguished-looking, shy, and rather clumsy, when they reach the station and he is suddenly lost to her in the crowd, "as the crooked pin dropped by a child into the wishing-well twirls in the water and disappears for ever."[27] Virginia Woolf identifies for the moment with Mrs. Norman in the frustrated effort to define the real Jacob. Yet the scene curiously anticipates her essay "Mr. Bennett and Mrs. Brown," where she berates what she alleges would be Arnold Bennett's failure to characterize an old lady across from him in a railway carriage. Much of *Jacob's Room* concerns the novelist's inability to catch her hero. We may note the young man's attitudes and gestures, but these, we are told, are insufficient, for always "there remains over something which can never be conveyed to a second person save by Jacob himself." But Jacob reveals very little to anyone; he is lonely and silent, sadly persuaded that each man must learn to live in his ineluctable isolation. And his elusiveness is made the more emphatic by a constant shifting of focus and a technique fashioned to register simultaneity, to offer a multiple response to a single event or a sudden shared impression of the weather or Mrs. Durrant's evening party or possibly Jacob Flanders.

None of his friends comes much closer than the stranger on the train to an understanding of Jacob or a rounded estimate of his apparently not very complex personality. Mrs. Durrant arrives at Mrs. Norman's judgment: " 'He is extraordinarily awkward,' she thought, noticing how he fingered his socks. 'Yet so distinguished-looking.' " Sandra Williams likewise finds him "very distinguished-looking." Fanny Elmer, an artist's model, thinks him "very awkward" but admires his beautiful voice. The Reverend Andrew Floyd, his old tutor, has trouble recognizing him, grown so tall, "such a fine young fellow." Even his mother cannot approach him; she senses only that he is a man and no longer a boy when his letters home tell her "really nothing" that she wants to know. Like the others, she misjudges and is content with her verdict. Typically, writing to a friend, she describes him as "hard at work after his delightful journey," while Jacob at the same instant is strolling aimlessly across Kensington Gardens.

The name of Jacob Flanders may be intended to reflect his destiny, his death in France, and Jacob may then be taken as representative of a generation of young intellectuals sacrificed to a rapacious war. But as depicted, he is too shadowy a figure to be a tragic hero or even to inspire deep sympathy. Having eluded our view for most of his short life, he dies off-stage. On the next to the last page of the novel, his mother reflects that all her sons are fighting for their country. The last page shows her going through his possessions with his friend Bonamy in the London flat to which he will not come back. "Such confusion everywhere!" she exclaims and in bewilderment holds out a pair of Jacob's old shoes. We are left then with what Virginia Woolf accused Wells and Bennett of offering: an impression of the house, the room, rather than the man. Yet the houses in *Tono-Bungay* are symbols of Uncle Teddy's ambition and not simply places. And Jacob's room, too, has a larger meaning; it stands for the young man's little living space in the world; it is the room of one's own, where the lonely self may or may not ever find its purpose and direction; and in the end it is nothing without its occupant.

As developed by Joyce in *Ulysses* and Virginia Woolf in *Mrs. Dalloway* and *To the Lighthouse*, the "new novel" of the 1920's turned away from the content as well as the form of the Bildungsroman, and interest in the genre seems to have shifted from England to America.[28] At any rate, by the thirties the most notable recent fictions of the kind were Thomas Wolfe's huge, sprawling, confessional *Look Homeward, Angel* and the Studs Lonigan trilogy of James T. Farrell with its new insistence on the social and economic determinants of character. British authors of the same time and for some years later, on the other hand, continued to probe aspects of the psychology of youth with little interest in the larger themes of adjustment to society or general apprenticeship to life.

Forrest Reid, for example, who wrote of children and young adults for nearly forty years, devoted his most ambitious work, the Tom Barber trilogy, exclusively to the wide-eyed, dreaming boyhood of his hero. The title of the second Tom novel, *The Retreat* (1936), derives from Henry Vaughan's poem on a child's sinless pre-existence and suggests Reid's deep nostalgia for a lost innocence, the same yearning for a far country as he announced on the first page of his autobiography:

> The primary impulse of the artist springs, I fancy, from discontent, and his art is a kind of crying for Elysium, . . . that same longing for an Eden from which each one of us is exiled. . . . It is a country whose image was stamped upon our soul before we opened our eyes on earth, and all our life is little more than a trying to get back there, our art than a mapping of its mountains and streams.[29]

L. P. Hartley preferred a delicate irony and symbolism to Reid's lyrical engagement. Yet his Eustace and Hilda books, *The Shrimp and the Anemone* and its sequels, are likewise limited in focus, concerned as they are with phases in the growing up of a brother and sister and the tragic tensions of their love for each other and their half-conscious destructive rivalries. And Denton Welch's tense novels of adolescence are even more highly specialized; *Maiden Voyage, In Youth Is Pleasure,* and *A Voice through a Cloud*[30]—the last written under the shadow of untimely death—celebrate the physicality of vigorous young manhood as observed with naive precision by a sensitive self-torturing invalid.

Not until after the Second World War was the English

novel returned to the broad realistic tradition and indeed brought directly under the influence of the Edwardians whom Mrs. Woolf had dismissed. Rejecting aesthetic experiment and subtle psychologizing and substituting fast-paced narrative for quiet reverie, the Angry Young Men of the fifties created young men very like themselves, determined, as George Ponderevo had been, to make their way in a social jungle where only the assertive might survive. In their fictions reappear many motifs of the conventional Bildungsroman: the hero, alienated from his parents and dissatisfied with his middle-class education and the narrow ethic of the province, declares his independence, achieves his sexual initiation (fiercer now, or at least more bluntly described), serves some sort of vocational apprenticeship, grubs about for money, and faces up eventually to the burden of self-interest and the problem of "success"—what it can mean and whether in the end it is worth the striving.

John Wain's *Strike the Father Dead* (1962)—to cite but one of the Angry books—announces a familiar theme in its title and in the epigraph drawn from *Troilus and Cressida:*

> Strength shall be lord of imbecility,
> And the rude son shall strike the father dead.

The father here is Alfred Coleman, Professor of Classics at a red-brick university, a man as rigid as a Greek declension, precise and self-approving, yet sadly inhibited and haunted by a guilt he long hesitates to confess. The rebellious son is Jeremy, who runs away from home and school and even society (he is a draft-dodger during the war), comes to London, loses what innocence he has left, and finds his real fulfillment as a jazz pianist. Alfred, Jeremy, and the boy's

Aunt Eleanor all serve as narrators, each offering a separate view of Jeremy's conduct, but of the three Jeremy is the one convincing character. Stylistically the novel seems at times a bit flat in its breezy colloquialism and overfacile in its brash humor. Yet it sustains its theme and brings it to full resolution: father and son are finally reconciled when Alfred admits his own past weakness and rebellion and Jeremy recognizes in a dazzling "moment of revelation" how much alike they really are; and in the end the son perceives that all mature dedication—to Greek poetry no less than to jazz—has an equal sanctity:

> I saw, now, that my way was really the same as the old man's. You played music, you studied the classics, because you had chosen it as your own particular skill, the contribution you were going to make, the thing you were good at. . . . You had to do a job: that was what it came down to.[31]

Entering middle age, the Angry novelists, like Jeremy Coleman, have found ways of accommodating themselves to the establishment and less energy to register the protest of youth. Later young writers, however, have continued to invoke the Bildungsroman as a means of explaining their own disenchantment or despair. Melvyn Bragg's *For Want of a Nail* (1965), for example, is sufficient evidence that the form retains its vitality. Tom Graham, the hero, grows up in Wordsworth's Cumberland, influenced less by the beauty of the setting than by the indifference and misconduct of his abrasive working-class family. From early childhood he craves an affection and security denied him by his preoccupied and promiscuous mother; and as he enters adolescence, his yearning for a father becomes an actual quest, for he rightly suspects that Edward Graham, his putative parent, has no real claim upon him. Tom is an alert, perceptive lad, intelligent enough eventually to win an Oxford scholarship, which at the last he is too embittered to accept. From the beginning he is pathetically alone; in no way an artist able to sublimate his loneliness, he takes refuge in fantasy, imaginative games, dreams of a bolder self, and we are reminded persistently of his "double-consciousness, double vision, double existence." His falling in love and later sexual initiation bring no reassurance or satisfaction; Betty as his soul-mate—or could she be his sister? —remains a remote ideal; Lena, easily attained, proves merely an available mindless body. His disillusion is complete, his moral shock shattering, when he identifies his "uncle" as his father and finds him continuing a cynical and sordid affair with his mother. By now he is seventeen and already very tired, "heavy with a constantly pincering nothingness," convinced that nothing matters and nothing exists "outside his own obsession with his own emptiness." In such a state he arrives, at the end of his story, in London, a young man from the provinces indeed but one without hope, purpose, or ambition. His final freedom carries with it the bondage of defeat. The novel of youth, once the chronicle of self-discovery, has here become yet another sad testament of modern anomie.

William Golding's *Free Fall* (1959) is no less bleak in its commentary: as the title may suggest, modern man flounders like an astronaut in a space ship beyond gravitational pull. But the author assigns to his hero, Sammy Mountjoy, a greater responsibility for his action than Bragg grants his heavily conditioned Tom Graham. Sammy is an altogether more complex character, and his story, though published several years earlier, better repays detailed consideration as our final example of the genre. Stronger in its intellectual framework than any of the "Angry" books, *Free Fall* raises fundamental moral and philosophical questions about the meaning or possible pattern of life and all the complexities of conduct. Like other post-war novelists, Golding looks back to the Edwardians, especially H. G. Wells; yet he seems also to know twentieth-century Continental writers, to draw on the expressionistic method of Kafka and to share the existential concerns of Camus and Koestler.[32] His *Bildungsroman*, the fourth of his novels, combines narrative realism and psychological analysis, the prose of science and the somber poetry of religion. Sammy, as narrator, is aware of the two forces and self-consciously alert to the styles in which he describes their power over him. His confession has therefore a tautness and austerity of design we have not encountered in the genre since Joyce's *Portrait*.

At the beginning of *Free Fall* Sammy insistently asks, "When did I lose my freedom? . . . How did I lose my freedom?" In search of an answer, seeking in effect to confront his real "self," to isolate "the point where *I* began," he traces his growth from his earliest childhood (he was born in 1917), through his troubled adolescence and a harrowing interment in a Nazi prison camp, to his present, two or three years after the war, when he is already a well-established painter about thirty years old. His review departs from the typical Bildungsroman in that it does not unfold in strictly chronological order. Recollection, he explains at the outset, proceeds by "a sense of shuffle fold and coil, of that day nearer than that because more important, of that event mirroring this, or those three set apart, exceptional and out of the straight line altogether."[33] But, however new may be the discontinuity of narrative, the flashbacks and leaps forward and omissions (frequent enough in other kinds of fiction and in cinema), Sammy's purpose—to orient himself by discovering through memory how he has become what he now is—differs very little from that of Wordsworth in *The Prelude* or David Copperfield or George Ponderevo. *Free Fall* indeed achieves its distinction less by technical innovation than by the skill with which it revitalizes familiar motifs and devices, the power with which it recapitulates the conventions of the form.

Like Julien Sorel and Harry Richmond and many a hero of legend and romance, Sammy as a child is led to believe, by his own wishes and by adult evasions about his origin, that he may be of noble ancestry, perhaps indeed a prince of the blood or at least the son of a gentleman. Yet he suspects before long that his slovenly Ma, who hints at a royal liaison in her past, is no devotee of fact; and he has little reason to credit his own dreams. When Ma abruptly (within less than half a page) sickens and dies, he is forced like other orphans of the Bildungsroman to seek a surrogate mother and father, the "parents not in the flesh" he finds in his schoolteachers, Miss Pringle and Nick Shales. Though the book is not a novel of "education" (in the narrow sense of that word), the school, as we shall see, contributes a good deal to the shaping of Sammy's character and conduct. If not precisely a young man from the provinces, Sammy has some attributes of the type; he belongs by birth to a semi-rural slum beyond the pale of a sophisticated society, which he one day will aggressively enter. His larger education, rather like Pip's, is his gradual movement into a corrupt world, his progress from Rotten Row, which has a certain innocence and warmth in its squalor, to Paradise Hill with all its urban and urbane hypocrisies. The two loves we have come to expect, the ideal and the sensual, are represented respectively by Beatrice Ifor, whom Sammy seduces and abandons, and the freespoken Taffy, whom he summarily marries. Beatrice is fragile, frightened, and chilly, recalling now Sue Bridehead, now Miriam Leivers, most of all perhaps George Ponderevo's Marion, though she is less intelligent than the first two and much more vulnerable than the last. Taffy seems a more intellectual Arabella or a simpler Clara Dawes, but she is far less realized than either; she is but a dim background shadow, little more than an alleged source of physical satisfaction.

Like Wordsworth of *The Prelude* and most of the Bildungsroman heroes, Sammy learns his deepest lessons from rare moments of insight, "spots of time" that reveal to him new levels of life and meaning. Three epiphanies especially stand out in his memory. As a small child he is struck by the configuration of a great cedar (much as the mature Mary Olivier is seized by the sense of ultimate reality in her lime tree); and remembering, he comments, "Later, I should have called the tree a cedar and passed on, but then, it was an apocalypse."[34] As an adolescent he plunges naked into "the providential waters" of a weir and, as if baptized or initiated into manhood,[35] emerges with a sudden sharp recognition of the self, his sexuality and his commitment to selfish desire even at the price of freedom. And as a young adult released from the torture cell in the prison camp, he experiences a mystical elation, a feeling of harmony in all living things and the presence of love as life's fourth dimension: "Standing between the understood huts, among jewels and music, I was visited by a flake of fire, miraculous and pentecostal; and fire transmuted me, once and for ever."[36] Sammy's true mode of vision is intuitive, for Sammy, like Paul Morel, is essentially the artist intent on discovering patterns which more prosaic minds have not imagined. And as such, like Paul or Stephen

Dedalus or Pater's Marius, he clearly voices some of the attitudes and aesthetic concerns of his author.

Like *Of Human Bondage, Free Fall* is explicitly not an autobiography but "to a considerable degree" an auto-biographical fiction—though in a less literal way, we may suppose, than the later, slighter stories that make up Golding's *Pyramid*. In an interview Golding took pains to distinguish his own career and person from Sammy's: "All the terms of my life were turned upside down. My boyhood and most of my life—I might say *all* of my life—have been hideously respectable. . . . But I set these things up: for example, I said to myself, 'You were in the navy; well, this man has to be in the army. You are a writer; you'll have to make this man a painter.' "[37] At the same time he admitted that Sammy shared his troubling concern "with the question of freedom of action"—and the effort itself to spell out differences in act and circumstance should suggest some measure of identity with Sammy's mind or spirit. Golding's father, like Nick Shales, Sammy's father "not in the flesh," was a selfless saintly man of limited vision, a scientific rationalist who had no religious belief and saw "no place in this exquisitely logical universe for the terror of darkness."[38] As a youth going up to Oxford, Golding accepted the optimistic humanism of the scientist, the bias of H. G. Wells in his most sanguine phase, much as Sammy assumes the sufficiency of Nick's naive rationalism. Experience as a naval officer in a brutal war, however, convinced Golding of the reality of illogic, unreason, and evil and utterly destroyed any lingering complacency about the human condition. The army provides Sammy a similar initiation; in the internment cell he learns the terror of darkness and finds the darkest dark of all at the center of his own being. The essential subjectivity of *Free Fall* lies in the author's personal commitment to his theme.

In T. S. Eliot's *Cocktail Party* Reilly the psychiatrist tells Edward the errant husband,

> Your moment of freedom was yesterday.
> You made a decision. You set in motion
> Forces in your life and in the lives of others
> Which cannot be reversed.[39]

Sammy must sort out his memories to discover for himself his own irreversible decision, the emergence of his discrete self-conscious self. "I am looking," he declares, "for the beginning of responsibility, the beginning of darkness, the point where I began."[40] Considered in such terms, the birth of self is clearly a falling from grace—and the notion of a theological lapse brings us back to the ambiguous title. The denotation of "free fall" in a space age, Golding explains, is first of all scientific, and the primary connotation follows immediately from the image of the weightless spaceman: "Where for hundreds of thouands of years men have known where they were, now they don't know where they are any longer." But there are other overtones of meaning, too: "There is also," we are told, "the Miltonic idea; there is also the Genesis idea; there is also the ordinary daily life idea of something which is 'for free,' and something which is also 'fall.' "[41] The conflict of the novel is the clash between the scientific or rationalistic assumption and the Miltonic or religious view of life; the theme is the loss of freedom attendant upon the denial of an open faith. Golding's avowed purpose is to reaffirm "the patternlessness of life before we impose our patterns upon it."[42] The stultifying patterns are the rigid, rationalized systems of Marxism or science or any narrow orthodoxy, the conformities that claim an exclusive hold on the truth. Freedom, as Sammy must understand it, is possible only when men are prepared to live in a world of incompatibles, of both determinism and choice, where both predictable science and unrestricted moral judgment are realities and facts of experience. Sammy loses his freedom when he yields to a compelling obsession in the light of which he attempts to rationalize or "pattern" his self-interest.

As a child Sammy is tough and ill disciplined, far from angelic, trailing, he says, no Wordsworthian clouds of glory. Yet his mischief leaves no stain; he is innocent of calculated evil and unconscious of his innocence and so, whatever his misdemeanors, essentially free. As the young adult reviewing his past, he is anxious, regretful, and oppressed by feelings of helplessness and guilt. Unable to see the relationship between his present self and "the infant Samuel," who seems another person altogether, he turns to the space between, the last adolescent year or two at school. In retrospect the influence of his teachers, his surrogate parents, becomes abundantly clear. Miss Pringle, who teaches Scripture, quickens Sammy's moral sense and stirs his imagination as long as she does not attempt reasonable or commonplace explanations of myth and miracle. Passionate by nature, now frustrated and neurotic, she should have real insight into the temptations and dark desires that beset Sammy; but her self-distrust, vindictive piety, and sadistic ridicule alienate his sympathies and drive him toward Nick Shales. Miss Pringle instinctively hates Nick because he finds it "easy to be good." Nick for his part is patient, kindly, imperturbable, and scrupulously fair, a good man indeed who properly wins the boy's respect and affection; but he has no personal knowledge of sin, no place in his orderly universe for wayward emotion, and accordingly no understanding of Miss Pringle's self-torment or Sammy's quickening sensuality; he resembles Piggy in *Lord of the Flies*, whom Golding depicts as "naive, short-sighted, and rationalist, like most scientists."[43] Apart from both teachers and above the conflict stands the headmaster, a neutral voice of intelligence, who recognizes Sammy's weakness and strength, his doubt, dishonesty, and selfishness and his rapidly developing talent as a draftsman. It is the wise headmaster who has the last word as Sammy leaves school:

> "I'll tell you something which may be of value. I believe it to be true and powerful—therefore dangerous. If you want something enough, you can always get it provided you are willing to make the appropriate sacrifice. Something, anything. But what you get is never quite what you thought; and sooner or later the sacrifice is always regretted."[44]

Sammy almost immediately determines his objective, the seduction and complete possession of Beatrice; his resolve is sealed by his unholy baptism in the weir, and at that point freedom itself seems not too great a sacrifice. Nick of course would not approve the decision, but Nick's scientific humanism nonetheless provides a sanction: "There are no morals," Sammy concludes, "that can be deduced from natural science, there are only immorals. . . . I transformed Nick's innocent, paper world. Mine was amoral, a savage place in which man was trapped without hope, to enjoy what he could while it was going."[45] The naive good man thus proves the bad influence.

Sammy's violation of Beatrice reaches beyond the limits of sexual aggression. It is an attempt to coerce a mind, to appropriate and consume another's integrity and personal identity. Sammy seeks more than physical excitement (he makes it clear that he has already had a sexual initiation, which he does not trouble to describe): "I said I loved you," he tells Beatrice; "oh God, don't you know what that means? I want you, I want all of you, . . . I want to be you!"[46] His sin, like that of Pincher Martin in Golding's preceding novel, has implications larger than the act; it reflects the condition of a soul savagely, hopelessly committed to its own selfishness. This is the core of selfhood that Sammy must confront in the Nazi prison. Dr. Halde, his Satanic tormentor, is apt in his diagnosis; Sammy is in a state of free fall, without direction, without belief in any reality beyond the self: "There is no health in you, Mr. Mountjoy. There is no point at which something has knocked at your door and taken possession of you. You possess yourself. . . . You wait in a dusty waitingroom on no particular line for no particular train."[47] It is no comfort to Sammy to know that his sickness is common, that the war itself is "the ghastly and ferocious play" of aimless children whose "wrong use of freedom" has lost them their freedom. He must still suffer his own bondage. In his darkened cell of solitary confinement he gropes in terror toward a mysterious center, a damp shapeless object of horror, tangible symbol of the center of his own being. At length reduced by unendurable fear, he cries out for help, in "an absolute of helplessness," knowing very well that no help can come from Dr. Halde or his kind, yet changed by the cry and ready now to leave all living behind, to let his own center perish, to burst through the door of death itself. Physical release soon follows the psychological liberation, and Sammy, having glimpsed the reality of a moral world, sees the need of a "vital morality" in individual relationships and the impossibility of his ever again living contentedly with his own nature.

Yet he is not wholly absolved of guilt, for as he tells his story he declares himself still "violently searching and self-condemned" and confesses, "My yesterdays walk with me."[48] After the war he must face the consequences of what he may have done as a selfish adolescent. He visits Beatrice in a mental hospital, where she has been a patient since he deserted her seven years before, now degraded to a mere animal, incurably deranged, incontinent, shrilling like a marsh-bird. He is told that he might have caused or hastened the girl's collapse or that, possibly, her sanity in any case was too precariously balanced to endure. But he is prepared without further proof to accept responsibility for the hideous result. This is to be the final mark of his maturity, his completed initiation. Like other Bildungsroman heroes, wiser for his self-discovery, he may now return to his "parents." He will persuade Nick Shales that rationalism is wrong in its facile rejection of a moral order; he will remind Miss Pringle that she shares his guilt and deserves his forgiveness. But Nick is dying of a tired heart and beyond all instruction, and Miss Pringle in her happy retirement is impervious to regret and glad to delude herself about the past. In the end Sammy is left convinced that, though science is true within its limits and morality is likewise pertinent, there can be no bridge between the two worlds, only the awareness, in moments of insight, that both worlds exist. The affirmation brings with it a last sharp memory, which serves as an enigmatic epilogue. On release from the prison cell Sammy discovers that the dreadful center is simply a damp floorcloth, a drab enough correlative of his soggy soul, and the commandant speaks briefly to him:

> "Captain Mountjoy. You have heard?"
> "I heard."
> The commandant indicated the door back to the camp dismissively. He spoke the inscrutable words that I should puzzle over as though they were the Sphinx's riddle.
> "The Herr Doktor does not know about peoples."[49]

What Sammy has heard must have been the voice of awakened faith assuring him that love and moral choice and freedom, despite all evidence to the contrary, are essential realities. What Herr Doktor Halde does not know is that human beings cannot be contained by his or anyone's self-confident rational system.

The ending of *Free Fall*, as of many other Bildungsromane, is inconclusive. Sammy is mature but shaken by his experience and still in search of inner peace. Insofar as he carries his guilt with him, his only victory is his acceptance of the burden. He is now a distinguished painter, but, unlike Paul Morel, he does not claim exemption from blame as a sort of aesthetic superman beyond good and evil. Indeed he explicitly denies that there can be a separate and more capacious moral standard for the artist. But he does value his creative instinct and the honesty of vision it demands. Art, he insists, is as much discovery as communication; and in art he has discovered the meaning of disinterested purpose. Like Wordsworth, who felt "chosen" for his mission, he has been able to say, "I was intended" (perhaps as the Biblical Samuel was intended for the Lord). Though he has too often allowed self-will to distract him, he has nonetheless found his proper work and glimpsed a way to truth. Whatever the mistakes of adolescence, he grows at last steadily into his vocation.

None of these later novels of youth, not even *Free Fall*, impressive as it is, achieves the total impact of *Great Expectations* or *The Mill on the Floss*, *Jude* or *A Portrait of the Artist*, for none of the later novelists matches Dickens in fertility of invention, or George Eliot and Hardy in compassion, or Joyce in verbal command. Several of the later books, nevertheless, testify to both the persistence and the vitality of the genre in our time. Though each differs in approach, all reflect the constant concern of the Bildungsroman with the dark passages of selfhood that the young Keats determined to explore. Like their predecessors, all are subjective and self-conscious to a high degree, and far as some may be from literal autobiography, each gains its measure of strength, as the earlier examples drew their power, from the novelist's personal stake in his materials and his considerable identification with the sensibility of his hero. Each of the heroes, whatever his accomplishment, shares something of the imaginative energy of his author, who, turning to the Bildungsroman to assess his own development, has drawn from his private experience as much or as little as he will, but who all the while, by the very act of writing, is himself an artist.

In commitment to his craft Sammy Mountjoy stands close to the most gifted of the older protagonists; by the end of *Free Fall* he is as strenuously the draftsman as David Copperfield is the writer, or Ernest Pontifex the Butlerian essayist, or George Ponderevo the designer of splendid gliders, or Stephen Dedalus the poet-aesthete. All of the novelists of youth from Dickens through Joyce and many of their heroes would have endorsed Sammy's conviction that art can demonstrate what science or mere analysis cannot prove. And all would have appreciated Sammy's astonished response to the schoolroom sketch of Beatrice Ifor that first certified his talent:

> The line leapt, it was joyous, free, authoritative. It achieved little miracles of implication so that the viewer's eye created her small hands though my pencil had not touched them. That free line had raced past and created her face, had thinned and broken where no pencil could go, but only the imagination.[50]

As he reaches maturity the hero of the Bildungsroman, old or new, will typically feel his bondage, the multiple constraints of living, often represented by the pressures of the cruel delusive city toward which his career has carried him. But from time to time the creative vision, the leaping line, or, failing that, simply the quiet intuition may restore as much of his lost freedom as is still recoverable. In book after book ever since *Wilhelm Meister* some such vision, a sharp epiphany or a more gradual imaginative enlightenment, has been essential to the hero's initiation and continuance. Wilhelm must sacrifice his illusions and welcome a secret revelation from the heights. David Copperfield will heed the voice of "great Nature" in an Alpine village rebuking his undisciplined heart and recalling him to life. Richard Feverel could be redeemed by the same voice speaking in a Rhineland storm, if only his cleansed imagination equaled his resurgent egoism. Pip is overwhelmed—destroyed and reborn—by his sudden awareness of the strength of love in the poor suffering criminal who has been his benefactor. Maggie Tulliver is saved—at least in spirit—by her natural piety, her will to imagine the unity of her own character and experience. Harry Richmond learns by a slow process to pity the father he can no longer respect. Marius finds escape from a time of sophisticated brutality in a timeless meditation and a new ritual of sympathy. Ernest Pontifex seeks imaginative release in independence of thought, and George Ponderevo, in bold invention. Jude's manhood brings only disillusion, but Hardy contrives to make the darkest "seemings" of the life a source of tragic catharsis. Paul Morel has frequent painterly perceptions of truth and meaning, though his possible final faith lies with Lawrence somewhere outside the novel. And Stephen Dedalus proudly affirms the vision that Joyce rather than Stephen will eventually body forth in art. Each of these brings his own inner resources of sensitivity to confront a hostile and insensitive environment. From the beginning the English Bildungsroman respects Wordsworth's confidence that the child questioning sense and outward things is father of the understanding man; and so the intuition persists, despite the world's confusions, that the individual life may find some ultimate coherence. In hero and author alike, it is the quickened imagination, moral or aesthetic, that animates and eventually outlives the troubled season of youth.

NOTES

INDEX

NOTES

Acknowledgment is made to several publishers and literary executors for quotation from books still under copyright protection. The passages from *Free Fall* by William Golding and the lines from *The Cocktail Party* by T. S. Eliot are quoted by permission of Faber and Faber, Ltd., London, and Harcourt Brace Jovanovich, Inc., New York. Passages from *A Portrait of the Artist as a Young Man* by James Joyce appear by arrangement with Jonathan Cape, Ltd., London, and the Executors of the James Joyce Estate. Selections from *Sons and Lovers* by D. H. Lawrence are included by permission of William Heinemann, Ltd., and with acknowledgment to Laurence Pollinger, Ltd., and the Estate of the late Mrs. Frieda Lawrence. The lines from Hardy's "Thoughts of Phena" are quoted by permission of the Macmillan Publishing Company, Inc., New York, from *Collected Poems of Thomas Hardy* (copyright 1925 by Macmillan Publishing Company, Inc.); the stanza from "Childhood among the Ferns" is reprinted by permission of the Macmillan Company, Inc., from *Winter Words* by Thomas Hardy (copyright 1928 by Florence E. Hardy and Sydney E. Cockerell, renewed 1956 by Lloyds Bank, Ltd.); and both these passages are reproduced with the further permission of the Trustee of the Hardy Estate, the Macmillan Company of Canada, and Macmillan, London and Basingstoke.

I. INTRODUCTION: THE SPACE BETWEEN

1. Letter of May 3, 1818, Hyder Edward Rollins, ed. *The Letters of John Keats*, 2 vols. (Cambridge, Mass., Harvard University Press, 1958), I, 280–281.

2. Letter of May 1, 1805, to Sir George Beaumont, Philip Wayne, ed., *Letters of William Wordsworth* (London, Oxford University Press, 1954), p. 72.

3. All quotations from *The Prelude* come from the 1805 text, Ernest de Selincourt, ed. (London, Oxford University Press, 1933). Here Bk. I, ll. 238–247, 352–361.

4. This was Mrs. Wordsworth's subtitle for *The Prelude* in its final version, posthumously published in 1850.

5. Bk. XI, ll. 326–328.

6. The epithet "lost" recurs (in all versions) at crucial moments; see 1805 text, Bk. VI, l. 529, Bk. VII, l. 608, Bk. XI, l. 330.

7. Bk. V, ll. 473–481.

8. Keats, *Letters*, I, 387.

9. Edgar Johnson, *Sir Walter Scott: The Great Unknown*, 2 vols. (New York, Macmillan, 1970), I, 524.

10. *Waverley*, Chaps. 4, 5.

11. See P. Hume Brown, *Life of Goethe*, 2 vols. (London, Murray, 1920), II, 671.

12. Hume Brown, II, 667n.

13. "Preface," *Wilhelm Meister's Apprenticeship and Travels*, 2 vols. (Boston, Cassino, 1884), I, 9; this title covers two quite distinct novels: the *Lehrjahre* of 1796 (*Apprenticeship*) and the much later *Wanderjahre* (*Travels*). Carlyle translated the latter in 1826 from a fragmentary version of 1821. Goethe then reorganized and greatly expanded the *Wanderjahre* for publication in 1829—and Carlyle did not translate the longer, final version. The *Apprenticeship* was always far better known in England than the *Travels;* and it is the *Apprenticeship* alone that is to be regularly understood by later references in my notes to *Meister* and by subsequent allusions in the text to *Wilhelm Meister*.

14. *Meister*, Bk. III, Chap. 2. Goethe slyly adds that Wilhelm had another less articulated motive for his visit to the count: "he durst not confess how greatly he wished again to be near the beautiful countess."

15. *Meister*, Bk. I, Chap. 10; see also the following chapter, which spells out Wilhelm's rejection of the tradesman's world.

16. *Meister*, Bk. VII, Chap. 9.

17. Quoted by George Henry Lewes, *The Life of Goethe* (New York, Ungar, 1965), p. 399.

18. Carlyle's preface, I, 10.

19. Susanne Howe (Nobbe), *Wilhelm Meister and His English Kinsmen* (New York, Columbia University Press, 1930), p. 6. Mrs. Nobbe offers much useful information on the Bildungsroman and its variants, as I discuss them below. In tracing the genre in England, however, she adheres to her restricted definition of the term and excludes nearly all of the novels with which I am concerned in the chapters that follow. Parts of the present paragraph are adapted or lifted directly from my essay "Autobiography in the English *Bildungsroman*," Morton W. Bloomfield, ed., *The Interpretation of Narrative: Theory and Practice* (Cambridge, Mass.,

Harvard Universitiy Press, 1970), p. 95. Hans Wagner's short study, *Der englische Bildungsroman bis in der Zeit des ersten Weltkrieges* (Bern, Francke, 1951), contains some bibliographical suggestions. François Jost discusses the derivation of the term in his stimulating article, "La Tradition du *Bildungsroman*," *Comparative Literature*, XXI (1969), 97–115. See also G. B. Tennyson, "The Bildungsroman in Nineteenth-Century English Literature," Rosario P. Armato and John M. Spalek, eds., *Medieval Epic to the "Epic Theater" of Brecht* (Los Angeles, University of California Press, 1968), pp. 135–146. Professor Tennyson points out how loosely the term is used as applied to the English novel, where the distinction is seldom made between an *Entwicklungsroman* ("merely the novel of development") and a Bildungsroman ("the novel of harmonious cultivation of the whole personality"), p. 142. In the novels I am discussing the problem of integration and maturity is certainly an issue, but few of the heroes set out self-consciously to achieve a well-rounded Goethean fulfillment, a *Vielseitigkeit* such as John Stuart Mill in his autobiography recognized as a worthy ideal.

20. Justin O'Brien in *The Novel of Adolescence in France* (New York, Columbia University Press, 1937) argues that there are really no good novels of youth in France before 1890. Balzac's early novel *Louis Lambert* and Flaubert's early *Novembre* are both cited as unsuccessful efforts to make an autobiographical hero a convincing character. Later French novels of adolescence are seldom Bildungsromane.

21. In terms equally well suited to Joyce's *Portrait*, Harry Levin describes *Henry Brulard* as informed by "the conflict between esthetic impulses and moral inhibitions within an awakening mind." See Levin, *The Gates of Horn* (New York, Oxford University Press, 1963), p. 94 (the whole chapter on Stendhal is richly perceptive). See also Victor Brombert's excellent study, *Stendhal: Fiction and the Themes of Freedom* (New York, Random House, 1968), esp. Chap. 1, "The Temptations of Autobiography," pp. 3–26.

22. In his admirable edition and translation of the novel, *Red and Black* (New York, Norton, 1969), Robert M. Adams calls attention to many details apparently drawn from Stendhal's experience and allusions to his reading and political opinions; but the main story-line is, of course, not autobiographical, however close may be the parallels between Stendhal's character and his hero's.

23. On arrival in Paris, Julien tells the Abbé, "My father has hated me from the cradle; it was one of my great misfortunes, but I shall no longer complain of fortune, I have found another father

in you, sir" (Chap. 31). Throughout my discussion of the novel I use my own translations from an 1870 two-volume edition of *Le Rouge et le Noir*.

24. *The Red and the Black*, Chap. 30. The French reads, "Il allait enfin paraître sur le théâtre des grandes choses."

25. Chap. 71. He also behaves as the dandy when he first enters the courtroom and pauses to admire its architecture: "It was pure Gothic, with a group of pretty little columns carved in stone with the utmost care. He imagined himself in England." Of his confinement in prison he can make a paradox worthy of Oscar Wilde: "The worst thing about a prison is that one cannot shut one's door."

26. Chaps. 36, 43, 56.

27. Except Stendhal himself, who invented many of the epigraphs and assigned them to many authorities from Machiavelli to Sainte-Beuve. At any rate there are seven genuine epigraphs from *Don Juan*, two of them from the late Canto XIII.

28. The "Romantic ironies" in *The Red and the Black*—the sudden shifts or breaks in moods, the undercutting of emotion, the intrusion of the author commenting on his style and his publisher (Chap. 52)—seem clearly indebted to the method of *Don Juan*. The poem, said Stendhal elsewhere, rested on Byron's real knowledge of men and society, which contrasted sharply with the provinciality of Lamartine: "No stupidity at present to be found in France can be compared with the stupidity of the provincial noble, living, as he has done for the last thirty-five years, in a state of perpetual anger against everything happening around him." See Geoffrey Strickland, ed., *Selected Journalism from the English Reviews of Stendhal* (London, Calder, 1959), "Lamartine and Byron," p. 43, and also "Memories of Lord Byron" and "Lord Byron in Italy," pp. 294–321.

29. Chap. 75. The French reads, "Allons, tout va bien, se dit-il, je ne manque point de courage."

30. *Sinister Street*, I (London, Secker, 1913), "Dedication."

31. *Sinister Street*, II (London, Secker, 1914), "Epilological Letter," pp. ii–iii.

32. *The Way of All Flesh*, Chap. 85 (Howard edition, see note 10 to my Chapter V, below). Cf. Butler's notebook entry: "QUARRELING WITH ONE'S FATHER: A man begins to do this about nine months before he is born. He then begins worrying his father to let him have a separate establishment, till the father finds him a nuisance and lets him have his own way." See *Notebooks* (London, Cape, 1951), p. 71.

33. Lionel Trilling uses this phrase to describe the English hero as well as the French. Though they do share much in common, the latter seems to me much more the calculating self-conscious opportunist. See Trilling, *The Liberal Imagination* (Garden City, N.Y., Doubleday, 1953), pp. 58–61.

34. At least in America. The *OED* lists no English usage of the idiom (in this sense) earlier than the twentieth century. The phrase occurs in *Tono-Bungay* (1908).

35. "Success" in the sense of "one who succeeds": the earliest example of this cited by the *OED* dates from 1882.

36. "Expectations" as "prospects of inheritance" (*OED*), a well-established sense of the word by the beginning of the Victorian period (and probably earlier).

37. *Meister*, Bk. VI, Chap. 8.

38. *Sinister Street*, II, 1122.

39. So does the hero of Henry Handel Richardson's *Maurice Guest* (1908), a solid Bildungsroman of an English youth without real talent who aspires in vain to a musical career in Germany.

40. Maugham, *The Summing Up* (New York, Literary Guild, 1938), pp. 193–194.

41. Maugham, p. 191.

42. Conrad, *Youth and Gaspar Ruiz* (London, Dent, 1930), "Author's Note," p. 167. *Youth* is, of course, much too short to be mistaken for a novel. I am concerned here merely with the difference in tone between an autobiography and a work of fiction.

43. *Youth*, pp. 56–57.

II. DICKENS, DAVID AND PIP

1. Letters of May 1849, Gordon N. Ray, ed., *The Letters and Private Papers of William Makepeace Thackeray*, 4 vols. (Cambridge, Mass., Harvard University Press, 1945–1946), II, 531, 533.

2. Gordon N. Ray, *Thackeray: The Age of Wisdom* (New York, McGraw-Hill, 1958), p. 110.

3. Thackeray's daughter, Anne T. Ritchie, comments on the autobiographical elements in her preface to *Pendennis*, vol. II, The Biographical Edition, 13 vols. (New York, Harper, 1898).

4. *Pendennis*, Chap. 61 ("The Way of the World"). Ray (*Thackeray*, p. 120) quotes the passage, with apparent approval, as an example of Thackeray's "Sadducceeism."

5. Quoted by Ray, *Thackeray*, pp. 113, 114.

6. Preface to *Pendennis*, written as soon as the novel was completed, dated Nov. 26, 1850. The same problem mars *Esmond*

(1852), Thackeray's next major work, a nearly perfect historical novel, but a Bildungsroman (insofar as it is one) with a dull and bloodless hero. In his introduction to the Rinehart *Esmond* (New York, 1962), G. Robert Stange skillfully relates the book both to the tradition of the Bildungsroman and to the tradition of the historical novel.

7. Walter Dexter, ed., *The Letters of Charles Dickens*, 3 vols. (Bloomsbury, The Nonesuch Press, 1938), II, 240.

8. On the date of the autobiographical fragment, see Edgar Johnson, *Charles Dickens: His Tragedy and Triumph*, 2 vols. (New York, Simon and Schuster, 1952), I, Notes iv (#63).

9. Autobiography, quoted by John Forster, *The Life of Charles Dickens*, 3 vols. (Philadelphia, Lippincott, 1873), I, 53, 57–58, 69.

10. Letter of Feb. 15, 1855, to Maria Beadnell Winter, Dexter, *Letters*, II, 629. Edgar Johnson, who gives a vivid account of the affair with Maria, comments on its effect: "All the rest of his emotional life he lay under the shadow of this lost love, which in its darkest places merges with the shadow cast by the spiked wall of the Marshalsea and the imprisoning shades of the blacking warehouse" (I, 83).

11. Frederick W. Dupee, ed. *The Selected Letters of Charles Dickens* (New York, Farrar Strauss and Cudahy, 1960), p. 219.

12. Cf. the comment of Robert Hamilton, "Of course, the adult David is completely unlike the adult Dickens, as unlike as a lamb to a fiery steed." See Hamilton, "Dickens's Favourite Child," *The Dickensian*, XLV (1949), 141.

13. Quoted by Johnson, II, 911. Insofar as the restless Byronic Dickens enters the novel at all, he may be seen in the character and conduct of Steerforth.

14. Johnson makes a similar comment on David as husband, II, 689.

15. Alternate trial titles listed by Forster, II, 465.

16. *David Copperfield*, Chap. 2.

17. *David Copperfield*, Chaps. 10, 55, 9. J. Hillis Miller discusses the book as a novel of memory in his *Charles Dickens: The World of his Novels* (Cambridge, Mass., Harvard University Press, 1958), pp. 152–158.

18. *David Copperfield*, Chaps. 26, 60.

19. *David Copperfield*, Chap. 39.

20. *David Copperfield*, Chap. 45. For a sensitive treatment of the theme, see Gwendolyn Needham, "The Undisciplined Heart of David Copperfield," *Nineteenth-Century Fiction*, IX (1954), 81–107.

21. *David Copperfield*, Chaps. 48, 53, 58.
22. *David Copperfield*, Chaps. 4, 21, 22.
23. *David Copperfield*, Chap. 26.
24. *David Copperfield*, Chap. 15.
25. The plan notes for Chap. 15 include the jotting, "Introduction of the real heroine." Agnes is always "the good angel"; Dickens keeps her in mind even at the time of David's courtship of Dora. His note to the plans for Chaps. 25-27 reads, "Carry the thread of Agnes through it all." See John Butt and Kathleen Tillotson, *Dickens at Work* (Fair Lawn, N.J., Essential Books, 1958), pp. 128, 150. The reality of Agnes has of course been frequently questioned. G. K. Chesterton thought her far less convincing than Dora. George Orwell called her "the most disagreeable of Dickens's heroines, the real legless angel of Victorian romance, almost as bad as Thackeray's Laura." See Orwell, *A Collection of Essays* (Garden City, N. Y., Doubleday, 1954), p. 109.
26. For want of a more convenient term, I use my own. See *The Victorian Temper* (Cambridge, Mass., Harvard University Press, 1951), Chap. 5, which discusses the pattern in Carlyle and the imagery of conversion in other Victorian works. See also the essay by G. B. Tennyson (cited above, Chap. 1, note 19), in which *Sartor Resartus* is called "that handbook of the Victorian *Bildungsroman*" (p. 143).
27. Butt and Tillotson, p. 172.
28. *David Copperfield*, Chap. 58 ("Absence").
29. To put the matter in terms of Adlerian psychology, one must make three principal adjustments—to sex, to work, to society,—failing any one of which a man becomes a neurotic personality. In turning to Agnes, David completes all three adjustments and achieves integration.
30. *David Copperfield*, Chap. 62.
31. *David Copperfield*, author's preface.
32. Dexter, *Letters*, III, 186.
33. See Bernard Shaw's letter to *The Dickensian*, XLV (1949), 118, following Humphry House, "G. B. S. on *Great Expectations*," XLIV (1948), 64.
34. *Great Expectations*, Chap. 27.
35. *Great Expectations*, Chap. 14.
36. *Great Expectations*, Chap. 56.
37. Ada Nisbet ably describes the "obsessive passions" in her essay, "The Autobiographical Matrix of *Great Expectations*," *Victorian Newsletter*, no. 15 (Spring 1959), 10-13; I here follow her reading of the novel.

38. The end of *Paradise Lost* is clearly echoed by the last sentence of Chap. 19, which marks "the end of the first stage of Pip's expectations": "And the mists had all solemnly risen now, and the world lay spread before me."

39. *Great Expectations*, Chap. 2.

40. Biddy's hands are always clean when she is an adult, always dirty when she is a child. When speculating on hands as a leitmotif in the novel, I came upon a full discussion of the subject by Charles R. Forker, "The Language of Hands in *Great Expectations*," *Texas Studies in Literature and Language*, III (1961), 208–293. The instances, however, that I have cited above are those that most struck me in my own reading.

41. Harry Stone makes a convincing analysis of the elements of fairy-tale and allegory in *Great Expectations* in his essay, "Fire, Hand, and Gate," *Kenyon Review*, XXIV (1962), 663–691.

42. *Great Expectations*, Chap. 8.

43. *Great Expectations*, Chap. 19.

44. *Great Expectations*, Chap. 20. Pip's experience in London is prefigured in the comic song Biddy teaches him years before he leaves the village:

When I went to Lunnon town, sirs,
    Too rul loo rul
    Too rul loo rul
Wasn't I done very brown, sirs?
    Too rul loo rul
    Too rul loo rul.   (Chap. 15)

45. *Great Expectations*, Chap. 27.

46. *Great Expectations*, Chap. 19.

47. Estella's sneering remark comes in Chap. 8, where the epithets are repeated several times. They recur in Chaps. 9, 10, 11, 15, and 16. In 18 Pip refuses to show the villagers his genteel new outfit since they "would make such a business of it—such a coarse and common business." In 29 he returns to Satis House "in lighter boots than of yore," and Miss Havisham asks Estella, "Less coarse and common?" Later (Chap. 24) his rowing instructor praises him for having "the arm of a blacksmith." Pip comments, "If he could have known how nearly the compliment had lost him his pupil, I doubt if he would have paid it."

48. Comments on gentlemen and gentility from Chaps. 17, 18, 8, 15, 22. Herbert Pocket is probably Dickens's—as well as Pip's—ideal gentleman, scarcely robust but spontaneous in his good taste, effort-

less in his superiority. "He was still a pale young gentleman, and had a certain conquered languor about him in the midst of his spirits and briskness, that did not seem indicative of natural strength. He had not a handsome face, but it was better than handsome: being extremely amiable and cheerful. . . . Whether Mr. Trabb's local work would have sat more gracefully on him than on me, may be a question; but I am conscious that he carried off his rather old clothes much better than I carried off my new suit." This passage, which may reflect some of Dickens's social insecurity or at least his envy of those who could take the gentlemanly graces for granted, is, I think, a fine example of the way in which the personal has become objective in *Great Expectations*.

49. *Great Expectations*, Chaps. 24, 41.

50. See John Henry Newman, *The Idea of a University* (1852: New York, Longmans, 1947), pp. 107, 185–186. Cf. Charles Kingsley's sermon, "The True Gentleman," written about the same time as Newman's discourse and not dissimilar in idea: "To be always thinking of other people's feelings and always caring for other people's comfort is the only mark of a true gentleman"—*Sermons for the Times* (New York, Dana, 1856), p. 311.

51. On the gentleman, *Great Expectations*, Chaps. 39, 54, 29.

52. Orwell (p. 82) considers the child's speech an absurdity, which he ascribes to some bias he finds in Dickens against the working classes; his complaint would be more persuasive if *Great Expectations* had been narrated in the third person by an omniscient novelist.

53. *Great Expectations*, Chap. 56.

54. *Great Expectations*, Chap. 28.

55. *Great Expectations*, Chap. 2.

56. On secret guilt, *Great Expectations*, Chaps. 22, 16.

57. The most ingenious reading in these terms is that of Julian Moynahan, "The Hero's Guilt: The Case of *Great Expectations*," *Essays in Criticism*, X (1960), 60–79. Mr. Moynahan argues that Pip indulges in destructive fantasies which come true, and in this way is responsible for Miss Havisham's death and for harming most others he meets, until in the end, living abroad, he may do "the least possible harm to the smallest number of people." Despite elements of allegory, the novel does not, I think, sustain so psychological an interpretation.

58. On Pip's candor, Chaps. 43, 14, 35.

59. *Great Expectations*, Chap. 35.

60. *Great Expectations*, Chap. 6.

61. On Estella, Chaps. 49, 29, 22.

62. *Great Expectations,* Chap. 29.

63. *Great Expectations,* Chap. 17.

64. *Great Expectations,* Chap. 49.

65. *Great Expectations,* Chap. 53.

66. *Great Expectations,* Chap. 54.

67. *Great Expectations,* Chap. 57.

68. *Great Expectations,* Chap. 57.

69. *Great Expectations,* Chap. 59.

70. Martin Meisel argues persuasively that this is indeed the "true ending" of the novel: "The Ending of *Great Expectations,*" *Essays in Criticism,* XV (1965), 326–331.

71. *Great Expectations,* Chaps. 25, 39.

III. GEORGE MEREDITH: HISTORIES OF FATHER AND SON

1. Meredith, quoted from *Fortnightly Review* (July 1909), by S. M. Ellis, *George Meredith, His Life and Friends* (New York, Dodd Mead, 1920), p. 81.

2. See Lionel Stevenson, *The Ordeal of George Meredith* (New York, Scribners, 1953), p. 183.

3. See Jack Lindsay, *George Meredith* (London, Bodley Head, 1956), p. 91.

4. *Richard Feverel,* Chap. 19. This and subsequent chapter numbers refer to the 1859 version of the novel rather than to Meredith's later revision, which cuts and telescopes the opening chapters and makes a few other changes.

5. See Mona E. Mackay, *Meredith et la France* (Paris, Boivin, 1937), pp. 237–238. Meredith had a copy of *The Red and the Black* in his library, but I cannot tell when he first read the novel. My suggestion that it may have influenced *Richard Feverel* presupposes that he knew it before 1859. The earliest reference to Stendhal in Meredith's letters (to the essay "De l'amour") appears in 1861; the last in 1906.

6. See Maria Krusmeyer, "Goethe's Influence on George Meredith" in Guy B. Potter, ed., *George Meredith and His German Critics* (London, Witherby, 1939), pp. 127–131, and René Galland, *George Meredith: les cinquante premières années* (Paris, Les Presses françaises, 1923), p. 315. Galland sees both *Wilhelm Meister* and *Harry Richmond* as histories of education through error: "*dans les deux cas, c'est l'illusion et l'erreur qui lentement pétrissent les héros.*"

7. *Richard Feverel,* Chap. 4.

8. *The Adventures of Harry Richmond,* Chap. 50.

9. On publication *Richard Feverel* was attacked by some reviewers as indecent and dropped from Mudie's list and banned by some parish libraries; the reviewer for *The Critic* concluded from many passages in the novel that Meredith's mind was "none of the purest" (see Stevenson, pp. 71–72). Few characters in respectable nineteenth-century English fiction speak as bluntly of sex as Squire Beltham in *Harry Richmond*, who here argues with his chaplain-tutor: "Peterborough defended his young friend Harry's moral reputation, and was amazed to hear that the squire did not think highly of a man's chastity. The squire acutely chagrined the sensitive gentleman by drawling the word after him, and declaring that he tossed that kind of thing into the women's wash-basket" (Chap. 36).

10. Harry Richmond's mother dies when he is a small child; Aunt Dorothy serves as a kindly substitute. Richard Feverel's mother, when the novel opens, has already deserted his father. Late in the novel, intent upon rescuing "fallen" women, Richard finds his mother and takes her into protective custody, where she is apparently soon forgotten both by Richard and by Meredith.

11. See Stevenson, p. 8.

12. *Harry Richmond*, Chap. 14 (Colonel Goodwin, a gentleman, is trying to persuade Harry not to jeopardize his status by returning to his father).

13. After 1861 the "gentleman" subtitle was dropped.

14. Meredith had previously published a volume of poems and two longish tales in prose, *The Shaving of Shagpat* and *Farina*, both more or less exotic fantasies.

15. See Stevenson, pp. 72–73.

16. *Richard Feverel*, Chap. 46.

17. At the time of Mary Meredith's last illness, in 1861, Meredith was finally prevailed upon to let Arthur visit her. See Stevenson, pp. 67, 96.

18. *Richard Feverel*, Chaps. 16 ("The Magnetic Age"), 18 ("Ferdinand and Miranda").

19. *Richard Feverel*, Chap. 26.

20. Cf. Adrian's comment on Richard's marriage (Chap. 35): "So dies the System! . . . And now let prophets roar! He dies respectably in a marriage-bed, which is more than I should have foretold of the Monster."

21. *Richard Feverel*, Chap. 37.

22. Letter of July 7, 1859, to Samuel Lucas, C. L. Cline, ed., *The Letters of George Meredith*, 3 vols. (Oxford, Clarendon Press, 1970), I, 40.

23. *Richard Feverel*, Chaps. 8, 7.

24. *Richard Feverel*, Chap. 15.

25. *Richard Feverel*, Chap. 37.

26. Cf. V. S. Prichett's comment: "Unlike, say, Tom Jones who merely commits follies, Richard is a sort of handsome anti-hero who is selfish, hot-tempered, and blinded by a youthful egoism disguised as principle. His pride is more forgivable than his father's and is relieved by the engaging, growing powers of youth." See *George Meredith and English Comedy* (New York, Random House, 1969), pp. 65–66; this little book is the most sensitive and sensible recent revaluation of Meredith's fiction.

27. *Richard Feverel*, Chap. 42.

28. *Richard Feverel*, Chaps. 3, 4, 9.

29. Cf. *Richard Feverel*, Chap. 13, and "Lucifer in Starlight" (published in 1883). I take it that the phrase "old Rebellion" must, like "the old revolt," refer to Satan's war in Heaven.

30. *Richard Feverel*, Chap. 43.

31. *Richard Feverel*, Chap. 17.

32. *Richard Feverel*, Chap. 38.

33. *Richard Feverel*, Chap. 45.

34. *Richard Feverel*, Chap. 30.

35. *Richard Feverel*, Chaps. 28, 29.

36. J. S. Mill, *Autobiography*, Chap. 5. Mill completed the first draft of the *Autobiography* before Meredith began *Richard Feverel*, but the book was not published until 1873. I suggest a parallel between the two works rather than an influence. (Indeed no direct influence seems possible; Meredith could not have known Mill's manuscript before 1859, and it is most unlikely that Mill, having read the novel, worked verbal echoes into the final version of his life history.) But Meredith may very well have known of the education James Mill gave his son and possibly have had it in mind when he wrote of Sir Austin's System (though there are sharp differences), for J. S. Mill was the assistant and later the successor to Thomas Love Peacock, Meredith's father-in-law, at the East India Company.

37. *Richard Feverel*, Chap. 38.

38. *Richard Feverel*, Chap. 46.

39. Cf. *David Copperfield*, Chap. 58, and *Richard Feverel*, Chap. 46 ("Nature Speaks"). It is less likely that Meredith is here indebted to Dickens than that both are using Wordsworthian language, though Dickens may not have known *The Prelude* (1850), which appeared shortly before the last installments of his novel. In any case, in *The Prelude* (Bk. I, ll. 586–588, 1850 version),

"the earth / And common face of Nature spake to me / Remember-
able things."

40. *Richard Feverel,* Chap. 48 ("The Last Scene").

41. See, for example, Gladys Ekeberg, "*The Ordeal of Richard
Feverel* as Tragedy," *College English,* VII (1946), 387–393, and
William E. Buckler, "The Artistic Unity of *Richard Feverel:* Chapter XXXIII" (i.e., Chap. 36 in the 1859 edition), *Nineteenth-
Century Fiction,* VII (1952), 119–123. Buckler sees the chapter in
question, "Nursing the Devil," as crucial to the ending, and his
premise is that Sir Austin's System rather than Richard's own failings causes the tragedy.

42. Cf. *The Princess* (Part I, ll. 233–234): "In such a hand as
when a field of corn / Bows all its ears before the roaring East."

43. Meredith's account of his intentions in the novel, in a letter
of Nov. 2, 1871, to William Hardman, *Letters,* I, 453.

44. *Harry Richmond,* Chap. 56.

45. *Harry Richmond,* Chap. 55.

46. Arthur Meredith was eighteen years old by the completion
of *Harry Richmond.* Though there are traces perhaps of Arthur
in Harry, Meredith has already made the necessary provisions for
his education, and Arthur's lonely, unhappy boyhood is over.

47. See Stevenson, p. 17.

48. Lindsay (p. 180) says "169 characters in it have been listed,"
though he does not indicate who made the count.

49. On conspicuous wealth, *Harry Richmond,* Chaps. 44, 29, 37.

50. *Harry Richmond,* Chap. 2.

51. *Letters,* I, 453.

52. *Harry Richmond,* Chap. 19.

53. *Harry Richmond,* Chap. 19.

54. *Harry Richmond,* Chap. 50. Cf. Roy's hubris or sense of
"divine right" in a comment to Harry, later in the same chapter,
when he chides him for being tired: "You drink no wine, you
cannot stand dissipation as I do. . . . I am a God, sir, inaccessible
to mortal ailments! Seriously, dear boy, I have never known an
illness in my life. I have killed my hundreds of poor devils who
were for imitating me. This I boast—I boast constitution. And I
fear, Richie, you have none of my superhuman strength. Added to
that, I know I am watched over. I ask—I have: I scheme—the tricks
are in my hand."

55. *Harry Richmond,* Chaps. 24, 30.

56. *Harry Richmond,* Chaps. 30, 39.

57. *Harry Richmond,* Chaps. 43, 47, 50, 54.

58. *Harry Richmond,* Chap. 50.

59. On Janet, *Harry Richmond*, Chaps. 33, 36.

60. In the last chapter Harry speculates on the difference between his view of himself and that of his friends: "Supposing that my idea of myself differed from theirs for the simple reason that I thought of what I had grown to be, and they of what I had been through the previous years?"

61. Cf. Norman Kelvin, *A Troubled Eden* (Stanford, Stanford University Press, 1961), p. 82: "Harry removed from his father's ways is Harry without an interesting future. There is really no suggestion at the end of the novel that his life is going to mean very much. It will consist of rational compromise, of seeking the sensible way, in all departments of existence."

IV. GEORGE ELIOT: A DOUBLE LIFE

1. The essay, "Evangelical Teaching: Dr. Cumming," appeared in October 1855. For Lewes's comment, see J. W. Cross, *George Eliot's Life as Related in Her Letters and Journals*, 3 vols. (New York, 1855), I, 384, and also the definitive modern biography by Gordon S. Haight, *George Eliot* (New York, Oxford University Press, 1968), p. 186.

2. "The Morality of *Wilhelm Meister*," reprinted from the *Leader*, July 21, 1855, by Thomas Pinney, ed., *Essays of George Eliot* (London, Routledge and Kegan Paul, 1963), p. 144. George Eliot and Lewes had read *Meister* together in 1854 and were to read it again, aloud, in 1870; see Gordon S. Haight, ed., *The George Eliot Letters*, 7 vols. (New Haven, Yale University Press, 1954–1955), II, 186n3, and V, 124. Since Lewes was the able biographer of Goethe, George Eliot was probably more familiar with the "first" Bildungsroman than any other English novelist attempting the genre.

3. Letter to D'Albert Durade, *Letters*, III, 231, quoted by Haight, *George Eliot*, p. 331.

4. See Haight, *George Eliot*, pp. 310–311.

5. The description of Mr. Pullet—and his name, too—also may suggest derivation from the flat characters in Dickens: "Mr. Pullet was a small man with a high nose, small twinkling eyes, and thin lips, in a fresh-looking suit of black and a white cravat that seemed to have been tied very tight on some higher principle than that of mere personal ease. He bore about the same relation to his tall, good-looking wife, with her balloon sleeves, abundant mantle, and large be-feathered and be-ribboned bonnet, as a small fishing-smack bears to a brig with all its sails spread" (*The Mill on the Floss*, Bk. I,

Chap. 7). But Dickens would have sketched the figure more eco-
nomically, with greater attention to the import of the white cravat
or to the image of the ships, which he would probably have developed as a metaphor rather than an incidental simile.

6. See Henry James, "The Novels of George Eliot," *Atlantic
Monthly*, XVIII (1866), 489, reprinted by Gordon S. Haight, ed.,
A Century of George Eliot Criticism (Boston, Houghton Mifflin,
1965), p. 51.

7. *Mill*, Bk. I, Chap. 7.

8. *Mill*, last paragraph of Bk. II; cf. *Great Expectations*, end of
Chap. 19.

9. Marian Evans: the original name was Mary Anne, which Miss
Evans changed to Marian on coming to London. I use the latter
form to avoid confusion.

10. "Brother and Sister," George Eliot, *Complete Poems* (Boston,
n.d.), pp. 391–397. The sonnet sequence is dated 1869.

11. The comment, though made about *Adam Bede*, is also pertinent to the *Mill:* "There is not a single portrait in the book, nor will
there be in any future book of mine" (*Letters*, III, 99).

12. A French study explores in detail George Eliot's interest in
Defoe and possible indebtedness; see P. G. Maheu, *La Pensée
religieuse et morale de George Eliot* (Paris, Didier, 1958).

13. Maggie is not named in the prologue (Bk. I, Chap. 1) but is
identified by her bonnet and her dog, "that queer white cur with
the brown ear." Later (Chap. 4) the dog is introduced as "Yap,
the queer white-and-brown terrier with one ear turned back."
When Maggie first enters (she has been seen through the parlor
window, at the river edge), she immediately throws off her bonnet.
The narrator carefully conceals her own (some critics says *his*)
identity, but there is no effort to establish a persona as narrator and
no reason to think of her as other than the omniscient author.
Henry Auster makes an excellent case for equating the narrator and
the author in his *Local Habitations: Regionalism in the Early
Novels of George Eliot* (Cambridge, Mass., Harvard University
Press, 1970), pp. 171–172.

14. *Letters*, III, 267.

15. W. J. Harvey, for example, one of George Eliot's ablest
critics, charges a "want of economy" in Bk. II, which describes
Tom's schooldays. He considers Tom's education largely irrelevant
to the "education" of Maggie, which he regards as the main theme
of the novel. See Harvey, *The Art of George Eliot* (London,
Chatto and Windus, 1961), p. 87.

16. *Mill*, Bk. I, Chap. 2.

17. *Mill*, Bk. IV, Chap. 1.

18. James, *Atlantic Monthly*, XVIII (1866), 490, and Dallas, *The Times*, May 19, 1860, p. 10, both reprinted in Haight, *Criticism*, pp. 9, 11, 52; George Eliot on Dallas, *Letters*, III, 299.

19. On St. Ogg's, see Auster, pp. 141–169, and U. C. Knoepflmacher, *George Eliot's Early Novels* (Berkeley, University of California Press, 1968), pp. 194–200.

20. *Mill*, "Conclusion."

21. *Mill*, Bk. VI, Chap. 4; Tom's attitude here is no doubt close to that of Isaac Evans, who was annoyed at his sister's religious heterodoxy and afraid that it would spoil her chance of making a good match; see Haight, *George Eliot*, p. 40.

22. *Mill*, Bk. VI, Chap. 6.

23. *Mill*, Bk. II, Chap. 3.

24. George Eliot attacks both the curriculum and the learning by rote at Mr. Stelling's but then with typical fairness adds: "Nevertheless, there was a visible improvement in Tom under this training, perhaps because he was not a boy in the abstract, existing solely to illustrate the evils of a mistaken education, but a boy made of flesh and blood, with dispositions not entirely at the mercy of circumstance" (Bk. II, Chap. 4).

25. *Mill*, Bk. VI, Chap. 3.

26. *Mill*, Bk. V, Chap. 2.

27. *Mill*, Bk. VII, Chap. 1.

28. *Mill*, Bk. VI, Chap. 5.

29. Gerald Bullett, *George Eliot: Her Life and Books* (New Haven, Yale University Press, 1948), pp. 194, 197.

30. *Mill*, Bk. V, Chap. 5.

31. *Mill*, Bk. I, Chap. 5.

32. *Mill*, Bk. II, Chap. 1.

33. *Mill*, Bk. III, Chap. 4.

34. *Mill*, Bk. IV, Chap. 3.

35. *Letters*, III, 299.

36. *Mill*, Bk. VII, Chap. 5.

37. *Mill*, Bk. I, Chap. 5.

38. *Mill*, Bk. II, Chap. 5.

39. Lawrence, quoted by "E. T." (Jessie Chambers), *D. H. Lawrence: A Personal Record* (London, Cass, 1965), p. 98.

40. *Mill*, Bk. IV, Chap. 3.

41. See Virginia Woolf, *The Common Reader* (New York, Harcourt Brace, 1953), pp. 173–174, and F. R. Leavis, *The Great Tradition* (Garden City, N.Y., Doubleday, 1954), pp. 55–58.

42. Cf. Knoepflmacher, p. 208.

43. See Knoepflmacher, pp. 210, 212: "Tom embraces the reality of St. Ogg's; Maggie yields to the fantasy life that was her father's destruction. . . . Like Mr. Tulliver, the girl possesses a 'soul untrained for inevitable struggles'; like the miller, she is deeply neurotic, incapable of accepting what Freud would call the 'reality principle.' "

44. *Mill*, Bk. III, Chap. 5.

45. *Mill*. Bk. VI, Chap. 3.

46. *Mill*, Bk. VI, Chap. 6.

47. Witness the Evangelical letters of 1840 to Mr. and Mrs. Samuel Evans, *Letters*, I, 39, 61, 73.

48. *Mill*, Bk. IV, Chap. 3.

49. *Mill*, Bk. V, Chaps. 1, 3.

50. *Mill*, Bk. VI, Chap. 7.

51. Swinburne, in his *Note on Charlotte Brontë* (1877), reprinted by Haight, *Criticism*, p. 127.

52. *Mill*, Bk. VI, Chap. 1.

53. "The Great Temptation," the title of Bk. VI.

54. *Mill*, Bk. VI, Chaps. 13, 14.

55. *Mill*, Bk. VI, Chap. 13.

56. *Mill*, Bk. VI, Chap. 14.

57. *Mill*, Bk. III, Chap. 6.

58. *Mill*, Bk. VI, Chap. 10.

59. *Mill*, Bk. VI, Chap. 14.

60. *Mill*, Bk. VII, Chap. 5.

61. See Thomas Pinney, "George Eliot's Reading of Wordsworth: The Record," *Victorian Newsletter*, No. 24 (Fall 1963), pp. 20–22.

62. *Poems*, p. 394.

63. *Mill*, Bk. VII, Chap. 5.

64. *Letters*, III, 269.

65. James, *Atlantic Monthly*, XVIII, 490.

66. *Letters*, III, 374.

67. George Levine relates the water symbolism to George Eliot's reading of Feuerbach; see "Intelligence as Deception: *The Mill on the Floss*," *PMLA*, LXXX (1965), 402–409. See also Knoepflmacher, pp. 164–178, and Harvey, pp. 234–236.

68. *Mill*, Bk. I, Chap. 10; cf. Bk. I, Chap. 2, as she sees Maggie through the window, "wanderin' up an' down by the water, like a wild thing: she'll tumble in some day," and then to Maggie, "You'll tumble in and be drownded some day, an' then you'll be sorry you didn't do as mother told you."

69. *Mill*, Bk. I, Chap. 3.

70. *Mill*, Bk. VI, Chap. 13.

71. Knoepflmacher (p. 220) also complains that there is "no causal connection" between Maggie's death and her flight with Stephen.

72. *Mill*, Bk. VII, Chap. 5.

V. THE WAY OF SAMUEL BUTLER

1. Letter of Jan. 15, 1908, in Evan Charteris, *The Life and Letters of Edmund Gosse* (London, Heinemann, 1931), p. 311.

2. *Father and Son* has often been taken as an indictment of Victorianism, but it is difficult to see how the father's creed, the strict fundamentalism of a narrow sect, could be construed as representative of the Victorian period, for it isolated the Gosses from all but a small congregation of zealots in a remote Devonshire village, and it gave the son a complacent sense of his difference as one of the elect. In the narrative the father's violent destruction of a plum-pudding, the "accursed" symbol of pagan idolatry, seems shockingly eccentric to the housemaids, who would typically be more at home in a world of Dickensian Christmas; and the son's predilection for graveyard poetry properly disturbs the nice normal adults at the Browns' party.

3. We have reason to believe that the young Edmund Gosse was much more smugly pietistic than he admits to being. See G. C. Williamson's account in *London Mercury*, XVIII (1928), 633–634, cited by William Irvine in his admirable introduction to the Riverside Edition of *Father and Son* (Boston, Houghton Mifflin, 1965), p. xxxviii n.

4. Irvine, ed., *Father and Son*, p. 142.

5. *Father and Son*, p. 216.

6. *Father and Son*, p. 210.

7. Gosse conceived of *Father and Son* long before he could have known of *The Way of All Flesh*. In 1890 when he wrote a more orthodox biography of his father (*The Life of Philip Gosse*), George Moore urged him to begin a book on his childhood. The actual writing, however, apparently did not long precede publication in 1907. By this time Gosse was undoubtedly familiar with Butler's novel, posthumously published in 1903. Whenever it began, his interest in Butler persisted for some years. In 1912 he presided at the fifth Erewhon dinner; see Henry Festing Jones, *Samuel Butler . . . a Memoir*, 2 vols. (London, Macmillan, 1919), II, 428. Gosse's critical comments on Butler appeared in his *Aspects and Impres-*

sions (London, Cassell, 1922) and *Leaves and Fruit* (London, Heinemann, 1927).

8. Gosse, "Samuel Butler," *Aspects and Impressions*, p. 63.

9. Butler is not very accurate in his dates. He cites Buckle's *History of Civilisation* and Mill's *Liberty* and remarks that "Ernest and his friends were ignorant of their very existence." This is not surprising in 1858, since *Liberty* did not appear till 1859 and, though the first volume of Buckle came in 1857, the second was not published till 1861. In the same paragraph (the second in Chap. 47) Butler assigns *Essays and Reviews* (1860) to 1859.

10. Quotations in this paragraph from Chaps. 9, 10, 47, 49, 89, of Daniel F. Howard's Riverside Edition, *Ernest Pontifex, or The Way of All Flesh* (Boston, Houghton Mifflin, 1964). This edition follows Butler's manuscript, which was revised for publication in 1903 by R. A. Streatfeild, who preferred the more general title. (Streatfeild also broke the chapters differently after Chap. 64). Since the novel has long had currency as *The Way of All Flesh*, I have not reverted to the manuscript title, though I have adopted the Howard text. In the last clause I have quoted, Streatfeild substituted "the High Priests of Science" for "the Huxleys and Tyndalls."

11. Claude T. Bissell has called it "Butler's attempt to give artistic embodiment to a moral philosophy that grew out of a scientific theory." See Bissell's useful essay on the relation of the theory to the novel, "A Study of *The Way of All Flesh*," Herbert Davis et al., eds., *Nineteenth-Century Studies* (Ithaca, Cornell University Press, 1940), p. 278.

12. Howard ed., Chap. 63.

13. Cf. P. N. Furbank's analysis of Butler's need to "possess," to make each of his enthusiasms distinctly his own, an extension of his own personality: *Samuel Butler (1835–1902)* (Cambridge, Cambridge University Press, 1948), pp. 21–30.

14. Butler dates the release in a footnote to his manuscript; see Howard ed., p. 250n and introduction, p. xviii.

15. That is, *Erewhon* (1872), the first book that Butler saw through the press. He refused to acknowledge *A First Year in Canterbury Settlement* (1863), which his father published without his authorization.

16. The memory is presented with unusual warmth, as if childhood, after all, did provide some happy security: " 'Don't you love the smell of grease about the engine of a channel steamer? Isn't there a lot of hope in it?' said Ernest to me, for he had been to Normandy one summer as a boy with his father and mother and

the smell carried him *back to days before those in which he had begun to bruise himself against the great outside world.*" Howard ed., Chap. 86 (Streatfeild, Chap. 80), italics mine.

17. See Arnold Silver, ed., *The Family Letters of Samuel Butler, 1841–1886* (Stanford, Stanford University Press, 1962). Silver's introduction, though hard on the father, presents a useful review of the relations between father and son.

18. Cf. Silver, pp. 18–19.

19. Howard ed., Chap. 3, p. 11 and note.

20. Letter of August 2, 1874, Geoffrey Keynes and Brian Hill, eds., *Letters between Samuel Butler and Miss E. M. A. Savage, 1871–1885* (London, Cape, 1935), p. 93, quoted also in part by Daniel F. Howard, "The Critical Significance of Autobiography in *The Way of All Flesh,*" *Victorian Newsletter*, No. 17 (Spring 1960), p. 3, an article to which my reading of the novel is much indebted. See also Howard ed., p. vi, on dating of composition.

21. V. S. Pritchett, *The Living Novel* (New York, Random House, 1964), p. 145.

22. Letter of July 2, 1878, *Letters between Butler and Miss Savage*, p. 188.

23. Quotations in this paragraph from Howard ed., Chaps. 28, 12, 89, 83, 16, 50.

24. Quotations from Howard ed., Chaps. 45, 47.

25. Howard ed., Chap. 63.

26. Quotations from Howard ed., Chaps. 24, 44, 86.

27. Letter of Nov. 6, 1874, *Letters between Butler and Miss Savage*, p. 98. Cf. the entry in his *Notebooks*, p. 135: "I do not think I ever disliked a book so much. I cannot call to mind a single character, or even passage, which does not disgust and depress me. I think I must have got hold of some other *Wilhelm Meister* by some other Goethe." Butler may have been led to Goethe's novel by the heavy praise of *Meister* in the preface to Bulwer Lytton's *Ernest Maltravers*, itself a sort of Bildungsroman. Though I do not know that Butler ever read the latter, Bulwer had been very popular throughout Butler's youth, and some reviewers in the early seventies thought him the author of the anonymous *Erewhon*. Butler, who had a number of derogatory things to say about Bulwer, thought the ascription absurd. I suggest that he may have glanced ironically at *Ernest Maltravers* (1837) sometime during the writing of "Ernest Pontifex." He tells us that the name Ernest was selected by George Pontifex at the time of the boy's birth

(1835), since "the word 'earnest' was just beginning to come into fashion." Bulwer's preface describes his novel as the story of an "apprenticeship" to "practical life"; Butler speaks of Ernest's "apprenticeship to life among the poor." The plots are quite dissimilar, but both Ernests have some literary aspirations, and Maltravers's guardian and guide, Frederick Cleveland, an affable, affluent bachelor, strongly resembles Overton.

28. On George Eliot, see letter of Mar. 1873 to Miss Savage, *Letters*, p. 40. On Meredith, who rejected *Erewhon* when Butler sent the manuscript to Chapman and Hall, see Jones, I, 148: "No wonder if his work repels me that mine should repel him." Silver (p. 23) compares Theobald Pontifex with Sir Austin Feverel. On Dickens, a typical slight is Butler's annoyance that Dickens should have been buried next to the great Handel (*Notebooks*, p. 73). But the influence of Dickens is apparent in *The Way of All Flesh:* Mrs. Jupp is clearly in succession from Mrs. Gamp; Aunt Alethea, Ernest's godmother and good angel, plays a role similar to Aunt Betsey's; Overton's return to Paleham for Alethea's funeral is suffused with the nostalgia we associate with David Copperfield's brooding on the past; and the late description of the visit to the home of the Thames bargeman has, it seems to me, a quite Dickensian cadence and animation: "It was a lovely April morning, but with a fresh air blowing off the sea; the tide was high, and the river was alive with shipping coming up with wind and tide. Seagulls wheeled around us overhead, seaweed clung everywhere to the banks which the advancing tide had not yet covered—everything was of the sea—sea-ey. . . ." (Chap. 91).

29. Howard ed., Chap. 68.

30. Howard ed., Chap. 69.

31. *Notebooks*, p. 63.

32. Howard ed., Chap. 86.

33. Howard ed., Chap. 61.

34. Howard ed., Chap. 57. Miss Savage, however, questioned Towneley's niceness (*Letters*, p. 301): "Your Towneley . . . must be toned down. A coarse creature with vicious propensities which he indulges in a slum such as you describe, Ashpit Place!"

35. Howard ed., Chap. 68.

36. Howard ed., Chaps., 73, 87.

37. On the names and "theology," see Sister Mary Bernetta Quinn, O.S.F., "Ernest Pontifex as Anti-hero," *English Fiction in Transition*, V, No. 1 (1962), 30–31. Joseph Bennett suggests that

the name Ernest Pontifex is a play on the pseudonym "Earnest Clergyman," with which Butler signed his letters to the *Examiner;* see Bennett's article, "The Devil in the Flesh: Samuel Butler's 'Confessional' Novel," *Victorian Newsletter,* No. 39 (Spring 1971), p. 28.

38. Letter from Miss Savage, Nov. 17, 1883, *Letters,* p. 302.

39. Howard ed., Chap. 53. In Chap. 52 Butler (or Overton) accuses Ernest of being misled by false analogies, but in 53 he himself makes a questionable analogy between biological evolution and the evolution of religious opinions—it is not clear how or why Methodism leads to Roman Catholicism as the cell becomes the vertebrate.

40. Ernest's "epiphanies," Howard ed., Chaps. 44, 57, 80.

41. Howard ed., Chap. 61.

42. Howard ed., Chaps. 84, 85.

43. Howard ed., Chap. 82.

44. Howard ed., Chaps. 90, 93.

VI. WALTER PATER: THE DISTANCE OF MARIUS

1. *The Renaissance* and *Marius the Epicurean* (Chap. 9), quoted from *The Works of Walter Pater,* 8 vols. (London, Macmillan, 1900), I, 235, II, 150, 154.

2. The young men misled by the hedonistic advice of the "Conclusion" are usually taken to be Pater's admirers, especially Oscar Wilde. I have argued that they were probably his detractors, particularly W. H. Mallock, who caricatured Pater as Mr. Rose in *The New Republic;* see my note, "Pater and the Suppressed 'Conclusion,' " *Modern Language Notes,* LXV (1950), 249–251.

3. Marius as spectator: *Marius,* Chaps. 19, 28, 6, 9. Cf. other references: "essentially but a spectator" (Chap. 4) and "his natural Epicureanism, already prompting him to conceive of himself as but the passive spectator of the world around him" (Chap. 8). On Pater's Brasenose, see A. C. Benson, *Walter Pater* (New York, Macmillan. 1906), pp. 15–20.

4. Marius as poet: *Marius,* Chaps. 4, 9.

5. For speculations on the religion of art and what Pater calls "this 'aesthetic' philosophy" as opposed to conventional morality, see esp. Chap. 9, "New Cyrenaicism."

6. *Marius,* Chap. 16.

7. On Stendhal, see Thomas Wright, *The Life of Walter Pater,* 2 vols. (New York, Putnam, 1907), II, 116. Pater studied Goethe with much care. Cf. Louise Rosenblatt, "The Genesis of Pater's

Marius the Epicurean," *Comparative Literature* XIV (1962), 248: "The repeated references to Wilhelm Meister may not be without significance in Pater's desire to write a *Bildungsroman.*"

8. Marius and education: *Marius,* Chaps. 3, 8, 9, 28.

9. *Marius,* Chap. 13.

10. *Marius,* Chap. 4.

11. *Marius,* Chap. 26.

12. Pater's account of the relationship (Chap. 4) might almost stand as a summary of David's dependence on Steerforth: "Over Marius too his dominion was entire. Three years older than he, Flavian was appointed to help the younger boy in his studies, and Marius thus became virtually his servant in many things, taking his humours with a sort of grateful pride in being noticed at all, and, thinking over all this afterwards, found that the fascination experienced by him had been a sentimental one, dependent on the concession to himself of an intimacy, a certain tolerance of his company, granted to none beside."

13. *Marius,* Chap. 7.

14. Quoted by Wright, II, 116.

15. So Mrs. Humphry Ward suggests in her review of *Marius,* *Macmillan's Magazine,* LII (1885), 133.

16. The following are among the post-classical figures and groups alluded to in *Marius:* Michelet, the *Vicaire Savoyard,* Wilhelm Meister, Swedenborg, Montaigne, Dante, St. Augustine, Louis XIV, Wordsworth, the German *Neuzeit,* "modern French romanticists."

17. *Marius,* Chap. 21, my italics.

18. Chap. 25 of *Marius* is given over to the diary. The phrase "passing by on the other side" comes of course from the parable of the Good Samaritan and seems out of place in the diary since Marius at the time has heard very little of Christian teaching.

19. On the place of the Cupid and Psyche story, there is a considerable difference of opinion. Gerald Cornelius Monsman, in his able study, *Pater's Portraits* (Baltimore, Johns Hopkins Press, 1967), pp. 71–75, gives the story an allegorical reading and argues that it "supplies the key to the novel, for it pinpoints the quest of Marius for the God of Love." It may indeed, I should agree, have some such purpose, but it still seems to me obtrusively long and very oblique. See other articles on the problem: James Hafley, "Walter Pater's *Marius* and the Technique of Modern Fiction," *Modern Fiction Studies,* III (1957), 99–109; Eugene Brzenk, "Pater and Apuleius," *Comparative Literature,* X (1958), 55–60; and Paul Turner, "Pater and Apuleius," *Victorian Studies,* III (1960), 290–296.

20. We must deduce the dates. At the time of Flavian's death (Chap. 8) Marius is eighteen. At nineteen he is ready to go to Rome to study rhetoric and to serve Marcus Aurelius (Chaps. 9, 10). Chap. 17 describes a visit to the palace a year after the first (Chap. 13), presumably when Marius is twenty, just after the death of Lucius Verus, i.e., A.D. 169. Four years apparently elapse, for Chap. 18 dates the "ceremony of the dart" at "the beginning of the year one hundred and seventy-three." Part IV transpires "some years later" (Chap. 20), but not more than four years later, for Marius makes his last journey immediately after the triumph of Marcus Aurelius, which takes place two years after Faustina's death (i.e., in 177—history tells us that the empress died in 175). Marius dies not long after his visit to White-nights. Marcus Aurelius published his first edict against the Christians in 177, but Pater makes no reference to this act. Presumably Marius was a victim of the persecutions in the villages shortly before the edict. Pater may not be strictly accurate in his dating, for he suggests that Marius at the time of his death is somewhat older than this time scheme allows.

21. *Marius*, Chap. 16.

22. *Marius*, Chap. 14. The later and closer parallel would be to the violence in cinema and television.

23. *Marius*, Chap. 11.

24. *Marius*, Chap. 9.

25. *Marius*, Chap. 14, "Manly Amusement," the whole of which is of climactic importance.

26. On style, *Marius*, Chaps. 5, 6.

27. See Chap. 9: "For the male element, the logical conscience asserted itself now, with opening manhood—asserted itself, even in his literary style, by a certain firmness of outline, that touch of the worker in metal, amid its richness. Already he blamed instinctively alike in his work and in himself, as youth so seldom does, all that had not passed a long and liberal process of erasure."

28. *Marius*, Chaps. 14, 27.

29. *Marius*, Chap. 27. The sentiment of this passage recalls Pip's acceptance of Magwitch, which is the mark of his own regeneration: "For now my repugnance to him had all melted away" (*Great Expectations*, Chap. 54).

30. *Marius*, Chap. 2. Pater shared Marius's aversion to snakes; see Wright, II, 89, for his horrified reaction to a snake bracelet worn by Mrs. William Sharp.

31. At least, I assume that Marius is remembering Flavian's death

and the "feeling of outrage, or resentment against nature itself, mingled with an agony of pity" (Chap. 7). Pater, with characteristic indirectness, repeats the phrasing but not Flavian's name; as Marius contemplates the likely end of his own sickness, "a consciousness of waste would come with half-angry tears of self-pity, in his great weakness—a blind, outraged, angry feeling of wasted power, such as he might have experienced himself standing by the deathbed of another, in condition like his own" (Chap. 28). Another novelist would have made it quite clear that Marius has his friend in mind, not just the vague and general "deathbed of another."

32. *Marius*, Chap. 3.

33. "The impression thus forced upon Marius connected itself with a feeling, the inverse of that, known to every one, which seems to say, *You have been just here, just thus, before!*—a feeling, in his case, not reminiscent but prescient of the future, which passed over him afterwards many times, as he came across certain places and people" (Chap. 7).

34. *Marius*, Chap. 19.

35. Monsman (pp. 78–79) calls attention to the parallel to St. Paul's warrior against the devil (Ephesians 6:11–17) and points out that Cornelius was also the name of the centurion baptized by St. Peter (Acts 10). We should not push the parallel too far, for it is difficult to see how Cornelius, in his capacity as a Roman soldier, can war "against the rulers of the darkness of this world."

36. *Marius*, Chaps. 10, 14.

37. Letter of Mar. 1, 1885, Lawrence Gove Evans, ed., *Letters of Walter Pater* (London, Oxford University Press, 1970), pp. 86–87.

38. *Marius*, Chap. 16.

39. *Marius*, Chap. 28.

40. T. S. Eliot, "Arnold and Pater," *Selected Essays* (New York, Harcourt Brace, 1932), p. 356.

41. Pater may have seen Jules Lemaître's *Serenus*, published in France in 1883, before he wrote the last chapters of *Marius* (see Rosenblatt article, cited above, p. 7). Pater reviewed the translation of *Serenus* in *Macmillan's Magazine* in 1887; see *Uncollected Essays by Walter Pater* (Portland, Me., Mosher, 1903), pp. 15–48. Pater's own attitude toward Christianity, however, was quite different from Lemaître's; in 1885, shortly after the publication of *Marius*, he wrote: "The supposed facts on which Christianity rests, utterly incapable as they have become of any ordinary test, seem

to me matters of very much the same sort of assent we give to any assumption, in the strict and ultimate sense, moral" (Evans, pp. 95–96, letter of Dec. 23, 1885, to Mrs. Ward).

VII. THOMAS HARDY: THE OBSCURITY OF JUDE

1. Rubric College is identified as Brasenose by a note in Hardy's hand, reproduced by Clive Holland, *Thomas Hardy: The Man, His Works and the Land of Wessex* (London, Jenkins, 1933), p. 144. See also William R. Rutland, *Thomas Hardy* (Oxford, Blackwell, 1938), p. 247. The relevant passage in *Jude the Obscure* occurs in Part VI, Chap. 2.

2. Hardy met Pater soon after the publication of *Marius,* and Pater visited him several times in London during his illness in July 1888; for Hardy's comment and other details, see Florence Emily Hardy, *The Early Life of Thomas Hardy* (New York, Macmillan, 1928), pp. 236, 275, 278.

3. *Marius,* Chap. 25; *Jude,* Part I, Chap. 2.

4. *Jude,* Part I, Chap. 2.

5. In view of the title of the last chapter of *Marius* ("Anima Naturaliter Christiana"), it is interesting that Walter Allen—without reference to Pater's novel—speaks of Hardy as "a soul naturally Christian." We may readily describe Jude Fawley in the same terms. See Allen, *The English Novel* (New York, Dutton, 1957), p. 288, and cf. David Cecil, who contrasts Hardy's pessimism and Christianity, *Hardy the Novelist* (Indianapolis, Bobbs-Merrill, 1943), p. 222.

6. F. E. Hardy, *Early Life,* pp. 272–273.

7. On the publication of *Jude,* see Richard L. Purdy, *Thomas Hardy: A Bibliographical Study* (London, Oxford University Press, 1954), pp. 86–91. On the difference between the serial and the novel, see Mary Ellen Chase, *Thomas Hardy from Serial to Novel* (Minneapolis, University of Minnesota Press, 1927), pp. 113–177.

8. See F. E. Hardy, *The Later Years of Thomas Hardy* (New York, Macmillan, 1930), p. 196. Like much else in the two F. E. Hardy volumes, this is Hardy's own comment dictated to his wife or paraphrased in her words.

9. See Evelyn Hardy, *Thomas Hardy* (London, Hogarth Press, 1954), p. 249. Rutland (p. 246) also remarks on the subjective element in *Jude:* "Hardy wrote no autobiography; but there is more to be seen of his inner life, by those who have eyes to see, in *Jude the Obscure* than in any other novel."

10. See Purdy, p. 89.

11. *Jude*, Part I, Chap. 2; F. E. Hardy, *Early Life*, p. 19; "Childhood among the Ferns," *Human Shows and Winter Words* (London, Macmillan, 1931), p. 263. A number of scholars, with a purpose rather different from mine, have called attention to these parallels—e.g., Purdy (p. 255) or Evelyn Hardy (p. 17).

12. See Carl J. Weber, *Hardy of Wessex* (Hamden, Conn., Archon Books, 1962), p. 144. Robert Heilman also lists parallels between Hardy and Jude in his introduction to the novel (New York, Harper and Row, 1966), p. 21.

13. "Thoughts of Phena," from *Wessex Poems, The Collected Poems of Thomas Hardy* (New York, Macmillan, 1928), p. 55.

14. See Lois Deacon and Terry Coleman, *Providence and Mr Hardy* (London, Hutchinson, 1968), an expansion of Miss Deacon's 1962 pamphlet *Tryphena and Thomas Hardy*. The authors present a fairly convincing case for some sort of affair between Hardy and Tryphena Sparks, but they have only quite questionable evidence to support their contentions that the lovers had a natural son, Randy (the original of little Father Time?), and that a marriage proved impossible since Tryphena was the illegitimate daughter of the illegitimate daughter of Hardy's mother! The main support for such speculation was an interview with Tryphena's daughter, a sadly confused old lady of eighty-six. F. R. Southerington repeats the tale and even includes photographs of Tryphena and the alleged son in his edition of *Jude* (Indianapolis, Bobbs-Merrill, 1972), along with some new and still highly dubious "evidence."

15. Citing *Wilhelm Meister* and *Faust*, Hardy ranks Goethe with Sophocles and Milton in "Candour in Engish Fiction," in the *New Review*, January 1890, reprinted by Harold Orel, ed., *Thomas Hardy's Personal Writings* (Lawrence, University of Kansas Press, 1966), p. 131n.

16. See Hardy's late reminiscence of Meredith, Orel, pp. 151–155.

17. F. E. Hardy, *Early Life*, p. 129.

18. I base the date on internal evidence. When Jude first comes to Christminster, we find Sue reading Swinburne's "Hymn to Proserpine," which was published in 1866 in *Poems and Ballads*, though Sue may not have acquired the volume until a year or two later. Jude returns, he himself tells us (Part VI, Chap. 1), to Christminster "eight or nine years later." Hardy of course may not have the precise Swinburne date in mind. Weber (p. 182) gives the action the earliest possible dates, 1855–1874. I suggest a death date of 1876 or 1877.

19. Letter of November 10, 1895, in F. E. Hardy, *Later Years*,

p. 40. Hillis Miller also briefly compares Jude to Pip but suggests that Hardy's protagonists, generally, live in a world where they are not wanted. See his *Thomas Hardy: Distance and Desire* (Cambridge, Mass., Harvard University Press, 1970), p. 3.

20. *Jude*, Part I, Chap. 2.
21. *Jude*, Part I, Chap. 7.
22. *Jude*, Part IV, Chap. 5. "Convention" here is public opinion, but Sue has also attacked conventional theology and has undermined many of Jude's old illusions about the sacredness of Christminster traditions.
23. *Jude*, Part V, Chap. 3.
24. *Jude*, Part V, Chap. 8.
25. *Jude*, Part VI, Chap. 1.
26. *Jude*, Part V, Chap. 8.
27. Wells, unsigned review of *Jude*, *Saturday Review*, Feb. 8, 1896, p. 154.
28. *Jude*, Part V, Chap. 1.
29. Letter of Nov. 10, 1895, F. E. Hardy, *Later Years*, p. 41.
30. Hardy belonged to the Independent Theatre Association founded in 1891 to promote knowledge of Ibsen, and in 1893 he attended performances of *Hedda Gabler, Rosmersholm,* and *The Master Builder* (see Rutland, pp. 252–253). Cecil (pp. 188–189, 189n) suggests that *Rosmersholm* was an influence on *Jude* and that Sue may derive from the character of Rebecca West in that play.
31. *Jude*, Part V, Chap. 1. Other Victorian novels suggest that divorce even for the humble was often a long, complicated, and expensive process.
32. *Jude*, Part V, Chap. 5.
33. *Jude*, Part VI, Chap. 8.
34. *Jude*, Part VI, Chap. 4.
35. *Jude*, Part 1, Chap. 6.
36. Letter of Sept. 20, 1926, F. E. Hardy, *Later Years*, p. 249.
37. *Jude*, Part VI, Chap. 3.
38. *Jude*, Part I, Chap. 7.
39. *Jude*, Part IV, Chap. 1.
40. *Jude*, Part II, Chap. 6.
41. *Jude*, Part IV, Chap. 1.
42. *Jude*, Part IV, Chap. 4.
43. *Jude*, Part V, Chap. 5.
44. *Jude*, Part V, Chap. 7.
45. *Jude*, Part VI, Chap. 3.
46. *Jude*, Part VI, Chap. 4.
47. See, for example, Cecil, p. 120, or Desmond Hawkins,

Thomas Hardy (London, Barker, 1950), p. 17, and esp. D. H. Lawrence, "A Study of Thomas Hardy," reprinted in part from Lawrence's *Phoenix* (1936) by Albert J. Guerard, ed., *Hardy* (Englewood Cliffs, N.J., Prentice-Hall, 1963), pp. 71–76. Cf. the judgment of Arthur Mizener, "*Jude the Obscure* as a Tragedy," *Southern Review*, VI (1940), 208: "Sue has twice Jude's quickness of wit and half his strength of character."

48. Letter of Nov. 20, 1895, F. E. Hardy, *Later Years*, p. 42.

49. See Part V, Chap. 5, which describes the visit to the Stoke-Barehills fair: "Sue adored roses, . . . and put her face within an inch of their blooms to smell them. 'I should like to push my face quite into them—the dears!' she had said."

50. *Jude*, Part III, Chap. 7.

51. *Jude*, Part VI, Chap. 3, and Part IV, Chap. 5.

52. *Jude*, Part V, Chap. 5.

53. *Jude*, Part I, Chap. 3.

54. See *Jude*, Part II, Chap. 6, and Part VI, Chap. 1.

55. *Jude*, Part I, Chaps. 2, 11 and Part V, Chap. 4.

56. Jude as a child discovers nature's cruelty (Part I, Chap. 2). Sue tells Phillotson that the universe is "horrid and cruel" (Part IV, Chap. 3). Phillotson tells Arabella that "cruelty is the law pervading all nature and society" (Part V, Chap. 8). Jude reflects on "the scorn of Nature" (Part III, Chap. 8).

57. *Jude*, Part VI, Chap. 3.

58. *Jude*, Part VI, Chap. 1.

59. *Jude*, Part VI, Chaps. 3, 10.

60. H. C. Webster, *On a Darkling Plain: The Art and Thought of Thomas Hardy* (Chicago, University of Chicago Press, 1947), p. 187.

61. A diary note, "probably about the end of August" (1895), quoted by F. E. Hardy, *Later Years*, p. 37.

62. A diary entry of Oct. 1892, quoted by F. E. Hardy, *Later Years*, p. 14. We may assume that Hardy is thinking of *Jude* since earlier in the same month he made his visit to Great Fawley, Berkshire, the Marygreen of the novel.

63. John 15:17–19. October 28 is the feast of Saint Simon and Saint Jude. I have no evidence that Hardy actually had this text in mind, though he was of course familiar with the Anglican Prayer Book. Some association between Jude and St. Jude seems to me far more likely than the relation that Norman Holland, Jr., tries to establish between Jude and "Jew," on the basis of the German word for the latter, *Jude*. Holland offers an interesting though often far-fetched and ultimately unconvincing reading of

the novel as a sustained attack on Christianity: *"Jude the Obscure:* Hardy's Symbolic Indictment of Christianity," *Nineteenth-Century Fiction,* IX (1954), 50–60.

64. Aunt Drusilla quotes Job to Jude (Part I, Chap. 2). Jude writes a verse from Job on the wall of Biblioll College (Part II, Chap. 6). Jude dreads the thought of his son's ever having to say, "Let the day perish wherein I was born" (Part V, Chap. 3), ironically one of the verses he repeats on his own deathbed, Part VI, Chap. 11).

VIII. H. G. WELLS: THE HERO AS SCIENTIST

1. *Tono-Bungay,* last sentence of Bk. II and first sentence of Bk. III.

2. *Tono-Bungay,* Bk. I, Chap. 1, sec. 2.

3. That is, self-consciously opposed to the practice of Henry James, whose authority Wells was beginning to resist. See Wells, *Experiment in Autobiography* (New York, Macmillan, 1934), p. 423.

4. Cf. Wells's own comments on *Tono-Bungay, Experiment,* p. 33, and "Preface" to the Atlantic Edition (1925): "The writer is disposed to regard it as the finest and most finished novel upon the accepted lines that he has written or is ever likely to write."

5. Efforts at verisimilitude, *Tono-Bungay,* Bk. III, Chap. 1, sec. 2, and III, 3, secs. 1 and 4.

6. *Tono-Bungay,* Bk. I, Chap. 1, secs. 1 and 2.

7. One small detail seems a close parallel to *Great Expectations.* When Beatrice first meets George, she snobbishly asks, "Is he a servant boy?" and remarks, "He's got dirty hands. . . . And there's a fray to his collar" (Bk. I, Chap. 1, sec. 7). With this compare Estella's introduction to Pip and her comment to Miss Havisham, "Why, he is a common labouring-boy! . . . And what coarse hands he has! And what thick boots!" (*Great Expectations,* Chap. 8). On hands in Dickens's novel, see above, Chap. II, n. 40.

8. *Tono-Bungay,* Bk. I, Chap. 2, sec. 1.

9. *Tono-Bungay,* Bk. I, Chap. 1, sec. 1.

10. *Tono-Bungay,* Bk. I, Chap. 1, sec. 9, and I, 2, sec. 3.

11. There are autobiographical elements in many of Wells's novels and stories, e.g., "A Slip under the Microscope," *Love and Mr. Lewisham, Kipps, Mr. Polly,* "The Door in the Wall," *The New Machiavelli, Joan and Peter, The World of William Clissold.*

12. Compare the gastronomic adventures of Teddy and Aunt Susan, Bk. III, Chap. 2, secs. 3 and 4, with the less ambitious sam-

pling by Wells and the second Mrs. Wells, described in *Experiment*, pp. 447–449, 541.

13. The chronology of *Tono-Bungay* is a bit confused. If we assume that George is writing his narrative at the same time as Wells is at work on the novel, the year is 1908. Since George announces that he has now reached forty-five (Bk. II, Chap. 4, sec. 2), his birth date would be 1863. Unless he is speaking in loose general terms, he is therefore slightly older than Wells, who was born in 1866. George says that he was twenty-four when he married Marion and at that time he had already read Grant Allen's novel *The Woman Who Did*. But since that immensely popular book did not appear until 1895, George at the end could not be more than thirty-seven if indeed he read it before his marriage. I take it that this is merely a careless slip and that in approaching *Tono-Bungay* we are wisest to assume that George and Wells are approximately the same age.

14. See the account of Uppark, with illustrations, including a photograph of the kitchen where Wells wrote his *Uppark Alarmist*, in Nigel Nicolson, *Great Houses of Britain* (London, Spring Books, 1965), pp. 152–157. ("Uppark" is usually so spelled, though it appears in Wells's *Experiment* as "Up Park.")

15. *Tono-Bungay*, II, Chap. 1, sec. 6.

16. Geoffrey West, *H. G. Wells* (London, Howe, 1930), p. 89.

17. See the note in Bennett's journal quoted by Reginald Pound, *Arnold Bennett* (New York, Harcourt Brace, 1953), p. 262. Wells's recent biographer Lovat Dickson presents him as a persistent and rather vulgar amorist all through the years of his second marriage (1895–1927); see Dickson, *H. G. Wells, His Turbulent Life and Times* (New York, Atheneum, 1969).

18. George on his love life: Bk. II, Chap. 4, secs. 1 and 11; III, 3, sec. 7; IV, 2, sec. 2.

19. *Tono-Bungay*, Bk. I, Chap. 4, sec. 10.

20. *Tono-Bungay*, Bk. I, Chap. 3, sec. 3.

21. *Tono-Bungay*, Bk. II, Chap. 4, sec. 10; I, 1, sec. 8.

22. *Tono-Bungay*, Bk. IV, Chap. 1, sec. 2.

23. *Tono-Bungay*, Bk. II, Chap. 2, sec. 2.

24. All quotations in this paragraph from Bk. II, Chap. 4, sec. 10. With the last, cf. J. S. Mill (*Autobiography*, Chap. V): "I was in a dull state of nerves, . . . the state, I should think, in which converts to Methodism usually are, when smitten by their first 'conviction of sin.'" The passage in *Tono-Bungay* seems a direct echo. George continues, "I sought salvation—not perhaps in the formulae a Methodist preacher would recognise—but salvation nevertheless."

25. *Tono-Bungay*, Bk. II, Chap. 1, sec. 6; I, 3, sec. 3; III, 3, sec. 1.

26. David Lodge sees England as the principal character of the novel; see Lodge, "Tono-Bungay and the Condition of England," in his *Language of Fiction* (London, Routledge and Kegan Paul, 1966). Kenneth B. Newell sees the life cycle of the organism, especially the social organism, as one of the unifying metaphors of the novel; see Newell, "The Structure of H. G. Wells's *Tono-Bungay*," *English Fiction in Transition*, IV² (1961), 1–8.

27. Quotations in this paragraph from Bk. I, Chap. 3, sec. 5; III, 1, sec. 3; IV, 1, sec. 2. On Whitaker Wright and parallels to Teddy, see Ingvald Raknem, *H. G. Wells and His Critics* (Oslo, Universitetsvorlaget, 1962), pp. 255–258.

28. See Virginia Woolf, "Mr. Bennett and Mrs. Brown," *The Captain's Deathbed and Other Essays* (New York, Harcourt Brace, 1950), p. 112: "They [Wells, Bennett, Galsworthy] have laid an enormous stress upon the fabric of things. They have given us a house in the hope that we may be able to deduce the human beings who live there."

29. *Tono-Bungay*, Bk. III, Chap. 4, sec. 5; IV, 1, secs. 4 and 8.

30. Wells's son, Anthony West, comments revealingly on his father's disposition: "He was by nature a pessimist, and he was doing violence to his intuitions and his rational perceptions alike when he asserted in his middle period that mankind could make a better world for itself by an effort of the will." See West, "H. G. Wells," *Encounter*, VIII (1957), 53. This passage is also cited by R. H. Costa, *H. G. Wells* (New York, Twayne, 1967), p. 149.

31. *Tono-Bungay*, Bk. IV, Chap. 3, sec. 1.

32. See J. Kagarlitski, *The Life and Thought of H. G. Wells*, trans. Moura Budberg (London, Sidgwick and Jackson, 1966), p. 167: "He sails away to return later to his native shores [George actually returns the next morning] and Wells leaves us in no doubt against whom his ship's guns will be turned—against Vulgarity, Meanness, Mediocrity, Spiritual Slavery, against the System." In a less doctrinaire fashion Patrick Parrinder also discusses the sick society of the novel, in his *H. G. Wells* (Edinburgh, Oliver and Boyd, 1970), pp. 66–78.

IX. D. H. LAWRENCE: THE BURDEN OF APOLOGY

1. Lawrence on *Tono-Bungay*, letters to Blanche Jennings, Harry T. Moore, ed., *The Collected Letters of D. H. Lawrence*, 2 vols. (New York, Viking, 1962), I, 51, 54; cf. I, 60. See also James

T. Boulton, ed., *Lawrence in Love: Letters to Louie Burrows* (Nottingham, University of Nottingham Press, 1968), p. 31.

2. See Jessie Chambers, "E. T.," *D. H. Lawrence*, p. 121. On meeting Wells in November 1909, however, Lawrence was less intimidated; the great man in fact disappointed him—"There is no glow in him," Lawrence told Louie Burrows (*Lawrence in Love*, p. 46).

3. On Borrow, Chambers, p. 110.

4. On *Wilhelm Meister*, letter of March 27, 1928, to Aldous Huxley, *Collected Letters*, II, 1049. Edward Engelberg also cites this passage and comments on Lawrence's view of *Wilhelm Meister* and Lawrence's general awareness of the Bildungsroman and its development in England; see his perceptive study of *The Rainbow* (with some pertinent remarks on *Sons and Lovers*, too) as a variation of the genre, "Escape from the Circles of Experience: D. H. Lawrence's *The Rainbow* as a Modern *Bildungsroman*," *PMLA*, LXXVIII (1963), 103-113.

5. On Stendhal, see *Lawrence in Love*, p. 100 (letter of April 28, 1911): "It is a terrible book which almost makes me laugh. Life seems such an escapade. And I feel so much like Julien Sorel— except that, of course, I am English and sentimentalist. . . . I marvel at Stendhal's wonderful cleverness. . . . Yet he misses out the religion, the philosophy, if you like, of life. He is not a bit metaphysical. He doesn't satisfy my sentimentality."

6. On *David Copperfield*, see Harry T. Moore, *The Intelligent Heart: The Life of D. H. Lawrence* (New York, Grove Press, 1962), p. 88. For a useful list and chronology, see Rose Marie Burwell, "A Catalogue of D. H. Lawrence's Readings from Early Childhood," *D. H. Lawrence Review*, III (1970), 193-324. *David Copperfield* is cited as early as 1904, though Lawrence probably read it much earlier still.

7. On George Eliot, see Moore, *Intelligent Heart*, pp. 89, 95, and Chambers, p. 98 (quoted above, Chap. IV, p. 105).

8. On *Richard Feverel*, letter of Dec. 27, 1910, to Louie Burrows, *Lawrence in Love*, p. 73.

9. On *Jude*, see Burwell, p. 219, and "A Study of Thomas Hardy," written shortly after *Sons and Lovers*, posthumously published in *Phoenix* (New York, Viking, 1936).

10. *Sons and Lovers*, Chap. 5.

11. *Sons and Lovers*, Chap. 10.

12. *Sons and Lovers*, Chaps. 11, 12, 13.

13. *Sons and Lovers*, Chap. 7.

14. *Sons and Lovers*, Chap. 8.

15. In addition to Jessie Chambers's memoir and the appendix to the 1965 edition by her sister May, see esp. Ada Lawrence and G. Stuart Gelder, *Young Lorenzo* (Florence, Orioli, 1931); Helen Corke, *D. H. Lawrence: The Croydon Years* (Austin, University of Texas Press, 1965); Frieda Lawrence, *Not I, But the Wind* (New York, Viking, 1934); W. E. Hopkin's memoir in Edward Nehls, ed., *D. H. Lawrence: A Composite Biography*, 3 vols. (Madison, University of Wisconsin Press, 1957–1959); and Lawrence's atuobiographical sketch, "Nottingham and the Mining Countryside," written in the last years of his life and first published in *Phoenix*. Some of these items and a good deal of other interesting material are included in Julian Moynahan's edition of *Sons and Lovers* in the Viking Critical Library (1968). See also the collection of sources and criticism edited by E. W. Tedlock, Jr., *D. H. Lawrence and "Sons and Lovers"* (New York, New York University Press, 1965).

16. See Chambers, appendix, p. 235. Cf. also May's report (p. 234) of Mrs. Lawrence's comment on her son's relation to his father: "He hates his father. . . . He keeps his distance, he never goes near him if he can help it." Jessie reports a similar statement by Mrs. Lawrence (p. 138). Lawrence himself (*Collected Letters*, I, 69) wrote at the time of his mother's last illness, "I was born hating my father: as early as I can remember, I shivered with horror when he touched me."

17. See Corke, p. 20.

18. Quotations from Chambers, pp. 133, 128, 136, 69, 184, 203. The real epilogue to Jessie's story may be Helen Corke's account (Corke, p. 45) of meeting her years later, in 1940, as a bitter broken woman, resentful of anyone who had known Lawrence.

19. Chambers, p. 216, also in *Collected Letters*, I, 127. On Jessie's collaboration and her notes, see Harry T. Moore, *Life and Works of D. H. Lawrence* (New York, Twayne, 1951), pp. 365–387, also in Tedlock, pp. 45–62.

20. I am not sure that I should go quite as far as Frank O'Connor, who asserts of *Sons and Lovers*, "Absolutely, the opening half is the greatest thing in English fiction." See O'Connor, *The Mirror in the Roadway* (New York, Knopf, 1955), p. 272.

21. *Sons and Lovers*, Chap. 4.

22. For Lawrence's opinions of *Sons and Lovers*, see his letters to Edward Garnett, Mar. 11, May 19, July 16 (?), Dec. 30, 1913, *Collected Letters*, I, 193, 205, 213, 259; the last of these declares, "I shan't write in the same manner as *Sons and Lovers* again, I think—in that hard, violent style full of sensation and presentation."

23. Lawrence, "Morality and the Novel" (1925), *Selected Literary Criticism* (New York, Viking, 1966), p. 111.

24. *Sons and Lovers*, Chap. 2.

25. Both of these epiphanies occur in Chap. 7.

26. *Sons and Lovers*, Chap. 7.

27. *Sons and Lovers*, the ending of Chap. 13.

28. Letter of Oct. 27, 1913, to A. D. McLeod, *Collected Letters*, I, 234.

29. Tedlock suggests (p. 73) that the final title readily invites a psychological, especially a Freudian, reading of the novel, whereas *Paul Morel* implies a "traditional hero-centered, picaresquely plotted narrative."

30. Letter of Nov. 14, 1912, *Collected Letters*, I, 160–161.

31. Jessie Chambers, reported by Helen Corke, p. 43.

32. Lawrence's poem "Last Words to Miriam" makes a similar charge: Miriam is blamed for enduring the speaker's love rather than responding to it. The last stanza, however, goes beyond the novel with the admission, "I should have been cruel enough to bring / You through the flame." See Vivian de Sola Pinto and F. Warren Roberts, eds., *The Complete Poems of D. H. Lawrence* (New York, Viking Press, 1971), pp. 111–112.

33. *Sons and Lovers*, Chap. 13.

34. *Sons and Lovers*, Chap. 4.

35. *Sons and Lovers*, Chap. 5.

36. *Sons and Lovers*, Chap. 9.

37. *Sons and Lovers*, Chap. 8.

38. *Sons and Lovers*, Chap. 13.

39. See Frieda Lawrence, p. 56, and Tedlock, pp. 36–37.

40. Letter of Sept. 11, 1916, to Barbara Low, *Collected Letters*, I, 475.

41. Preface sent to Garnett in January 1913, in Aldous Huxley, ed. *Letters of D. H. Lawrence* (New York, Viking, 1932), p. 104.

42. Alfred Booth Kuttner, "*Sons and Lovers:* A Freudian Appreciation," *Psychoanalytic Review*, III (1916), 295–317.

43. *Sons and Lovers*, Chap. 14.

44. The homosexual implications are clear but not as pervasive as in *Women in Love*, where Rupert Birkin is fiercely drawn to Gerald Crich (though even *Women in Love* is evasive). For whatever reason, the young Lawrence was fascinated by the theme. Frank O'Connor (*Mirror*, p. 276) comments on the confused motives in the latter part of *Sons and Lovers:* "The real trouble is that Paul Morel is not in love with Clara, but with Dawes."

45. *Sons and Lovers*, Chaps. 9, 15.

46. On flowers, see *Sons and Lovers*, Chaps. 7, 9, 11. Cf. Frieda Lawrence, p. 35. Richard Aldington also comments on Paul's communion with flowers, in his *Portrait of a Genius, But* . . . (London, Heinemann, 1950), pp. 40–41. Gudrun in *Women in Love* (Chap. 18) also caresses flowers with a "reverential, almost ecstatic admiration" and is not censured for doing so.

47. *Sons and Lovers*, Chap. 15.

48. *Sons and Lovers*, Chap. 9.

49. *Sons and Lovers*, Chap. 10.

50. It has been suggested that Lawrence's own early ethic owes something to such sources in Nottingham; see John Beer, "Ford's Impression of the Lawrences," *Times Literary Supplement*, May 5, 1972, p. 520.

51. Jessie Chambers in a letter to Helen Corke after Lawrence's death, Corke, p. 40.

52. Cf. *Sons and Lovers*, Chap. 15: "He could not paint. The picture he finished on the day of his mother's death—one that satisfied him—was the last thing he did."

53. *Sons and Lovers*, Chap. 15. Though it appears as "whispered" in some editions, "whimpered" is apparently the correct reading, and as such it detracts from the sense of affirmation that some critics have tried to read into the lines that follow, the last short paragraph of the novel. On "whimpered" see Harry T. Moore, "A Postscript," Tedlock, pp. 63–65. Professor Moore does not point out that the line must be an echo of one in Chap. 6: " 'Mother!' Paul whimpered, his hand round her waist." This early passage, like the late one, describes how death comes between mother and son, here the death of William, which for a time makes Mrs. Morel neglect Paul. On both occasions Paul feels abandoned and betrayed.

54. Boulton, *Lawrence in Love*, p. 73.

X. PORTRAIT OF JAMES JOYCE AS A YOUNG AESTHETE

1. Chester G. Anderson, ed., *A Portrait of the Artist as a Young Man* (New York, Viking, 1968), p. 215. All references that follow are to this excellent critical edition, which contains, in addition to the text, many useful ancillary materials.

2. On Joyce and Goethe, see Edmund L. Epstein, *The Ordeal of Stephen Dedalus* (Carbondale, Ill., University of Southern Illinois Press, 1971), pp. 128–129, 200. Epstein cites three mentions of Goethe in *Stephen Hero* and one in the published *Portrait*. He argues that the battle of the puppets David and Goliath in *Meister*

suggested to Joyce the struggle of the artist against a hostile public. I suggest the theme of self-directed *Bildung* as the most striking parallel between *Meister* and the *Portrait*.

3. Ezra Pound's comment appears in a letter of Aug. 3, 1915, recommending Joyce for a grant from the Royal Literary Fund, Richard Ellmann, ed., *James Joyce: Letters*, 3 vols. (New York, Viking, 1966), II, 359. I do not know when Joyce first read Stendhal, but in the 1920's he told George Antheil to begin his serious reading of fiction with *Le Rouge et le Noir* and *La Chartreuse de Parme:* see Ellmann's biography, *James Joyce* (New York, Oxford University Press, 1959), p. 568n (hereafter cited as Ellmann).

4. On Hardy, see Stanislaus Joyce, *My Brother's Keeper* (New York, Viking, 1958), pp. 74–75, and Ellmann, p. 54.

5. On Butler, see Epstein, *Ordeal of Dedalus*, pp. 3–4, and Epstein's article, "James Joyce and *The Way of All Flesh*," *James Joyce Quarterly*, VII (1969), 22–29.

6. On Meredith, see Ellsworth Mason and Richard Ellmann, eds., *The Critical Writings* of *James Joyce* (London, Faber, 1959), pp. 88–89 (Joyce curiously claims that Meredith's novels lack "the lyrical impulse" but adds that they have "a distinct value as philosophical essays"). See also Ellmann, p. 54. Joyce was annoyed when his friend C. P. Curran detected the influence of Meredith on *Stephen Hero;* see Curran, *James Joyce Remembered* (London, Oxford University Press, 1968), pp. 32, 50. Donald Fanger, reviewing Meredith's influence, sees a parallel between Lucy and the seaside girl and points to a foreshadowing of the interior monologue in Meredith's late novel *One of Our Conquerors;* see Donald S. Fanger, "Joyce and Meredith," *Modern Fiction Studies*, VI (1960), 125–130. Joyce remembered *Richard Feverel* well enough, when writing *Ulysses*, to quote (almost accurately) an epigram from Chap. 28: "Sentimentalists . . . are they who seek to enjoy Reality without incurring the Immense Debtorship for a thing done." (In *Ulysses* the epigram is turned against Stephen Dedalus.)

7. "A Portrait of the Artist," reprinted by Anderson, *Portrait*, p. 259. The essay was first published by Robert Scholes and Richard M. Kain in the *Yale Review* (Spring 1960) and then in their useful gathering, *The Workshop of Dedalus* (Evanston, Ill., Northwestern University Press, 1965), pp. 60–68.

8. Quoted by Anderson, *Portrait*, 492.

9. Eliot, quoted by Virginia Woolf, *A Writer's Diary* (New York, New American Library, 1968), p. 57 (entry of Sept. 26, 1922).

10. On copying out *Marius*, see W. Y. Tindall's note to his edition of Joyce's *Chamber Music* (New York, Columbia University Press, 1954), p. 23.

11. *Portrait*, pp. 158–159, 176.

12. *Marius*, Chap. 6. Pater goes on to describe Flavian's principle that to command an audience he must first know his own standards and interests (and we can readily see Stephen endorsing Flavian's belief and deportment): "It was a principle, the forcible apprehension of which made him jealous and fastidious in the selection of his intellectual food; often listless while others read or gazed diligently; never pretending to be moved out of complaisance to other people's emotions: it served to foster in him a very scrupulous literary sincerity with himself."

13. On Wordsworth, see postcard to Stanislaus Joyce, June 11, 1905, *Letters*, II, 91; see also II, 90, where Joyce selects Wordsworth, Shakespeare, and Shelley for heaviest emphasis in the literature course he designs for the Trieste school.

14. Ellmann, p. 307.

15. *Portrait*, pp. 164–165.

16. In *Ulysses* Stephen perhaps does learn what the heart is, but that lies outside the *Portrait* and is not to be predicted by what the *Portrait* tells us.

17. *Portrait*, p. 98.

18. On the gentleman, *Portrait*, pp. 9, 83–84, 91.

19. Theodore Spencer, ed., *Stephen Hero* (Norfolk, Conn., New Directions, 1963), p. 248.

20. *Stephen Hero*, p. 211.

21. *Portrait*, pp. 150–151.

22. *Portrait*, p. 84.

23. On words, *Portrait*, pp. 9, 62.

24. Cf. Harry Levin's interesting analysis of the ending of Chap. 4 and his comment on the girl by the sea: "This is incantation, and not description. Joyce is thinking in rhythms rather than metaphors." Levin, *James Joyce* (London, Faber, 1960), p. 55. Frank O'Connor also passes stringent judgment on the passage as "insufferably self-conscious": O'Connor, *The Mirror in the Roadway* (New York, Knopf, 1956), p. 304. Others argue that Joyce's overwriting is deliberate and intended to mock Stephen.

25. Hugh Kenner's close analysis of the opening supports his belief that the first two pages "enact the entire action in microcosm": Kenner, *Dublin's Joyce* (Bloomington, Ind., Indiana University Press, 1956), p. 114. See also William York Tindall, *A*

Reader's Guide to James Joyce (New York, Noonday Press, 1959), pp. 86–93.

26. See Julian B. Kaye, "Who is Betty Byrne?" *Modern Language Notes*, LXXI (1956), 93–95, and also C. G. Anderson, "The Sacrificial Butter," *Accent*, XII (1952), 3–13. One of Joyce's late letters, however, suggests that Betty Byrne was in fact a very old woman (clearly not J. F. Byrne's mother and not St. Elizabeth) who sold Joyce delectable sweets when he was a small boy (*Letters*, III, 428).

27. On *Stephen Hero*, see Theodore Spencer's introduction (1944) to the text and also Joseph Prescott, *Exploring James Joyce* (Carbondale, Ill., Southern Illinois University Press, 1964), pp. 17–28.

28. See marked proof of *The Egoist* serial version and typescript of later corrections in British Museum (BM/C116/h6 and BM/C116/c6). Most of the corrections show Joyce's eagerness to attain greater precision and continuity; Joyce deletes many commas, drops many capitals, runs compounds together like new words to render a more immediate single impression (e.g., "ivy-twined," "greasestrewn," "churchdoor," "lateblossom," "knee-deep").

29. Kenner (p. 132) sums up Stephen's limitations, finds him "indigestibly Byronic," and charges a "total lack of humour." Tindall (*Reader's Guide*, pp. 55–56) severely rebukes Stephen's inhumanity and egoism. John Gross points to his "messianic delusions": Gross, *Joyce* (London, Fontana, 1971), p. 29, a well-balanced brief critical evaluation.

30. Yeats letter of July 29, 1915, *Letters*, II, 356.

31. According to Caroline Gordon, the novel is "the picture of a soul that is damned for time and eternity caught in the act of foreseeing and foreknowing its damnation. . . . Joyce is convinced that his hero is damned." See Gordon, "Some Readings and Misreadings," *Sewanee Review*, LXI (1953), 389, 393. Hugh Kenner's judgment is similar: "its central theme is Sin: the development of Stephen Dedalus from a bundle of sensations to a matured, self-conscious, dedicated, fallen being." See Kenner, "The Portrait in Perspective," Seon Givens, ed., *James Joyce: Two Decades of Criticism* (New York, Vanguard Press, 1948), p. 142. A. Walton Litz, who is much less severe on Stephen, also sees him as "a potential Icarus," in his *James Joyce* (New York, Twayne, 1966), p. 71.

32. See Mason and Ellmann, *Critical Writings*, p. 111.

33. Letter of Oct. 31, 1925, to Damaso Alonso, *Letters*, III, 129.

34. Letter of Apr. 9, 1917, *Letters*, I, 102.

35. See Curran, pp. 52–60, 105–115.

36. Quoted by Ellmann, p. 81.

37. Letter of Sept. 18, 1905, *Letters*, II, 107.

38. Letter of Oct. 27, 1909, to Nora Barnacle Joyce, *Letters*, II, 255.

39. Ellmann, whose knowledge of Joyce's life is surely unequaled, sees "no lack of sympathy" in the *Portrait* at any stage of its writing, though also a recognition that Stephen is frequently a callow youth (*Joyce*, p. 150). In his introduction to the *Letters* (II, lii), a finely balanced estimate of Joyce's character, Ellmann comments: "His dominant image of himself was one of delicacy and fragility, of perpetual ill health and ill-luck, of a tenor among basses."

40. *Portrait*, p. 65.

41. This is Hugh Kenner's reading, *Dublin's Joyce*, pp. 121–122.

42. *Portrait*, p. 162.

43. Diary entries, *Portrait*, pp. 247, 250, 251, 252.

44. Trieste notebook, printed by Anderson, *Portrait*, p. 293.

45. For a much more positive evaluation than mine, see Robert Scholes, "Stephen Dedalus, Poet or Esthete," *PMLA*, LXXIX (1964), 484–489. John Gross, on the other hand, succinctly dismisses the villanelle as something which "might almost have been written by Enoch Soames" (p. 42). Others might say that it was intended as a parody, but the similarity to Joyce's "serious" pieces in *Chamber Music* belies that suggestion.

46. *Portrait*, p. 221.

47. Anderson ("The Sacrificial Butter") goes to ingenious lengths in interpreting the chapter as a symbolic version of Christ's mission, trial, and passion. I cannot accept all of Anderson's readings, but some of them have called to my attention a good deal of probable Christian allusion I should not have detected.

48. Ellmann's apt phrase to describe Joyce's own view of the artist's vocation (*Letters*, II, xxxviii).

49. Letter of Aug. 22, 1912, to Nora Joyce, *Letters*, II, 311. Joyce must have remembered this letter as he wrote the penultimate entry in Stephen's diary—unless he habitually thought of his mission in such terms.

XI. OF BONDAGE AND FREEDOM: LATER NOVELS OF YOUTH

1. Beresford's three volumes telling Jacob's story are *The Early History of Jacob Stahl* (1911), *A Candidate for Truth* (1912), and

The Invisible Event (1915). Mackenzie's *Sinister Street* appeared in two volumes, 1913 and 1914. Other novels that might be grouped with these studies of youth are Hugh Walpole's *Fortitude* (1913), Oliver Onions's *Little Devil Doubt* (1910), and Gilbert Cannan's *Mendel* (1916).

2. A model of Edwardian realism, *Clayhanger* (1910) has many elements of the Bildungsroman (tension between father and son, problems of choosing a career, first love, a strong autobiographical component, the provincial setting and mores), but it differs from the novels I have been discussing in that it bypasses the hero's childhood and early adolescence and centers on a relatively short time span. It forms part of Bennett's trilogy, which also includes *Hilda Lessways* and *These Twain*.

3. For Maugham's view of his novel, see above, Chap. I, nn. 40, 41, and cf. his preface to the 1963 Penguin edition: "The book did for me what I wanted, and when it was issued to the world I found myself free from the pains and unhappy recollections that tormented me." See also Robin Maugham, *Somerset and All the Maughams* (New York, New American Library, 1966), p. 117, where Maugham is quoted as saying, "I wrote *Of Human Bondage* to rid myself of an intolerable obsession. . . . I wanted to lay all those ghosts, and I succeeded." For a brief review of the autobiographical elements in *Of Human Bondage*, see Richard A. Cordell, *Somerset Maugham: A Writer for All Seasons* (Bloomington, Ind., Indiana University Press, 1969), pp. 91–95.

4. *Of Human Bondage*, Chap. 59.

5. *Of Human Bondage*, Chap. 74.

6. *Of Human Bondage*, Chap. 59.

7. *Of Human Bondage*, Chap. 53.

8. Philip argues this in conversation with Macalister (Chap. 67), who has been defending Kant's categorical imperative. Philip's words, ironically, echo Cronshaw's attack on free will, which long before (Chap. 45) has made Philip's brain reel: "When an action is performed it is clear that all the forces of the universe from all eternity conspired to cause it."

9. *Of Human Bondage*, Chap. 106.

10. *Of Human Bondage*, Chap. 121.

11. *Of Human Bondage*, Chap. 122; cf. Pater's use of the same quotation in *Marius* (Chap. 8), cited above.

12. *Of Human Bondage*, Chaps. 27, 75.

13. See Maugham's own statement in a 1946 address, Klaus A. Jonas, ed., *The Maugham Enigma* (New York, Citadel Press, 1954), p. 126.

14. May Sinclair, "The Novels of Dorothy Richardson," *The Egoist*, V (1918), 57, 58, reprinted as introduction to the 1919 reissue of *Pointed Roofs*. The phrase "stream of consciousness" was previously used by William James, but Miss Sinclair gave it literary meaning and currency; see Walter Allen's introduction to a new edition of the *Pilgrimage*, 4 vols. (London, Dent, 1967), p. 5.

15. *Mary Olivier*, Bk. I, Chap. 2, sec. vii.

16. *Arnold Waterlow*, Chap. 21.

17. *Mary Olivier*, Bk. IV, Chap. 23, sec. vii.

18. *Mary Olivier*, Bk. IV, Chap. 25, sec. iv.

19. *Mary Olivier*, Bk. V, Chap. 35, sec. iv.

20. *Arnold Waterlow*, Chaps. 4, 7, 15.

21. *Arnold Waterlow*, Chap. 38.

22. *Arnold Waterlow*, Chap. 44.

23. *Arnold Waterlow*, Chap. 32.

24. Another of May Sinclair's books should be remembered for its psychological penetration, her *Life and Death of Harriet Frean* (1922), a frightening study of a "martyr complex," but, thanks to its rigid economy, a case history rather than a full-bodied Bildungs-roman.

25. Virginia Woolf, *A Writer's Diary*, pp. 32, 37, 54.

26. It is not clear how considerable may be Virginia Woolf's personal stake in the depiction of Jacob, but much of Jacob's career (his childhood summers by the sea, his Cambridge days, his trip to Greece) seems to run parallel to the experience of her elusive but much loved brother, Thoby Stephen (1880–1906). Just as the novel tries to assemble Jacob from the impressions of those acquainted with him, Virginia Woolf, after Thoby's untimely death, sought to find out all she could about him from his friends. See Quentin Bell, *Virginia Woolf*, 2 vols. (New York, Harcourt Brace Jovanovich, 1972), I, 112.

27. *Jacob's Room*, Chap. 3.

28. Cf. William York Tindall's comment on novels of adolescence after 1920, *Forces in Modern British Literature* (New York, Knopf, 1947), p. 179.

29. Forrest Reid, *Apostate* (London, Constable, 1926), p. 3. Reid's early novel, *The Garden God: A Tale of Two Boys*, very aesthetic and Paterian, dates from 1905. The Tom Barber books are *Uncle Stephen* (1931), *The Retreat* (1936), and *Young Tom* (1944). His *Following Darkness* (1912), revised as *Peter Waring* (1937), has been compared to Joyce's *Portrait* as an Irish novel of

adolescence, though Reid's Ireland is Ulster; see Roger Burlingham, *Forrest Reid* (London, Faber, 1953), pp. 79–81.

30. Denton Welch (1915–1948) published the first of his novels in 1943; his last, *A Voice through a Cloud*, appeared posthumously in 1950; all are heavily autobiographical. See also Jocelyn Brooke, ed., *The Denton Welch Journals* (London, Hamilton, 1952).

31. John Wain, *Strike the Father Dead* (London, Macmillan, 1962), p. 327. Giving us very little notion of Jeremy's childhood, *Strike the Father Dead* falls short of being a full-scale Bildungsroman; we need to know more of Jeremy's early conditioning if we are fully to understand what motivates his adolescent rebellion. Other Angry novels with some of the same components are Kingsley Amis's *Lucky Jim* (1954), John Braine's *Room at the Top* (1957), Keith Waterhouse's *Billy Liar* (1959), and Wain's earlier novel, *The Contenders* (1958). On the Angry writers in retrospect, see Jerome Meckier, "Looking Back at Anger: The Success of a Collapsing Stance," *Dalhousie Review*, LII (1972), 47–58.

32. Bernard S. Oldsey and Stanley Weintraub compare *Free Fall* and *The Fall* of Camus, published three years earlier, *The Art of William Golding* (New York, Harcourt Brace, 1965), pp. 103–122. Peter M. Axthelm compares *Free Fall* (as "the search for a reconstructed order") with Koestler's *Darkness at Noon*, *The Modern Confessional Novel* (New Haven, Yale University Press, 1967), pp. 97–127. The crucial prison scene evokes a terror and psychological pain reminiscent of Kafka's *Trial*.

33. *Free Fall*, Chap. 1.

34. *Free Fall*, Chap. 2.

35. See *Free Fall*, end of Chap. 12, and cf. Howard S. Babb, who describes the experience as "a baptism in reverse," *The Novels of William Golding* (Columbus, Ohio State University Press, 1970), p. 112.

36. *Free Fall*, Chap. 10.

37. Jack I. Biles, *Talk: Conversation with William Golding* (New York, Harcourt Brace Jovanovich, 1970), p. 79.

38. See Golding's essay "The Ladder and the Tree," an autobiographical sketch, in his non-fictional volume *The Hot Gates* (London, Faber, 1965), p. 172. Cf. Biles, *Talk*, pp. 83, 85, 88.

39. *The Cocktail Party* (New York, Harcourt Brace and World, 1950), p. 71.

40. *Free Fall*, Chap. 2.

41. Golding on the title, *Talk*, pp. 81–82.

42. Golding, quoted by James R. Baker, *William Golding* (New York, St. Martin's Press, 1965), p. 56.

43. Golding on Piggy, *Talk*, p. 12; see also p. 13: "He's an in-nocent; he's a complete innocent. He is like scientists, who really think they're getting somewhere in real, genuine, human terms. . . . Piggy never gets anywhere near coping with anything on that island at all." The cautions seem necessary to Golding insofar as many readers of *Lord of the Flies* have taken Piggy as a wholly sympathetic character. We are apparently to regard Nick Shales as similarly limited.

44. *Free Fall*, Chap. 12.

45. *Free Fall*, Chap. 12.

46. *Free Fall*, Chap. 4. Mark Kinkead Weekes and Ian Gregor in their valuable *William Golding* (London, Faber, 1967), p. 176, detect "some sort of metaphysical dimension" in Sammy's violent love-lust.

47. *Free Fall*, Chap. 7.

48. *Free Fall*, Chap. 1.

49. *Free Fall*, Chap. 14.

50. *Free Fall*, Chap. 12.

INDEX

Titles of books, poems, and short stories are entered under the authors. Names of characters mentioned in the text without immediate reference to the novels in which they appear are listed in the index in parentheses following the titles.

Adams, Henry, *The Education*, 25
Adams, Robert M., 287
Aldington, Richard, 320
Allen, Grant, *The Woman Who Did*, 173, 315
Allen, Walter, 310, 326
Alonso, Damaso, 323
Amis, Kingsley, *Lucky Jim*, 327
Anderson, Chester G., 320, 321, 323, 324
Antheil, George, 321
Apuleius, 142, 153; "Cupid and Psyche," 142, 149, 307; *The Golden Ass*, 152
Armato, Rosario P., 287
Arnold, Matthew, 26, 150–151; *Literature and Dogma*, 260
Augustine, Saint, 307
Austen, Jane, *Emma*, 18
Auster, Henry, 299, 300
Autobiography, 6, 7, 25–26, 123
Axthelm, Peter M., 327

Babb, Howard S., 327
Baker, James R., 327
Balzac, Honoré de, 100; *Louis Lambert*, 287; *Père Goriot* (Rastignac), 20
Beadnell, Maria (Mrs. Winter), 32, 34, 290
Beaumont, Sir George, 285
Beer, John, 320

Beerbohm, Max, "Enoch Soames," 324
Bell, Quentin, 326
Bennett, Arnold, 193, 263, 265, 325; *Clayhanger*, 248, 325; *Hilda Lessways*, 325; *The Old Wives' Tale*, 18; *These Twain*, 325
Bennett, Joseph, 305–306
Benson, A. C., 306
Beresford, J. D., 248; *A Candidate for Truth*, 324; *The Early History of Jacob Stahl*, 248–249, 324; *The Invisible Event*, 325
Bildungsroman, meaning of the term, vii–viii, 13–14, 287; characteristics of the genre, 17–27
Biles, Jack I., 327
Bissell, Claude T., 303
Blackwood, John, 97, 113
Bloomfield, Morton W., 286
Borrow, George, 204; *Lavengro*, 204
Bossuet, Jacques B., 99
Boulton, James T., 316–317, 320
Bragg, Melvyn, *For Want of a Nail*, 268–269
Braine, John, *Room at the Top*, 327
Brombert, Victor, 287
Brontë, Emily, *Wuthering Heights* (Heathcliff, Cathy), 176
Brooke, Jocelyn, 327

329

330   INDEX

Brookfield, Jane (Mrs. W. H.), 28
Brookfield, William, 28
Brown, P. Hume, 286
Brzenk, Eugene, 307
Buckle, H. T., 120; *History of Civilisation*, 303
Buckler, William E., 297
Buckley, J. H., 286, 291, 306
Budberg, Moura, 316
Bullett, Gerald, 300
Bulwer-Lytton, E. B., 60, 304–305; *Ernest Maltravers*, 304–305
Bunyan, John, *The Pilgrim's Progress*, 134–135
Burlingham, Roger, 327
Burrows, Louie, 205, 210, 224, 317
Burwell, Rose Marie, 317
Butler, (Dr.) Samuel, 124
Butler, Samuel, 116, 119–139, 162, 288, 302–306; *Erewhon*, 125, 303, 305; *Evolution Old and New*, 121; *A First Year in Canterbury Settlement*, 125, 303; *Life and Habit*, 121, 122; *Life of Dr. Samuel Butler*, 124; *Luck, or Cunning*, 121; *Unconscious Memory*, 121; *The Way of All Flesh* (Ernest Pontifex), 8, 13, 17, 19, 20, 21, 22, 23, 97, 116, 119–139, 143, 169, 172, 188, 190, 227, 231, 248, 249, 253, 280, 282, 302–306
Butler, Mrs. Thomas, 125
Butler, Thomas, 125, 126
Butt, John, 291
Byrne, Betty, 237, 323
Byrne, J. F., 237, 323
Byron, George Gordon, Lord, 7–8, 16, 17, 19, 38, 146, 233, 239, 288; *Don Juan*, 7–8, 135, 244, 288, 290
Byron, Lady, 7

Camus, Albert, 270; *The Fall*, 327
Cannan, Gilbert, *Mendel*, 325
Carlyle, Thomas, 10, 12, 52, 79, 286, 291; *Sartor Resartus*, 40, 41, 291; translation of *Wilhelm Meister*, see Goethe
Cecil, David, 310, 312

Cecilia, Saint, 160
Cervantes, Miguel de, *Don Quixote*, 175
Chambers, Jessie, 204, 205, 206, 209, 210–212, 217, 222, 223, 300, 317, 318, 319, 320
Chambers, May, 210, 318
Chapman, John, 96
Chase, Mary Ellen, 310
Chesterton, G. K., 291
Cline, C. L., 295
Coleman, Terry, 311
Coleridge, Samuel Taylor, 5
Colum, Padraic, 228
Conrad, Joseph, *Lord Jim*, 18; *Youth*, 25, 289
Cordell, Richard A., 325
Corke, Helen, 318, 319, 320
Costa, R. H., 316
Cowap, Mr., 192
Cross, J. W., 298
Cumming, John, 92
Curran, C. P., 321

D'Albert, François, 96
Dallas, Eneas Sweetland, 100
D'Annunzio, Gabriele, 241
Dante, 307
Darwin, Charles, 121, 251; *The Origin of Species*, 121, 251
Darwinism, 121, 251
Davis, Harbert, 303
Deacon, Lois, 311
Defoe, Daniel, 105, 114; *History of the Devil*, 96
Degas, Edgar, 240
de Selincourt, Ernest, 285
Dexter, Walter, 290
Dickens, Charles, viii, 21, 28, 30–62, 63, 64, 65, 93–94, 99, 115, 131, 139, 146, 148, 162, 168, 189, 205, 226, 233, 249, 255, 280, 290, 291, 292, 293, 296, 298–299, 302, 305; *David Copperfield* (David, Micawber, Steerforth), 13, 19, 22, 29, 30–44, 45, 48, 60, 61, 63, 79, 82, 86, 93, 131, 141, 143, 144, 146, 168, 169, 172, 178, 189, 190, 195, 205, 206,